Nations at war provides an explanation of war in international politics grounded on data-based, empirical research. The book classifies and synthesizes the research findings of over 500 quantitative analyses of war at the analytic levels of the state, dyad, region, and international system. Because wars follow from political decisions, two basic decisionmaking models – the rational and the nonrational – are examined in relation to the explanatory framework of the volume. In addition, case analyses of two wars – the Iran/Iraq War (1980) and World War I (1914) – are provided as demonstrations of scientifically-based explanations of historical events. The primary structural factors responsible for the onset and seriousness of war are identified and the explanations are developed according to the scientific model of "covering laws." The conclusion presents a discussion of the potential for probabilistic predictions of conflict within the context of war and peace studies.

D1262479

CAMBRIDGE STUDIES IN INTERNATIONAL RELATIONS: 58

Nations at war

Editorial Board

Cambridge Studies in International Relations is a joint initiative of
Cambridge University Press and the British International Studies
Association (BISA). The series will include a wide range of material,
from undergraduate textbooks and surveys to research-based
monographs and collaborative volumes. The aim of the series is to
publish the best new scholarship in International Studies from
Europe, North America and the rest of the world.

CAMBRIDGE STUDIES IN INTERNATIONAL RELATIONS

Series list continues after index

Nations at war
A scientific study
of international conflict

Daniel S. Geller
University of Mississippi

J. David Singer
University of Michigan

 CAMBRIDGE
UNIVERSITY PRESS

PUBLISHED BY THE PRESS SYNDICATE OF THE UNIVERSITY OF CAMBRIDGE
The Pitt Building, Trumpington Street, Cambridge CB2 1RP, United Kingdom

CAMBRIDGE UNIVERSITY PRESS
The Edinburgh Building, Cambridge CB2 2RU, United Kingdom
40 West 20th Street, New York, NY 10011–4211, USA
10 Stamford Road, Oakleigh, Melbourne 3166, Australia

First published 1998

Printed in the United Kingdom at the University Press, Cambridge

Typeset in Palatino 10/12$\frac{1}{2}$ pt [CE]

A catalogue record for this book is available from the British Library

Library of Congress cataloguing in publication data
Geller, Daniel S.
Nations at war : a scientific study of international conflict / Daniel S. Geller,
J. David Singer.
　　p.　cm. – (Cambridge studies in international relations: 58)
Includes bibliographical references and index.
1. War – Mathematical models.
2. World politics – Mathematical models.
3. Iran-Iraq War, 1980–1988.
4. World War I, 1914–1918.
I. Singer, J. David (Joel David), 1925– .　II. Title.　III. Series.
U21.2.G436　1997
355.4'8–dc21　97–10267　CIP

ISBN 0 521 62119 4 hardback
ISBN 0 521 62906 3 paperback

Contents

Contents

Figures and tables

Figure

Tables

Acknowledgments

The systematic, quantitative empirical analysis of war has a history traceable to the third decade of the twentieth century in the works of Lewis Fry Richardson and Quincy Wright. This book seeks to draw together their findings and those of similarly motivated individuals by identifying consistent empirical patterns associated with the onset and seriousness of war. It is also an attempt to demonstrate how such patterns may be integrated to produce a scientific explanation of this most destructive of all human activities.

In such an endeavor, the first debt is to those scholars who have sought expansion of our knowledge of war through the application of scientific methodology. Their names are scattered throughout the pages of this book. Special thanks are due to friends and colleagues who read the manuscript and, with their criticism, attempted to steer us away from serious errors of both fact and interpretation. Here, we are indebted to Michael Nicholson, Erich Weede, James Lee Ray, Claudio Cioffi-Revilla, and Patrick James. Due to their efforts the final manuscript was much improved. However, we – and not they – are responsible for any and all errors that appear in this book.

Institutional support for this project should also be noted. Daniel Geller benefited from the generosity of the University of Mississippi – through the Office of the Dean, College of Liberal Arts and the Faculty Sabbatical Review Committee – for providing release time and research support for work on the manuscript during the 1995–1996 academic year. A research grant for mathematical conflict analysis from the University of Mississippi Foundation Associates' Fund in 1994 also permitted additional time and effort to be devoted to this project. The work of Graduate Assistants Daniel Jones, James Batt, Chi-Feng Hsu, and Joshua Brown at the University of Michigan and the University of Mississippi on a number of quantitative empirical analyses presented in this volume is also gratefully acknowledged. Royce Kurtz, Reference Bibliographer for the John D. Williams Library at the University of Mississippi, provided much-needed help in both locating and securing many of the studies cited in this book.

We also wish to thank John Haslam, Commissioning Editor, Social Sciences Group, Cambridge University Press and Steve Smith, Managing Editor of the Cambridge Studies in International Relations series for their support of this study both during and after the review process. Their steady involvement and interest in seeing the manuscript published was of immeasurable value. The copy-editing expertise of Barbara Docherty – in reading the original drafts and correcting the authors' innumerable errors – provided sorely needed assistance. With much gratitude, we note that a deep debt is owed to our friend and colleague, John Vasquez, who was instrumental in his role as an external reviewer for Cambridge in convincing the Editorial Board of the merits of this book.

Perhaps most importantly, we are grateful for the wisdom of Lynne and Diane, without whose counsel for compromise in their husbands' arguments this work might not have been completed.

Introduction

War is a rare event in world politics, but it is always with us. How can we say this? On the one hand, if we note that the number of territorial states in the global system has ranged from fewer than 30 after the Napoleonic Wars to nearly 200 at the end of the twentieth century, that gives us about 400 nondirectional pairs of states in 1816 and about 18,000 pairs today. And even if we recognize that most wars are between neighbors, and thus reduce the possible pairs at war in a given year to the 40 bordering neighbors in 1816 and the 317 in 1993, the potential is never even approached. There were no wars under way in 81 of the 180 years since the modern interstate system came into being, and seldom more than one in any given year. On the other hand, 75 interstate wars led to a total of more than 30 million battle-connected fatalities among combatants, not to mention tens of millions of additional deaths among civilians in the context of these wars.

Another way to make this point is by looking at the frequency of war involvement by the members of the interstate system. During the time period under consideration here, we find that 150 states never experienced international war, 49 saw only one or two wars during their tenure in the system, 16 had three or four, and only France, Britain, Germany, Italy, Russia, Greece, Egypt, and Turkey were involved in more than 10 during the nearly two centuries since the Congress of Vienna in 1815.

The paradox is that most societies are in continuous preparation for a very rare event – but of course, if the event occurs, the stakes can be enormous. Not only does war usually bring extraordinary destruction to combatants and civilians, and to their homes and farms and roads and factories, but all too often the losers may find their lands occupied or annexed, and their wealth confiscated by the victors.

Despite the costs of war, especially to the losers, the effort to avoid it nevertheless remains paradoxical. That is, the conventional wisdom says that "if you want peace, prepare for war," on the premise that potentially aggressive neighbors will be deterred and intimidated rather than provoked and encouraged to follow suit. This is not the place to add up the myriad costs of these near-universal and time-honored preparedness programs – in terms of money, skills, opportunity costs, environmental damage, economic decline, and psychic and moral deterioration – but it is impossible to estimate the imbalance between costs incurred over the decades and costs avoided. And, of course, what gives the paradox a sinister twist is the frequency of the self-fulfilling prophecy – to which we will return in our discussion of the war-proneness of dyads.

In any event, the terrible destructiveness of interstate war has led a good many scholars to seek the causes of this deadly human practice. We fall readily into that group. But as those familiar with the Correlates of War (COW) Project might surmise, our ambition is somewhat more modest; the project's title makes clear that social scientists need to know a fair amount about the *correlates* of war before we can speak with much authority about its *causes*. Until we begin to ascertain which conditions and events precede and co-vary with fluctuations in the incidence of war in world politics, it would be naïve as well as presumptuous to claim any grasp of its causes.

This proposition might seem self-evident, but a moment's reflection should remind us of how frequently it is violated; for every investigation devoted to the search for war's correlates, there are thousands of studies that hope or claim to identify its causes or origins or roots. This need not surprise us, however. In addition to the powerful human drive to understand and/or eliminate war, there is the sad fact that until quite recently no one thought to bring scientific methods to bear on the study of war. As a matter of fact, it is only in the past century that the intellectual strategies and observatorial procedures of the physical and biological sciences have been understood as germane to any social phenomena. As a result, the literature on armed conflict is full of interesting, suggestive, plausible, and provocative guesses, speculations, and assertions – often labeled "theories" in the less precise academic precincts.

On the other hand, the pioneering efforts of Bloch (1898), Sorokin (1937), Richardson (1960), and Wright ([1942], 1964) have not been without result; each of these scholars helped us to make the transition

2

(described in Singer 1990) from the promises of Condorcet (1794) and Buckle (1885) to the scientific peace research movement marked by the appearance of *Quantitative International Politics* (Singer 1968). Today, we have upwards of 600 data-based articles, largely found in five major journals – all in English – as well as two dozen or so book-length studies in which problems of world politics in general and armed conflict in particular are subjected to rigorous and systematic treatment. While much of this research follows from the Correlates of War Project that began at the University of Michigan in 1963–1964, it has by now expanded dramatically in theoretical orientation, substantive focus, and methodological predilection. It is from this far-from-homogeneous body of scholarship that the study at hand emerges; our aim is to summarize and synthesize a large proportion of these empirical findings and then to integrate them into as coherent an explanation of modern interstate war as possible.

Integrative problems

As anyone who has read – or better still, written – the sort of review article found in the physical or biological science journals can easily appreciate, this is no simple task. Despite the strong scientific norms in favor of reproducibility, the inducements away from reproducibility – and thus, comparability – are often powerful. That means that even though several studies are intended to test the same theoretical model, they often will not. Partly this is a data and measurement problem, with individual investigators measuring the same variables in different ways, observing different regions of the world or looking at different historical periods. Furthermore, we can use different research designs, postulating different time lags between predictor and outcome variables, computing moving averages over time spreads of differing lengths, using different transformations to cope with the historical outlier cases, and assuming the reciprocal effects of our predictor variables to be additive in some designs and multiplicative in others.

This lack of perfect – or even proximate – similarity from one study to the next means that even if they all point to the same conclusion, we cannot assume theoretical convergence, nor can we assume that they point to differing conclusions even if the statistical results are quite dissimilar. In disciplines that rely more on laboratory experiments (Campbell and Stanley 1963) rather than historical experiments

(Singer 1977) we typically find a much higher level of comparability and thus a stronger basis for treating their findings as cumulative. As a matter of fact, a set of methods known as meta-analysis has evolved in the social sciences, along with an increasing sensitivity to its strengths and weaknesses (Wolf 1986). In our field, the best known effort to explicitly compare and combine the statistical results of a fairly well defined set of studies (Rummel 1985) met with mixed success. But as the scientific world politics movement continues to grow, and especially as we adhere more closely to the historical experiment type of research design, we can expect greater attention to the canons of reproducibility and comparability (Singer 1975). Until then, faced as we are with rather idiosyncratic approaches to the measurement of our variables, empirical domain, and research design, what do we do?

We make do. More precisely, we do what all good scientists do at every stage in a given investigation. We think hard, looking first at what we and others claim to know about the query at hand, paying close attention to the larger class of studies to which we assign this one, distinguishing between those claims that rest on the revealed wisdom, professional folklore, or armchair "theory" on the one hand, and those that rest to an appreciable extent on reproducible evidence on the other. We then go on as suggested above, to ascertain the similarities and differences that characterize the more systematic studies. And if, for example, the findings for cases covering one region, type of society, or historical period turn out to differ from those for another empirical domain – and this may not be obvious in their published articles – we take careful note.

Our point here is that the most rigorous devotee of scientific methods is called upon, time and again, to make intuitive judgments. There certainly is a checklist of factors to consider when we evaluate and try to integrate disparate results from the data-based literature, but in the final analysis it is little more than a judgment call. In making such calls, we essentially fall back on our theoretical biases, which rest of course on our reading, recollection, and reinterpretation of that vast body of literature with which we are familiar. To be sure, a very large portion of that literature is a vague mix of historical anecdote, policy-induced hunch, contemporary fashion, and vague recall of some long-ago graduate seminar. This is quite acceptable as long as we keep the source of our intuition in mind and then go on to evaluate it in a truly skeptical fashion, and as long as we lay it

4

alongside the formal models in literature (not for empirical veridicality, but for logical consistency) and check it against the data-based generalities (many of which, so noted, will point in more than one direction).

Further confounding this hard-to-reproduce process is the personality or the mood or the immediate incentives that are at work. Statisticians like to distinguish between Type I and Type II errors and that distinction is germane here; in the Type II error, we overestimate the evidence that leads us to see a pattern when it may not exist in empirical reality, while the Type I tendency is more likely to infer randomness and to thus overlook a strong but nonobvious configuration. Both are, in principle, to be avoided, but those of us who assume that social phenomena are inherently systematic, patterned, and law-like – and who are therefore more positive about scientific method – normally will err in the Type II direction; a possible example might be the excellent and very flattering Vasquez article on "The Steps to War" (1987) in which the author carefully examines most of the Correlates of War findings on the alliance-to-war relationship and interprets them as more coherent and consistent than would those of us who carried out the studies. On the other hand, those who are excessively critical, or take a dim view of the social science enterprise, or see international history as little more than one unique event after another will tend to miss a potentially significant but less visible set of regularities. We dwell on this issue at some length because the scholarly worth of this volume is in part dependent on how rigorously, carefully, and creatively we handle this task.

Theoretical views

By now you have a rather clear sense of our methodological orientation, but little clue as to the theoretical predisposition. A decade ago, this would have been a relatively straightforward discussion, but due to conceptual carelessness, semantic insensitivity, and epistemological innocence, the theoretical waters are once again muddied beyond belief.

All of us have been exposed to quite a variety of normative and empirical orientations *vis-à-vis* the subject of world politics, and the dominant tendency has been toward agnosticism. That is, given the thin and scattered range of evidence-based findings, we have wisely taken the view that one or another of the theoretical schools may ultimately be vindicated, but that in the meantime our task should be to test the indicators of a variety of them against the historical record. Put differently, those of us with that orientation have urged considerable open-mindedness toward conflicting explanatory models of world politics, coupled with a strong commitment to systematically examining the evidence in support of them.

However, the field took a remarkably counter-productive direction in the early 1980s (Singer 1989b). The bootless and sterile debate that had absorbed some of us while in graduate school in the post-World War II decade – "realism" versus "idealism" – again surfaced as a topic of allegedly serious discussion. As we see it, the issue emerged out of the policy debate that marked the onset of the Soviet–American "cold war." Such scholars as E.H. Carr (1939) in Britain and Hans Morgenthau ([1948], 1967) in the United States – sharply criticizing Western policies of the inter-war period as naïve and idealistic because of their alleged reliance on international law, international organization, and collective security – argued for a more hard-nosed and Machiavellian view of international politics. For these self-acclaimed "realists," there were three basic premises: (1) the system is and would remain essentially anarchistic; (2) statesmen do and should think primarily in terms of their "national interests;" and (3) the dominant currency is and will remain that of military and industrial capabilities. Despite the telling critiques of Ernst Haas (1953, 1964) and others, not to mention the disastrous consequences – many of which are only now becoming apparent – of the superpowers' eager embrace of policies rooted in "realism," generations of students have been subjected to these arguments. This issue is still alive, with the contemporary version pitting neo-realism against neo-liberalism (Keohane 1986; Kegley 1995).

We express this view for several reasons, the first of which is semantic. There surely is a more honest label for this perspective, including power politics, realpolitik, machpolitik, balance of strength, etc. More substantively, even if one could call idealism or realism a theory, we would need to articulate and then put to the empirical test some of the behavioral consequences of their premises, and many of those who bandy about these terms have, to date, failed to do so. Others, including ourselves, *have* done so, and much of the data-based literature turns out to address a variety of the relevant consequences. In sum, it is time to get on with the articulation and testing of rival models and hypotheses regarding armed conflict and to move beyond the literary debate.

Later in the book we present further evidence, but for the moment we can summarize the factors that make us question certain elements within the "realist" paradigm. First, it usually assumes the territorial state to be not only the single most dominant actor in the system, but also a unitary one driven by considerations of expected utilities for the state as an entity, rather than a coalition of varying cohesiveness each of whose constituents pursues its own parochial interests in the familiar stew of domestic and foreign policy interactions. Second, it assumes a degree of anarchy in the system that ignores the web of institutional, legal, and pragmatic constraints; these "regimes," while expanding rapidly toward the close of this century were by no means absent even as far back as the Congress of Vienna. Third, it downgrades or even ignores the role of ethical criteria in security decision-making; international history is full of cases in which moral inhibitions mitigated or even prevented moves that would violate, or appear to violate, domestic or international standards. And, fourth, it pays far too little attention to the importance of competence, rectitude, credibility, and legitimacy, all of which interact with material capabilities to make for a state's power, understood here as the ability to both exercise influence and resist influence attempts by others.

Having said all of this, we have no intention of ignoring the theoretical implications of realpolitik and related orientations. As a matter of fact, we already have two excellent collections of rigorous and systematic articles that explicitly address such implications; the earlier is *Correlates of War II: Testing Some Realpolitik Models* (Singer 1980) and the more recent is *Reconstructing Realpolitik* (Wayman and Diehl 1994). More significantly, both the speculative and the more systematic literature using formal models and/or data-based investigations are full of alternative and more diverse theoretical points of departure. Nor can there be much ambiguity as to our position here: we are not going into the investigation committed to any one particular explanation of war and then subject it to careful scrutiny. Rather, we pursue here a search for consistent empirical patterns (Bremer and Cusack 1995), and do so despite the opposing view that theory should precede empirical investigation. An early critic of our project described it as "count first and think second," but that phrase is no more helpful than its opposite of "fantasize first and examine second."

Merely putting these alternatives so crudely is to illuminate the fact that few of us ever follow one or the other of these extremes; most of us spend our research careers working both sides of the street and crossing back and forth quite frequently. We get general ideas from all sorts of stimuli and try to think of historical examples that support or question these ideas, and we encounter all sorts of facts and ask which generalizations they undergird or undercut. We doubt that our colleagues do it any other way. When we reconstruct our research for our readers, we may present it *in extremis* – from either the inductive or deductive side of the street – but we doubt if such reconstructions ever capture what we really do.

Thus, it comes as no surprise if we confess that on the one hand we want to be very responsive to the empirical evidence generated by the data-oriented community of world politics scholars, while at the same time coming in with our own theoretical predilections. What might these latter be? As you might surmise from the above, our bias is towards the importance of realpolitik variables – but with questions as to their consequences. In studies reported in *Correlates of War II*, we find repeated support for the significance of system structure, relative capabilities, and geopolitical considerations, but we also find that these factors turn out to move the states toward war in certain contexts and away from war in others. Further, as we lay out our understanding of the decision processes by which governments deal with the issues that culminate in war or peace – or stalemate, crisis, or compromise – it will become apparent that we cannot completely embrace one or another of the contending models that dominate the literature.

Ex post facto experiment, or international history as social science laboratory

In our discussions so far, you have no doubt observed frequent reference to the importance of testing models and hypotheses against the empirical or historical evidence, but the rationale is by no means self-evident. To be sure, the objective is to generalize about world politics and interstate armed conflict, and it thus makes sense to examine these phenomena as they unfolded in the past. On the other hand, the global system and its relevant attributes are in a state of continuous change, thus making the system of the mid-twentieth century or the early nineteenth century little more than a rough analogy to today's system, and far from identical. One implication is that we might be equally justified in testing our models in such other empirical domains as pre-industrial societies, labor–management conflicts, or campus politics, and another is that there is *no* appropriate domain; every empirical domain offers at best a rough analogy to the global system of the present or the impending future.

This is, then, yet another argument against the possibility of a science of world politics; not only are no two cases sufficiently similar, but the context for every case will also turn out to be different. On the other hand, if the world offered perfect similarity from one case to the next, life would indeed be less interesting, and if every interstate war arose out of identical circumstances, our research task would be simple. More seriously, it is the very mix of similarity and difference from case to case that makes it possible to compare them and then go on to search for generalizations. In any experimental design, the essential task is to "control for" several factors by holding them constant in quite a few cases while varying one or two at a time to see which combinations of factors lead to which specific outcomes. Such manipulation of our predictor variables is partly provided by "nature" in the sense of the configurations given by history and partly by the ways in which we set up our research design. And to reiterate our thesis here, the global/international system is an evolving one, with some of its properties changing slowly over time, others rapidly fluctuating, and still others remarkably constant over the decades and centuries. As long as we are aware of this reality, have figured out how to measure these properties over time and across regions, and control for them in our analyses, this is not a handicap at all. Conversely, such evolution offers an interesting scientific challenge and at the same time creates the opportunity to carry out the sort of *ex post* or historical experiment essential to the development of solid knowledge on matters of war and peace.

Organization of the volume

From what has been said so far, our objective is quite clear: to offer a coherent synthesis of research findings leading to an explanation of interstate war for the historical period since the Congress of Vienna; but our motivation is not merely one of scientific curiosity but of securing knowledge that might be applicable to the relevant future as well. Thus our attention to cross-temporal comparisons over the past and our hope of coping with the developing system as it unfolds in the decades ahead. In pursuit of such an explanation, we reiterate that we build heavily on the results of prior data-based research – ours and that of our growing company of like-minded colleagues. But once again, a caveat. We will be strongly influenced by existing findings – some of which are abstracted in Jones and Singer (1972) and Gibbs and Singer (1993) – but, as noted earlier, these studies are far from perfectly convergent. And even if they were, we have lived through enough of this type of research to appreciate the ways in which it can go wrong. Thus, while taking second place to no one on the virtues of the data-based historical test of our theoretical models, there will be instances in which we come out disagreeing with some apparently solid and consistent findings; we need not apologize for this, but we will certainly try to explain. Sometimes the judgment will rest on reservations about certain aspects of the studies, sometimes we will conclude that the premises and reasoning of a formal model – or even a well-articulated essay – are more compelling, and with some frequency we will recognize the relative infancy of our science and go with the more intuitive judgment. We make these points explicit to counter the anti-scientific view that the scientific method is little more than rigid adherence to certain mechanistic procedures. Algorithmic computation is a virtue, but independent judgment of conflicting evidence is more virtuous still.

With these points spelled out, we turn to the rationale by which our material is organized and presented. In addition to the approach that claims to have already identified the major factors in the etiology of war, there seem to be three general ways of organizing one's material. First is the listing of groups of variables – such as economic, geographic, cultural, technological, etc. – all of which need to be considered. Second is one or another version of the "process model," in which we begin with an evaluation of the factors that are furthest from the moment at which war is chosen or rejected, as in Bremer (1993b). From the distal to the proximate, we typically examine historical background, the state of the regional system, the capabilities of the protagonists, the precipitating events, the decision context and personalities, on up to the immediate conditions at the "moment of truth." However, only a modest effort has been made to link these background and ecological phenomena to the onset of war. The work of Russell Leng (1983, 1984, 1993) – focusing on recurrent crisis interaction – is a notable exception in this area.

A third approach is based on the "level of analysis" at which one's outcome variable is found. While much ink has flowed around this question (Waltz 1959; Singer 1961), there still remains plenty of ambiguity; sociologists continue to find out about "emergent properties" of a system, political scientists are now bemused as to whether we should "select on the dependent variable," and anthropologists are far from closure as to how to most validly measure the attributes of a given culture. But for the purposes of this volume, such issues can safely be set aside; our task is simpler. Following the Overview in chapter 1, we begin with a brief chapter that lays out our views on decisionmaking – the process and calculation that serves to connect a complex range of background conditions into a policy move – and then go on to address what we know, or think that we know, about the correlates of war as it is found at four different levels of analysis. More specifically, we begin with a summary of the evidence that tells us what it is about territorial states that makes them more or less war-prone during the past two centuries (chapter 3). Moving up from the state level to that of the dyad (chapter 4), we then examine the evidence that allegedly makes certain pairs of states – whether contiguous neighbors or not – more war-prone, and others less so. Then in chapter 5 we do the same for regions, in that we compare the war-proneness of different geographical areas as well as the same ones at different points in their evolution. Finally, and perhaps most theoretically important, we turn to the interstate system from the Congress of Vienna until the present (chapter 6), and try to discover those periods and configurations that have turned out to be especially war-prone *vis-à-vis* those in which war occurred rarely or with lower levels of severity and magnitude.

In closing this Introduction, we want to suggest that the cumulative growth of a science of world politics has been impeded by a wide range of social, political, economic, and academic conditions over which the scholarly community may exercise little if any control. But one factor that has hampered our progress – and over which we have considerable control – is the way in which we use language. In most cases, our terminology will conform with accepted current usage. In those instances where different definitions of a term have obscured its meaning, we will provide a specific definition for its usage in this book. All natural languages evolve and all professions develop their own jargon, but we will do everything possible here to maximize clarity, precision, and accessibility.

1   Overview

This volume is designed to provide an explanation of war in international politics grounded on data-based, empirical research. The study is organized around research findings at the analytic levels of the state, dyad, region, and international system. Because wars follow from political decisions, two basic decisionmaking models – the rational and the nonrational – are examined in relation to the explanatory framework of the volume. In addition, case analyses of two wars – Iran/Iraq (1980) and World War I (1914) – are provided as demonstrations of scientifically-based explanations of historical events. The primary factors responsible for the onset and seriousness of both wars are identified and the explanations are developed according to the scientific model of "covering laws." The Conclusion presents a discussion of the potential for probabilistic predictions of conflict within the context of war and peace studies.

Principal among the objectives of this book is an effort to generate a series of probabilistic laws drawn from consistent empirical regularities at multiple analytic levels. Such probabilistic laws may then be subsumed within theories that explain the underlying processes of the empirical uniformities. Wars in the two case studies – Iran/Iraq (1980) and World War I (1914) – are explained logically by inductive probability given the empirical regularities (probabilistic laws) derived from the data-based research. In other words, the two case-study wars are explained by inductive subsumption under laws of probabilistic form. We view such explanations as intrinsic both to scientific inquiry and to the development of empirically grounded theory.

Epistemology

Methodology follows from epistemology. The procedures for developing knowledge are a function of how knowledge is defined. Hence, a brief discussion is required on the epistemological foundations underlying the empirical analysis presented in this book.

Empirical patterns

A principal objective of scientific inquiry is to provide "explanations" of empirical phenomena. However, the definition of the term "explanation" and the criteria by which explanations are evaluated are not universally agreed upon. In conventional language, to "explain" a phenomenon is to incorporate it within a "cause and effect" sequence – or, at minimum, to locate it within a pattern of existential regularity. The philosophical issue of causality is an enormously complicated one, with the work of David Hume ([1748], 1894) perhaps the most influential attempt at specifying criteria of causation. Hume's three criteria for a causal relationship are: (1) constant conjoining; (2) space–time contiguity; and (3) temporal ordering. However, whether causality governs the phenomenal universe and, if so, whether such causal principles can be known are a matter of philosophical (i.e., ontological and epistemological) debate. Hume maintained that experience alone and not *a priori* reasoning is the substantive basis for knowledge, though even observation (experience) is insufficient to demonstrate the operation of causal principles or even simple causal relationships. Rather, Hume argued that knowledge of associations is limited to the noncausal expression of the conjunction of events.[1]

---

[1] Immanuel Kant ([1781], 1966) carried Hume's argument further. Hume maintained that neither pure reason nor sensory experience can establish causal relationships; Kant questioned the objective nature of causality itself. Kant maintained that human understanding is based upon the organizing and unifying principles of its own intrinsic mechanisms. We cannot describe the world as it is; we can only impart to it the form in which we perceive it. Reality is filtered through the *a priori* mechanisms ("categories") of human understanding, of which one such mechanism is the notion of causality. Thus the mind may go beyond the mere unification of sensory data; it may create a system of metaphysical illusions which tend to organize sensory phenomena according to principles which are beyond the mind's apperceptive machinery. In other words, apart from the inability of the human sensory apparatus to establish causality, Kant raises the issue of whether such a principle operates at all outside of the mechanisms of the mind. Kant ([1781], 1966:106–109) states this position in book I, chapter II, section 2.4, "Preliminary Explanation of the Possibility of the Categories as Knowledge *a priori*."

The Humean position on causality[2] is the dominant view in the empiricist philosophy of science (Guttenplan and Tamny 1971:344), although it is certainly not beyond dispute. However, to question the empirical demonstrability of causation is not to deny that the phenomenal universe exhibits certain patterns or regularities. It is the principal ontological assumption of the scientific search for knowledge that such patterns exist and are discernible. To assume otherwise – that all phenomena occur randomly (i.e., without any order) – is to preclude scientific inquiry. This position on patterns is consistent with general models of scientific explanation based on either deductive–nomological or inductive–probabilistic forms of reasoning. Although there are substantive differences in the epistemologies of empiricist philosophers such as Carl Hempel (1966), Karl Popper (1959), R.B. Braithwaite (1953), Hans Reichenbach (1951), and Imre Lakatos (1970), all subscribe to the "covering law" model of explanation in one form or another. The epistemological foundation for the analysis presented in this volume is the covering law model of scientific explanation.[3]

Deductive–nomological explanation

A deductive–nomological explanation is an argument employing universal instantiation which demonstrates that the phenomenon to be explained (the conclusion or explanandum phenomenon) is a consequence to be expected given the explanatory facts (the premises or explanans). The explanans are comprised of two statements: (1) a general assertion (or law); and (2) an assertion about particular facts. As Hempel (1966:51) notes, a deductive–nomological explanation is an argument with the following form:

$$L_1, L_2, \ldots, L_r$$
$$C_1, C_2, \ldots, C_k \left.\right\} \text{ explanans sentences}$$
$$\therefore \quad E \qquad \text{explanandum sentence}$$

where

E = the explanandum (conclusion)

$L_1, L_2, \ldots, L_r$ = general law(s)

$C_1, C_2, \ldots, C_k$ = assertion(s) about specific fact(s)

---

[2] See David Hume ([1748], 1894) section IV, "Skeptical Doubts Concerning the Operations of the Understanding."

[3] See Nicholson (1996: chapter 2) for a discussion of the concepts of scientific theory and explanation and for a comparison of the application of covering law models in the physical and social sciences.

This type of argument by deductive subsumption under general laws ("covering laws") is one form of scientific explanation. An example of the application of universal instantiation to a debate in world politics is as follows:

> Democratic dyads do not engage in war.
> State A and State B were democracies.
> ∴ Dyad AB did not engage in war.

Given the deductive form, the explanandum must be true if the explanans are true.[4] However, in scientific explanation the truth of the explanans is determined through observational evidence. In other words, the argument above may be deductively valid but empirically false, if either of the explanans is false.[5]

Universal laws

Deductive–nomological explanations possess a structure whereby the explanandum follows logically from the explanans by universal instantiation. According to this model, an event is explained by subsumption under a universal (or "covering") law. The laws in deductive–nomological explanations must be statements of universal form which assert a uniform connection between aspects of an empirical phenomenon or between different phenomena (Popper 1959:69; Hempel 1966:51,54; Braithwaite 1953:9). Both the explanandum (conclusion) and the minor premise (specific case) of the explanans are simply particular examples of the universal (covering) law.

In sum, a universal law is a statement which specifies a set of conditions for a subject class that, if present, will invariably hold for conditions of any member of that class. Since scientific explanations based on the deductive–nomothetic model must not only possess logical (internal) validity but must also be true (possess external or

---

[4] Explanation and prediction are tightly connected with the deductive–nomothetic model. If there is a general law and a specific case or condition falling under the subject class of that law, then predictions of events which are subsumed under the subject class of the law can be established. For example, a prediction based on the previous deductive–nomothetic explanation would take this form:

> Democratic dyads do not engage in war.
> State A and State B are democracies.
> ∴ Dyad AB will not engage in war.

[5] See Russett (1995), Layne (1995), and Spiro (1995) debating this issue on the democratic peace proposition.

empirical validity), the universal law and minor premise of the explanans must be testable-in-principle.

Probabilistic explanation

Not all scientific explanations are of deductive form incorporating universal laws (Hempel 1966:58–59; Reichenbach 1951:233). The deductive–nomothetic model of explanation where the explanandum is invariably true given the truth of the explanans (which contains a universal law) is but one model of scientific explanation. Another form of explanation is probabilistic. In contrast to deductive–nomothetic explanation, with probabilistic explanation the explanandum is not deductively subsumed within the explanans. More specifically, with probabilistic explanations the explanans might be true but the explanandum false. In the probabilistic model, the explanans identifies a tendency or probability but does not assert a universal law, as in the deductive–nomothetic form. Hence, the explanans in probabilistic explanations implies the explanandum only with a certain probability. An example of the application of the probabilistic explanatory model to the debate over the democratic peace proposition is as follows:

The probability of democratic dyads engaging in war is low.
State *A* and State *B* were democracies.

——————————————————————————— [makes highly probable]
Dyad *AB* did not engage in war.

There are obvious similarities between the deductive–nomothetic and the probabilistic explanatory forms. Both models explain events by reference to laws. However, the deductive–nomothetic model employs laws of universal form, whereas the probabilistic model uses laws of probabilistic form. Deductive explanation implies the (internal or logical) truth of the conclusion with absolute certainty; probabilistic (inductive) explanation implies the truth of the conclusion only with a given probability.[6]

---

[6] Explanation and prediction are also closely connected with the inductive probabilistic model. For example, a prediction based on the previous inductive probabilistic explanation would take this form:

The probability of democratic dyads engaging in war is low.
State *A* and State *B* are democracies.

——————————————————————————— [makes highly probable]
Dyad *AB* will not engage in war.

For a discussion of the logic and philosophy of induction, see Swinburne (1974 *passim*). See Nicholson (1996:35–37) on the issue of prediction in scientific theory.

Probabilistic laws

A universal law is a statement which asserts a homogenic relation between different phenomena or between aspects of a single phenomenon that holds for all examined, unexamined, past, present, and future cases. It also implies the homogenic relation for counterfactual and hypothetical conditionals[7] which cover all possible cases. It is this structure which provides explanatory and predictive power to universal laws. A probabilistic law has a similar character. It asserts a probabilistic relation between different phenomena or between aspects of a single phenomenon that holds for any examined, unexamined, past, present, and future cases. It also implies the probabilistic relation for counterfactual and hypothetical conditionals which cover all possible cases. It is this structure which provides explanatory and predictive power to probabilistic laws.

The distinction between universal and probabilistic laws resides in form and in the resultant logics which they reflect. The former is an assertion covering all cases under the specified conditions; the latter is an assertion covering a given percentage of cases under the specified conditions. These two forms of assertion are logically different and distinct, irrespective of validity or evidence (Hempel 1966:66).

With deductive–nomological explanation the truth of the explanandum – based on the information contained in the explanans – is a logical certainty. With probabilistic explanation the truth of the explanandum – based on the information contained in the explanans – is not a statistical probability, but a logical (inductive) probability. Hempel (1966:67–68) argues that irrespective of whether or not a definite numerical (statistical) probability can be assigned to the explanandum, the support provided by the probabilistic law in the explanans is found in the logic of induction.

In sum, the distinction between deductive–nomological and probabilistic explanations resides in logical form. Deductive–nomological explanations of events rest on deductive subsumption under universal laws; probabilistic explanations of events rest on inductive subsumption under probabilistic laws. It is logical form (and the weaker conclusions of induction) that constitutes the principal difference between the two types of explanation.

---

[7] See Guttenplan and Tamny (1971:327–328) for a concise description of counterfactual and hypothetical conditionals in logic.

Theory

Empirical laws – whether of universal or probabilistic form – may be explained by theories that refer to structures and processes which produce the patterns described in the laws. Theories attempt to explain these patterns or regularities and to provide a more fundamental understanding of empirical phenomena. Theories treat phenomena as manifestations of underlying forces that are governed by theoretical principles through which the patterns may be explained (Popper 1959:59; Hempel 1966:51,70).

Theories contain theoretical terms (internal principles) which have no empirical referents. They also contain observation terms which are empirical entities or properties that the theory purports to explain, predict, or retrodict. The connection between theoretical terms and observation terms is made by correspondence rules (bridge principles). These rules cross the boundary between the unobservable structures and processes of theoretical terms and the empirical referents found in observation terms. Without correspondence rules (or bridge principles), theories would have no explanatory power and would be untestable (Hempel 1966:72–75). It should be noted that theories may be of either deductive–nomological or probabilistic form.[8]

Epistemological critiques

In recent years, critiques of empiricist epistemology have become more common. Much of this criticism flows from the philosophical school of "scientific realism" (e.g., Harre 1970; Bhaskar 1978, 1986). In the field of international politics, two of the more prominent proponents of scientific realism are Alexander Wendt (1987) and David Dessler (1991). The principal thrust of the scientific realist critique is that "empiricist" (Wendt 1987) or "correlational" (Dessler 1991) science is incapable of producing "causal knowledge" (Dessler 1991:345). As Wendt (1987:354) argues:

> whereas the empiricist explains by generalizing about observable behavior, the realist explains by showing how (often unobservable) causal mechanisms which make observable regularity possible *work*.

In Dessler's (1991:345) view:

[8] See Hempel (1966:68–69) for a discussion on this point and for examples of probabilistic theories.

causal knowledge cannot be captured within the confines of the deductive–nomological framework. Causal explanation shows the *generative* connection between cause and effect by appealing to a knowledge of the real structures that produce the observed phenomena, and it is this generative connection that gives the notion of cause meaning beyond that of simple regularity.

This distinction between "causal" and "correlational" science attributed to empiricist philosophy appears tenuous. The goal of Hempel's epistemology is to produce theory which explains empirical regularity in the most basic and fundamental way, utilizing unobserved entities and processes as mechanisms. Theory, according to Hempel (1966:75) is composed of "internal principles" (unobserved theoretical structures and processes) and "bridge principles" (theoretical rules connecting the internal principles to observable phenomena): "Without bridge principles, the internal principles of a theory would yield no test implications, and the requirement of testability would be violated." Therefore, Hempel seeks in theory construction the use of unobserved structures and processes that will account for the observed regularities of the empirical world.

Perhaps some of the basis for the dispute resides in the sequence presented by empiricists for the development of knowledge. For example, Hempel begins at the level of empirical observation, proceeds to the generation of empirical (deductive–nomothetic or probabilistic) laws, and finally comes to the level of theory – explaining empirical uniformities on the basis of unobserved structures and processes. In Hempel's own words (1966:75–77):

> In a field of inquiry in which some measure of understanding has already been achieved by the establishment of empirical laws, a good theory will deepen as well as broaden that understanding. First, such a theory offers a systematically unified account of quite diverse phenomena. It traces all of them back to the same underlying processes and presents the various empirical uniformities they exhibit as manifestations of one common set of basic laws . . . The insight that such a theory gives us is much deeper than that afforded by empirical laws; . . . for the laws that are formulated at the observational level generally turn out to hold only approximately and within a limited range; whereas by theoretical recourse to entities and events under the familiar surface, a much more comprehensive and exact account can be achieved . . . At any rate, the natural sciences have achieved their deepest and most far-reaching insights by descending below the level of familiar empirical phenomena.

In short, empiricist epistemology appears fully consistent with theoretical (i.e., causal) explanation based on unobserved structures and processes. In fact, this view of the development of knowledge insists on it.[9]

Levels of analysis

The organization of quantitative, data-based research on factors associated with both the onset of war and its characteristics (e.g., magnitude, severity, duration, etc.) will follow a levels-of-analysis framework. Specifically, descriptions and evaluations of empirical findings on patterns and sources of war will be grouped on the basis of the analytic level of the unit of observation (i.e., unit level of the dependent variable). The levels of state (monad), dyad, region, and international system have been selected for this purpose.

The level-of-analysis issue in the study of international politics and war was raised initially by Waltz (1959) and Singer (1961). Waltz chose to approach the subject in terms of war explanations drawn from the analytic levels of the individual, the structure of separate states, and the structure of the system of states, whereas Singer's discussion focused on the two levels of the state and international system, with the explanatory level of the individual subsumed within the state level. Moreover, Singer explicitly distinguished between studies examining state-level (i.e., foreign policy) behavior and those studies examining aggregate patterns of behavior in the international system. In a later work, Singer (1970) speculated that state attributes, relational characteristics within dyads, and system-level attributes might combine in creating a potent source of war.

---

[9] Another epistemological debate involves the subject of paradigms in the study of international relations and the issue of incommensurability. For example, it is frequently maintained that the field of international relations encompasses three basic paradigms: political realism, liberalism, and Marxism. Holsti's (1985) analysis contains the implication that the paradigms are different and (to a greater or lesser extent) incommensurable. The issues raised in the broader debate include the testability of theory (i.e., can propositions only be tested within the context of their own paradigm), and the questions concerning the "explanation" versus "understanding" controversy (i.e., are there two distinct epistemological approaches to the study of international relations, one "causal" and the other "interpretive," or only one approach that melds the two). See Hollis and Smith (1990), Nicholson (1996), and Patomäki (1996) for discussion on these post-modernist issues.

War-prone states

If all states do not act similarly in similar situations, then perhaps variation in foreign policies is due to variation in their internal attributes.[10] According to this logic, states with the same critical internal attributes will evidence similar patterns of foreign policy behavior, distinct from the patterns produced by states with different attributes. Examples of war explanations based on the internal characteristics of states would include Lenin's thesis that the structure of a state's economic system determines its war behavior and Kant's proposition regarding the inherent peacefulness of democratic governments.

Specifically, Lenin ([1916], 1939) argued that states with competitive, profit-driven capitalist economies must pursue an expansionist foreign policy in order to secure access to new sources of raw materials, cheap labor, and external markets; a natural concomitant of an imperialistic foreign policy is conflict and war. Kant's ([1795], 1939) thesis that nations with democratic governments would be less likely to engage in war than autocracies – due to the involvement of the general population in war decisions and a reluctance to pursue a foreign policy bound to bring hardship and suffering on itself – incorporates a similar attribute-based logic. In short, these two examples suggest that state-level attributes affect patterns of war: the probability of war initiation should be higher for states with capitalist economic systems than for states with socialist economies (Lenin); and the probability of war involvement should be lower for states with democratic political systems than for states with autocratic governing structures (Kant).

The subfield of the comparative study of foreign policy was created jointly by the Snyder, Bruck and Sapin (1962) and Rosenau (1966) propositions regarding the relevance of the internal attributes of states to foreign policy behavior. For example, in addition to his discussion of the impact of individual (leadership) idiosyncracies, formal roles, and systemic factors on foreign policy actions, Rosenau included a set of dichotomous variables based on state-level attributes postulated to affect patterns of foreign policy behavior. The variables included:

[10] Many foreign policy (state-level) analyses (e.g., Rosenau 1966; Allison 1969) focus on the influence of individual idiosyncracies, governmental roles, organizational structure and process, and bureaucratic politics in foreign policy decisionmaking models. The issue of decisionmaking will be examined in chapter 2.

geography and physical resources, or "size" (large/small); level of economic development (developed/underdeveloped); and type of polity (open/closed). Rosenau hypothesized that the "relative potencies" of his five factors (individual, role, governmental, societal, and systemic) on foreign policy behavior would vary according to the permutations of the three principal attribute dichotomies. Initial attempts to proceed with the comparative study of foreign policy in a systematic manner followed this outline (McGowan and Shapiro 1973), but expansion of the salient attribute set followed rapidly.

The set of state-level attributes postulated to affect patterns of war is extensive. These include such diverse factors as population pressure, business cycles, national culture, internal conflict, election cycles, power status, number of borders, and level of militarization, to name but a few.[11] Empirical findings relating to war-prone states are presented in chapter 3.

War-prone dyads

War is a form of interaction between two or more states. In contrast to monadic-level studies, dyadic analyses permit the examination of relational factors for pairs of states that engage in conflict. For example, dyadic studies of war allow for the analysis of patterns of contiguity/proximity between contending states, capability differentials, paired regime-types, trade patterns, and arms races. In fact, two-party conflicts have constituted approximately 72 percent of all militarized interstate disputes between 1816 and 1976.[12] Therefore, the study of the war patterns of dyads and the factors associated with those patterns appears to be a promising level of analysis.

One issue of importance involves the population of states in dyadic studies of war. For example, some analyses utilize the entire universe of state-pairs (e.g., Bremer 1992). Other studies focus on distinct subsets of the universe, such as major power dyads (e.g., Huth, Bennett and Gelpi 1992). A third option, arising from recent empirical

[11] For a discussion of the array of ontological, epistemological, and methodological issues raised by state-level analyses, see Singer (1961 *passim*). For a discussion of the reductionism of state-level explanations of international politics, see Waltz (1959: chapter IV; 1979:18–20, 60–73). See Buzan, Jones and Little (1993:102–113) for a synopsis of the related "agent-structure" debate in international relations.

[12] See Gochman and Maoz (1984:595–599) for distributions in both dyadic and multi-state dispute participation and for a description of the militarized interstate dispute database.

work, suggests the importance of a subset population defined by long-term conflicts. These conflict-prone dyads, or "enduring rivals," account for a disproportionately large amount of the violence which occurs in the interstate system. Two analyses by Goertz and Diehl (1992, 1993) note that long-term rival dyads are responsible for roughly half of the wars, violent territorial changes, and militarized disputes that occur in the nineteenth and twentieth centuries. By another estimate[13] (Wayman and Jones 1991), enduring rivalries between 1816 and 1986 constitute approximately 8 percent of all dyad-years but account for almost 40 percent of the militarized interstate disputes which occur during that period.

The observation that long-standing conflict dyads[14] interact differently from either single-event dyads or "proto-rivals" (Goertz and Diehl 1992) has led to a number of empirical analyses on capability balances (Gochman 1990a; Geller 1993; Wayman 1996), on the effect of system structure (Huth, Bennett and Gelpi 1992), and on deterrence conditions (Huth and Russett 1993) for rival states. In these studies, enduring rivalries are treated as a "contextual" factor (Goertz 1992) which can affect the dynamics of arms races, deterrence, and war.

Moreover, the impact of past interactions on future choices and behavior is noted in numerous areas of study. For example, game

[13] Multiple definitions of "enduring rivals" with widely varying criteria have been established for the construction of databases. For example, Wayman (1982, 1996) defines an "enduring rivalry" as any major power dyad which engages in two or more militarized disputes within a 10-year period. Diehl (1985), and Diehl and Kingston (1987) define a "major power rivalry" as any dyad involved in three or more militarized disputes within a 15-year period. Gochman and Maoz (1984) provide a rivalry data set that includes all dyads which have engaged in a minimum of seven militarized disputes during the period from 1816 to 1980. Jones, Huth and Maoz (Jones 1989) design a database with more elaborate criteria – specifically, they stipulate that for an enduring rivalry to exist, the conditions of "severity," "durability," and "intensity" must be satisfied. These criteria cover, respectively: the minimum number of militarized disputes engaged by the dyad; the minimum time span between the first and last disputes; and the maximum time span between consecutive disputes. The databases constructed from these definitions and criteria vary in terms of total rivalries, number of dyads by power status, average number of disputes, average duration of rivalry, and number of wars. Goertz and Diehl (1993) provide a description of the various definitions and criteria used in constructing sets of enduring rivalries by Wayman (1982, 1996), Diehl (1985), Diehl and Kingston (1987), Gochman and Maoz (1984), and Jones, Huth and Maoz (Jones 1989), as well as an empirical comparison of the contents of these databases. Also see Goertz (1994:196–222).

[14] For a critique of numerically-based rivalry identification methods, see Thompson (1995).

theory suggests the importance of the distinction between single- and multiple-play (iterated) games in the selection of strategies (Nicholson 1989:30). The coercive bargaining theories of Kahn (1962, 1965) and Schelling (1960, 1966) also assume that actions in prior confrontations and outcomes of prior confrontations influence future behavior. Singer's (1963) model of interstate influence explicitly incorporates the past behavior of opponents in the decisional calculus of strategic choice. The same logic is found in Leng (1983) who demonstrates empirically the effects of experiential learning through his analysis of dyads which have engaged in multiple disputes and shows that in a context such as this, decisionmakers tend to choose the coercive level of strategy based on the outcome of the previous confrontation. Leng's work on bargaining during extended crises also indicates the presence of learning patterns.

These observations suggest that the analysis of dyadic-level patterns of conflict may yield important insights into the processes of war. Empirical findings relating to war-prone dyads are presented in chapter 4.

War-prone regions

Considerable variation exists among the regions of the world in terms of the temporal period of both state formation and economic development. The contrast along these dimensions between Europe, North America, and Latin America in one group, and Africa, the Middle East, and portions of Asia in another is striking. The modern European-centered state-system is generally dated from 1648 with the end of the Thirty Years' War and the Congresses of Münster and Osnabrück which produced the Treaties of Westphalia. The boundaries of the state systems of North America and Latin America were essentially complete by the middle of the nineteenth century and, as in the European case, have maintained their basic political subdivisions through the end of the twentieth century. In contradistinction, political independence for much of Asia, Africa, and the Middle East occurred only after the collapse of the European colonial empires following the conclusion of World War II. Moreover, the older regional state-systems of Europe, North America, and Latin America have adopted predominantly democratic forms of government, whereas many of the states in Asia, Africa, and the Middle East exhibit more authoritarian political structures. This distinction has led some analysts (e.g., Weede 1995) to predict a bifurcation of world politics between "zones of peace" and "zones of turmoil." Other scholars (e.g., Rosenau 1990) foresee a period of turbulence and instability that will sweep the entire world arena as the traditional patterns of interaction established among the older state-systems are undermined through increasing contact with states and nonstate actors from the newer subsystems.

Congruent with the pattern of early versus late state formation is the regionally defined temporal pattern of economic development. It has been argued (e.g., Wallerstein 1984) that international politics has evolved along with the gradual spread of the capitalist world economy. Those states that achieved high levels of economic development first (i.e., in Europe and North America) constituted a "core" which shaped the political and economic structures of peripheral and semi-peripheral areas (i.e., Africa, Asia, Latin America, and the Middle East). To the extent that political and economic structures of states influence foreign policy, then sharp regional variations in patterns of behavior should be evident.

A third factor – strongly related to temporal period of both state formation and economic development – involves the distribution of capabilities by region. For most of the history of the modern state system, major powers have been concentrated in Europe, with the United States entering the central system in the late nineteenth century. Because economic and military capabilities constitute the foundation for interstate action, distinctions in regional patterns of behavior due to capability differentials may be evident in data analyses. It should be noted also that the "shatterbelt" concept (e.g., Kelly 1986) postulates a source of war through major power involvement and competition in less developed regions of the world. The Middle East, portions of Asia, and Sub-Saharan Africa have been identified as principal twentieth-century shatterbelts.

Empirical evidence pertaining to war-prone regions is presented in chapter 5. The analysis will be divided between sections focusing on inter-regional war comparisons and intra-regional patterns of war relating to time, spatial heterogeneity, and contagion.

War-prone systems

The thesis that the structure of the international system determines the general patterns of state behavior (e.g., Waltz 1959, 1979) rests on the simplifying assumption that all states react similarly to the same external situation. The structure of the international system creates incentives and disincentives for certain types of actions and is a force that serves both to constrain and to induce specific forms of state behavior. This shaping of behavior occurs in two ways: through socialization (i.e., specifying appropriate norms of behavior); and through competition.

Waltz (1979:79–101) defines the structure of the international system in terms of three characteristics: anarchy, functional homogeneity of units, and the distribution of capabilities. He argues that these attributes account for the general patterns of power balancing (through arms races and alliance) that have been evidenced throughout the history of international relations. Of the three attributes of system structure, Waltz (1979:161–163) maintains that the distribution of capabilities is the most important for explaining periods of international war and peace. He bases this statement on the observation that this characteristic (the distribution of capabilities) alone has varied over time. Anarchy and unit functional homogeneity have been structural constants throughout the period of the modern state system. Therefore, if patterns of interstate behavior change over time, the change must be attributed to variation in the system-level distribution of capabilities.

According to this logic, changes in polarity, alliances (formation or configuration), and capability concentration[15] all should be associated with changes in behavior patterns (Singer 1961). Precisely what direction or form these changes should be expected to take in the frequencies or characteristics of war is a matter of debate (e.g., Deutsch and Singer 1964; Rosecrance 1966; Waltz 1967), but this logic has driven the empirical search for war-prone systems based on differences in the number of major powers, the extent and configuration of alliances, and the systemic dispersion of capabilities.

The empirical findings on war-prone systems are presented in chapter 6. In addition to factors such as polarity, alliance, and capability concentration, the effects of other system-level variables including borders, Kondratieff economic cycles, war contagion/diffusion processes, nonviolent norms, and intergovernmental organization membership are also examined.

---

[15] The concentration of capabilities in the system and the polarity (the number of major states) of the system are different measures of the systemic distribution of power. Capability concentration is a statistical measure of the aggregate inequality of capabilities as distributed among all major powers in the system. See chapter 6, n. 6 for an example of this type of measure.

Empirical patterns

Below is a list of consistent and cumulative empirical uniformities on war that have been identified through quantitative, data-based research. These patterns have been drawn from a review of over 500 empirical studies and are discussed in detail in chapters 3–6.

■ **Onset (occurrence/initiation)[16] of war**
Factors increasing the probability of the onset (occurrence/initiation) of war:

Level of analysis: state
- Power status (major power)
- Power cycle (critical point if major power)
- Alliance (alliance member)
- Borders (number of borders)

Level of analysis: dyad
- Contiguity/proximity (common border/distance)
- Political systems (absence of joint democracies)
- Economic development (absence of joint advanced economies)
- Static capability balance (parity)
- Dynamic capability balance (unstable: shift/transition)
- Alliance (unbalanced external alliance-tie)
- Enduring rivalry

Level of analysis: region
- Contagion/diffusion (presence of ongoing regional war)

Level of analysis: system
- Polarity (weak unipolarity/declining leader)
- Unstable hierarchy
- Number of borders
- Frequency of civil/revolutionary wars

---

[16] The Correlates of War (COW) Project defines an "international war" as a military conflict waged between national entities, at least one of which is a state, and that results in at least 1,000 battle-deaths of military personnel. Unless otherwise noted, the following definitions apply throughout the book to these terms:
War occurrence – A dichotomous variable indicating either the presence or absence of war for the unit of observation.
War initiation – The war initiator is the state that started the actual fighting or first seized territory or property interests of another state.

■ **Seriousness (magnitude/duration/severity)[17] of war**
Factors increasing the probable seriousness (magnitude/duration/severity) of war:

Level of analysis: state
● Power status (major power)

Level of analysis: system
● Alliance (high polarization)

Case studies

Two case studies – presented in chapters 7 and 8 – will be used to demonstrate the structural forces that influence the onset of dyadic and multistate wars. More specifically, the historical cases of the Iran/Iraq War (1980) and World War I (1914) will be explained – scientifically – on the basis of empirical uniformities established through large-scale, quantitative analyses. As Hempel (1966:68) notes, explanations of individual events may be provided through inductive subsumption under probabilistic laws, as well as through deductive subsumption under universal laws. These explanations will demonstrate that the cases of the Iran/Iraq War and World War I are specific instances of a set of patterns that have appeared in a much larger number of cases.

The form of covering law model employed in this analysis involves explanation of an event as a result of the conjunction of a set of strong empirical patterns. The empirical patterns are not interrelated deductively, but rather are treated as inductive generalizations which, additively, increase the probability of the occurrence of the specified outcome. In other words, an event is explained by subsumption under a set of intersecting probabilistic laws.

---

[17] Unless otherwise noted, the following definitions apply throughout the book to these terms:

War magnitude – The sum of all participating nations' separate months of active involvement in each war.

War duration – The length in months from the inception of the war to its termination.

War severity – Total battle-deaths of military personnel in each war.

Iran/Iraq War (1980)

The Iran/Iraq War of 1980 conforms to a set of probabilistic laws based on empirical regularities identified at the dyadic level of analysis. These two states: shared a common border (contiguity); had nondemocratic regimes (absence of joint democracies); were economically underdeveloped (absence of joint advanced economies); and evidenced an unstable military balance (a capability shift in 1979 and a transition in 1980). Add to this the classification of the dyad as an "enduring rivalry" (based on the frequency of its previous militarized conflicts)[18] and the existence of an unresolved territorial dispute (over the Shatt al'Arab waterway), and the occurrence of dyadic war with initiation by the militarily superior challenger of the status quo (Iraq) was a high probability event consistent with a broad array of empirical war patterns. Although the nonoccurrence of the event is not precluded logically due to the inductive form of argument, nevertheless the war may be considered "explained" by its subsumption under probabilistic laws.

World War I (1914)

World War I conforms to a set of probabilistic laws based on empirical regularities identified at the state, dyadic, and systemic levels of analysis. The states involved in the onset (occurrence) of the war were contiguous or proximate major powers (Austria-Hungary, Russia, Germany, France, and Great Britain); three of these major powers (Germany, Great Britain, and Russia) were moving through critical points on their power cycles; two of these major powers had an unstable capability balance (Germany and Great Britain had recently experienced a power transition);[19] three of these major powers lacked democratic political structures (Austria-Hungary, Germany, and Russia); and the international hierarchy was unstable with a declining leader (Great Britain). Add to this the classification of the Germany/France dyad as an "enduring rivalry"[20] and the highly polarized alliance systems (Germany/Austria-Hungary and Great Britain/France/Russia), and the occurrence of a war of enormous magnitude,

---

[18] See chapter 7 for a complete description of this rivalry classification.
[19] See Doran (1989) and Houweling and Siccama (1991, 1993) for pre-1914 major power capability balances and critical points. See chapter 8 for a complete description of these variables.
[20] See chapter 8 for a complete description of this rivalry classification.

duration, and severity was a high probability event consistent with a broad array of empirical war patterns. Although the nonoccurrence of the event is not precluded logically due to the inductive form of argument, nevertheless the war may be considered "explained" by its subsumption under probabilistic laws.

Conclusion

The summary at the close of the volume presents a recapitulation of the principal points and arguments found in the preceding eight chapters. The policy-oriented issue of the generation of probabilistic predictions of conflict in specific cases and the implications of chaos theory for prediction in this field are also discussed. As a final note, the element of human choice in war decisions is examined with regard to both structural forces and predictive indeterminacy, and is placed within the context of the development of the scientific study of war.

2 Decision models

Introduction

Wars follow from decisions. Therefore, any explanation of war must incorporate, explicitly or implicitly, a model of decisionmaking. Decisionmaking models are distinguished by their assumptions about rationality. The two alternative assumptions undergirding these models are, simply, the rational and nonrational. Nonrational models, whether focusing on psychological variables or organizational interests and routines, maintain that decisions are frequently distorted by systematic perceptual, cognitive, or bureaucratic biases. Although the definition of "rationality" is a subject of both philosophical and conceptual debate, minimal criteria for an instrumentally rational decision would include the logical requirements of consistency and coherence in goal-directed behavior. Indeed, Singer (1981:14–15, 1989a:14) notes that:

> the most important difference amongst the contending causes of war models is that of the foreign policy decision process. That is, each model . . . postulates a different set of decision rules . . . [A]ny explanation of war – systemic, dyadic, or national – must attend to the ways in which the putative explanatory factors impinge upon and are affected by the decision process.

Nonrational models focus on psychological or bureaucratic factors associated with individuals or organizations and often require detailed information on specific people or bureaucratic structures and processes, whereas rational models offer the simplifying assumption that psychological or bureaucratic biases have little impact and that decisionmakers (or decisionmaking units) all calculate in more or less the same way. For example, Waltz's (1979:118) structural theory of

31

international politics assumes that "[decisionmakers] try in more or less sensible ways to use the means available in order to achieve the ends in view." However, Waltz (1959:232) also notes that while the structure of the international system influences the basic patterns of foreign policy, it may not account for specific events. Explanations of singular events may require the incorporation of elements located at subsystemic levels of analysis, including factors associated with decisionmaking. As Jervis (1976:17) argues, the external situation among the major powers of Europe in the early twentieth century would have led those states into war at some point in time, but decisionmaking analysis is required to explain why World War I began in August 1914. For this reason, the descriptive study of foreign policy decisionmaking has moved toward psychological or organizational explanations of specific events in case studies, whereas the search for general patterns of war in the attributes of states, dyads, regions, or systems implicitly assumes a degree of uniformity in decisionmaking. In other words, accepting the simplifying assumption of rational decisionmaking facilitates the examination of other, nondecisional elements among the causes of war located at the analytic levels of the state, dyad, region, and system and permits these structural factors to be incorporated in a general explanation of war without reference to specific leaders or bureaucratic/organizational factors within governments.

Singer (e.g., 1981:15, 1989a:10–11, 1992:270, 1995:229), among others, is skeptical of the validity of a rational choice model of foreign policy decisionmaking. He argues that a more empirically accurate description of governments and their national security elements depicts them in terms of coalitions and subcoalitions of individuals with different or opposing priorities. The priorities themselves may stem from individual self-interest, the parochial interests of bureaucratic organizations, or discordant conceptions of the "national" interest. These incongruent priorities often result in individual and group preferences for different foreign policies and there may be no coherent preference function for the decisionmaking group as a whole (i.e., Arrow's Impossibility Theorem [Olinick 1978:186–190]).[1] Conversely, in rational choice theory the decisionmaking unit is assumed to have a

[1] See Bueno de Mesquita (1981a:12–18) for a rational choice theorist's response to this critique and Ray (1995a:144, 149–151) for a discussion on the importance of the "as if" assumption of a single, dominant decisionmaker. See Farkas (1996) for an explanation (based on evolutionary models) of how collective actors, such as states, can behave

single, consistent utility function of rank-ordered preferences on which a choice will be based.

Singer also discusses the occurrence of war as a result of a process of miscalculation. In one case (e.g., Singer 1990:11), threats designed only to intimidate lead to a series of increasingly coercive and escalatory actions and counteractions until violence erupts; in the other case (e.g., Singer 1958:*passim*, 1979:31–34), war is the result of a long-term process whereby some basic dispute or perception of external threat provokes a self-reinforcing hostility spiral between two states accompanied by increasing militarization, tension, and conflict. Although neither of these accounts necessarily falls outside of an instrumentalist rational-choice framework of decisionmaking, they nevertheless do emphasize factors that in a broader sense are "extra-rational" (Singer 1992:269–276).

This chapter will discuss cognitive psychological models focusing on beliefs and perceptions as well as on group dynamics that affect cognitive processes, and will offer prospect theory as an example of a decisionmaking theory based on psychological principles which influence the perception of decision problems. Organizational bias that results from bureaucratic routines or interests and which leads to nonrational decisions will be approached in terms of organization theory, with its focus on standard operating procedures, parochial interests, and limited capacity for innovation or change. Lastly, rational models of decisionmaking will be examined through an analysis of expected-utility theory – a formal model of rational choice under conditions of risk, based on the axiomatic principles of transitivity and connectivity among elements in a preference function, with expected-utility maximization as the basic decision rule.

Nonrational models

Decisionmaking theories based on psychological and social psychological constructs can be classified dichotomously: one category encompasses cognitive psychological models that focus on an individual's beliefs, perceptions, and cognitive processes; the other category encompasses cognitive models involving group dynamics.

rationally even though the individuals who comprise the actors do not follow the rules of rational choice.

Cognitive psychology: beliefs, perceptions, and cognitive processes

Decisionmaking models based on cognitive psychology are grounded on the supposition that there are limits both to the cognitive abilities of individuals and to the cognitive efforts that will be devoted to a decision problem. The operative principle in such models is one of "cognitive economy." In other words, the complexity of the world requires the use of cognitive devices to minimize strain and to maintain a relatively simple, stable, and consistent set of beliefs and perceptions. However, maintaining a system of integrated beliefs and perceptions often leads to systematic errors and biases in the interpretation of information. For example, Jervis (1976:239) suggests that certain events in an individual's history are likely to create subsequent perceptual predispositions. An event will exert a particularly strong influence if it: (1) was experienced firsthand; (2) occurred early in adult life; (3) had important personal consequences; and (4) is unconjoined with other events offering alternative perceptions.[2]

Similarly, cognitive models predict that information that is emotionally exciting or vivid will be afforded greater credibility than information with more substance but less emotional impact (Kaufmann 1994:563). Cognitive models also predict that information which is inconsistent with existing beliefs will tend to be misinterpreted or ignored because the restructuring of belief-systems comes at considerable cognitive expense. This tendency varies with the importance of the belief in the individual's cognitive structure. Core beliefs are protected more vigorously than peripheral or instrumental ones (Kaufmann 1994:563). The foundation for these hypotheses is the psychological theory of cognitive dissonance and the resulting tendency toward dissonance reduction. Specifically, Festinger (1957:13, 31) postulates that:

> (1) The existence of dissonance, being psychologically uncomfortable, will motivate the person to try to reduce dissonance and achieve consonance. (2) When dissonance is present, in addition to trying to reduce it, the person will actively avoid situations and information which would likely increase the dissonance.

Jervis (1968) offers a number of hypotheses on misperception based

---

[2] Jervis (1976:239–243) provides historical instances of this cognitive dynamic in the area of foreign policy decisionmaking.

on cognitive mechanisms that may bias foreign policy decisions. For example: (1) decisionmakers tend to shade new information so that it is consistent with their existing beliefs and images; (2) decisionmakers are likely to adhere to an established view rather than to explore new interpretations of events; (3) misunderstanding is likely when there is incongruence in the background of concerns and information between the sender and receiver of messages. In short, cognitive processes may seriously distort perceptions and bias foreign policy decisions in nonrational ways.

Cognitive psychology: group dynamics

Group dynamic models posit that intra-group pressures also can bias the interpretation of information and thereby influence policy choices. The underlying assumption of these models is that ego defense constitutes a principal force in human cognition. Stress and debilitating emotions such as fear and anxiety also can strongly influence cognitive processes and may produce defensive mechanisms designed to avoid or minimize the emotional conflict and pressure. It is generally maintained that such processes operate only when decisionmakers grapple with high-intensity choices that involve threats to critical values or trade-offs between values which cannot be attained simultaneously. In order to minimize the stress and negative emotions produced by such decision problems, small-group decision units will tend to distort information or simply deny the existence of value trade-offs or value threat. The greater the interests at stake in the decision problem, the stronger the bias in assessments of the situation. In short, the group-dynamic models suggest that critical decisions produce defensive avoidance of uncomfortable facts and result in reality distortion.

Perhaps the best known analytic example of cognitive bias due to group dynamics in foreign policy decisionmaking is Janis' (1972, 1982) "groupthink" model. Specifically, Janis (1972, 1982), Janis and Mann (1977), and Herek, Janis and Huth (1987) argue that defective decisionmaking (groupthink) results from a small-group dynamic to which crisis decisionmaking units are particularly susceptible. The individual-level ego-defensive mechanisms become reinforcing within the context of small-group deliberations and produce the following set of dysfunctional symptoms in crisis decisionmaking units:

(1) Gross omissions in surveying alternatives

(2) Gross omissions in surveying objectives
(3) Failure to examine major costs and risks of the preferred choice
(4) Poor information search
(5) Selective bias in processing information at hand
(6) Failure to reconsider originally rejected alternatives
(7) Failure to work out detailed implementation, monitoring, and contingency plans.[3]

Among the effects of groupthink on foreign policy decisions are a greater propensity for risk-taking and the creation of simplistic stereotypes of leadership groups in the opposing state.[4]

In sum, both the individual-level and group-dynamic cognition models suggest that foreign policy decisionmaking will not conform to standards of rationality, but rather will be biased in terms of information reception and evaluation as well as option selection.[5]

Prospect theory

Instrumental rationality is usually defined in terms of a preference function governed by the logical rules of "connectivity" and "transitivity."[6] These elementary requirements of consistency and coherence in preference rankings form the basis of such formal rational choice models as expected utility. Indeed, expected-utility theory (e.g., Bueno de Mesquita 1981a) has been widely applied in the analysis of war decisions. However, prospect theory (e.g., Kahneman and Tversky 1979) holds that psychological principles determine both the perception of decision problems and the evaluation of options, and that

---

[3] See Herek, Janis and Huth (1987:204–205) for a discussion of these symptoms.

[4] For an application of the groupthink model to deterrence situations, see Morgan (1977:60–62).

[5] Vasquez (1993:65) postulates that different "types" of wars will be characterized by different modes (nonrational or rational) of decisionmaking. Specifically, he notes that "wars of rivalry" (i.e., wars between states with approximately equal capabilities) are often preceded by a growing mutual hostility:

> This makes both sides willing to hurt and harm the other side as an end in itself, often with minimal regard to the costs. Conversely, wars of inequality are more likely to be governed by rationalistic cost-benefit considerations especially when viewed from the perspective of the initiator. Here decisions by the stronger to initiate war are more apt to follow the kind of cool, calm, and collected calculations described by expected-utility theory.

[6] In effect, the two rules mean that the decisionmaker has, at minimum, an ordinal (rank-order) preference function. See Zagare (1990:240–243) for a discussion of the elements of instrumental rationality.

these principles often lead to systematic violation of the rules of connectivity and transitivity.

As Levy (1992a:172–173) notes, expected utility is a theory of decisionmaking under conditions of risk. The principle of expected utility states that decisionmakers are expected-utility maximizers when confronted with a set of risky options. In reaching a decision, the expected utility of each option is calculated in terms of the summed values of the outcomes multiplied by their probabilities, with selection based on the option that has the highest weighted sum. However, a decisionmaker's risk orientation (i.e., risk aversion, risk acceptance, or risk neutrality) will also affect choice. For instance, if a decisionmaker has a choice between two options of equal expected utility, where one has a definite (certain) outcome of 100 utility points and the other is a gamble with an expected utility of 100 utiles (for example, a 10 percent probability of winning 1,000 utiles and a 90 percent probability of winning nothing), a risk-acceptant decision-maker will prefer the gamble, a risk-averse decisionmaker will prefer the certain outcome, and a risk-neutral decisionmaker will be indifferent toward the two options. In dealing with risk orientation at the margins, expected-utility theorists assume a specific, stable risk attitude. As a case in point, when dealing with conflicts between major powers, Bueno de Mesquita (1981a:124–125) assumes decisionmaking risk neutrality or risk acceptance. Prospect theory, however, posits that risk orientations *vary* according to estimates of outcomes as deviations from a reference point. Specifically, it is posited that decisionmakers tend to be risk acceptant with respect to losses and risk averse with respect to gains. Moreover, prospect theory also posits that a change in the "framing" of the reference point can invert a preference order between options.

Tversky and Kahneman (1986:123) use the phrase "decision frame" to describe the decisionmaker's perception of the options, outcomes, and probabilities associated with a given choice; moreover, they note that it is frequently the case that a particular decision problem may be framed in multiple ways. Although prospect theory holds that choices involving gains are often risk averse and choices involving losses are often risk acceptant (Tversky and Kahneman 1986:124–125), a simple restatement of a decision problem shifting the reference frame from loss to gain (or vice versa) produces an empirical shift in risk orientation among experimental populations.

For example, consider the effects of framing shifts in this summary of a decision problem posed by Tversky and Kahneman (1986:124) in an experiment:

> The United States is considering two programs for dealing with a new disease expected to kill 600 people. If Program A is adopted, 200 people will be saved. If Program B is adopted, there is a 1 in 3 probability that 600 people will be saved, and a 2 in 3 probability that no one will be saved. Which program do you favor?

Tversky and Kahneman report that the majority response (72 percent) in this problem – for Program A – is risk-averse decisionmaking. The prospect of saving with absolute certainty 200 people is more attractive than the risky prospect of equal expected value – a 1 in 3 chance of saving 600 people. The identical decision problem was then posed for a second set of respondents with a different reference frame:

> The United States is considering two programs for dealing with a new disease expected to kill 600 people. If Program C is adopted, 400 people will die. If Program D is adopted, there is a 1 in 3 probability that nobody will die, and a 2 in 3 probability that 600 people will die. Which program do you favor?

In this portion of the experiment, Tversky and Kahneman report that the majority choice in the second formulation of the problem was strongly in favor (78 percent) of Program D. This is a risk-acceptant selection: the absolute certainty of 400 deaths is less attractive than the 2 in 3 probability that 600 people will die. In short, a shift in framing has produced a shift from risk aversion to risk acceptance in the valuation of the identical options.

This example shows how the intrusion of psychological principles associated with the framing of decision problems might violate basic logical rules of connectivity and transitivity.[7] The issue becomes even more complex when one considers whether the reference point for a choice problem is set as the asset position at the moment of decision or at some previous point in time. For example, Levy (1992a:177–178) notes how choice problems in international relations often revolve around the framing of asset positions either in terms of the status quo or the status quo ante. The selection of the reference point as the status

---

[7] Zagare (1990:241) argues that even though the context in which choices are framed may in fact influence the order of an individual's preference function, rational choice models are not necessarily disrupted by this phenomenon. See Nicholson (1995) for a discussion of the significance of preference function stability to models of rational choice.

quo or as the status quo ante may alter the valuation of outcomes (as potential gains or losses) and thereby shift actors' behaviors between risk aversion and risk acceptance.

Organization theory

Organization theory contributes another nonrational model to the set of nonrational decisionmaking models previously discussed. However, organization theory does not depend on psychological factors to produce nonrational decisions, but rather focuses on organizational processes and interests that may run counter to rational policy.

Perhaps the most widely known formulation of how organizational routines and interests can influence foreign policy is Allison's (1969) organizational process model as developed in his analysis of the actions of the United States before and during the 1962 Cuban missile crisis. Allison focuses on the influence of organizational routines (or standard operating procedures) in providing information, defining problems, and presenting options to decisionmakers. According to this model, decisionmakers nominally in charge of the massive civilian and military bureaucracies are in fact constrained in their choices by the operating procedures and parochial interests of their organizations.

Allison's (1969:702) own summary of the effects of organizational process on decisionmaking is as follows:

> If a nation performs an action . . . today, its organizational components must yesterday have been performing (or have had established routines for performing) an action only marginally different from this action. At any specific point in time, a government consists of an established conglomerate of organizations, each with existing goals, programs, and repertoires. The characteristics of a government's action in any instance follows from those established routines, and from the choice of government leaders – on the basis of information and estimates provided by existing routines – among existing programs.

These routines are largely fixed in format, impervious to short-term innovation or change, and are designed to serve the parochial interests of the organization. According to this model, the stronger the influence of such factors, the greater the likelihood of nonrational behavior.

A recent analysis by Sagan (Sagan and Waltz 1995:52–55) on the effects of the proliferation of nuclear weapons from the perspective of organization theory[8] strikes many similar chords. He argues that decisionmakers intend to construct rational policies, but their information, options, and actions are shaped by powerful bureaucratic forces. Organization theory holds that organizations operate on the basis of: (1) limited (or "bounded") rationality; (2) routines and organizational rules rather than calculated decisions; and (3) self-interest and competition with other bureaucratic units. As Sagan concludes, to the degree that organizational processes and interests determine state behavior, "a theory of 'rational' state action is seriously weakened" (Sagan and Waltz 1995:54).

Sagan's analysis of the prospects for peace under continuing proliferation of nuclear weapons – when viewed through the lens of organization theory – is disturbing. Sagan argues that the behavior of many new nuclear weapons states will be influenced heavily by their military organizations, and that the biases, routines, and parochial interests of these organizations will result in deterrence failures and accidental usage of nuclear weapons irrespective of strong national interests to the contrary.

Rational models

Procedural rationality

Critiques of the rational actor model abound in the literature of international politics.[9] For example, Morgan (1977:78–79) discusses three conceptions of rationality (i.e., "perfect," "imperfect," and "sensible" decisionmaking) and concludes that governments generally operate along the lines of the third (and least stringent) model. However, all three of these models involve, in varying degrees, a conception of rationality based on "procedure." Procedural rationality suggests that decisionmakers follow a series of steps for determining the selection of options in the pursuit of goals. Morgan (1977:80) describes "perfect," procedural rationality in this way:

> The perfect decision maker starts with objectives that are attainable; he does not pursue the impossible. To come to grips with a problem in relation to those objectives, the decision maker generates or obtains essentially all the necessary information about it, his re-

---

[8] Also see Sagan (1994) on this subject.
[9] This is particularly true with regard to deterrence theory (e.g., George and Smoke 1974; Morgan 1977; Jervis 1984; Levy 1996).

sources for dealing with it, the alternatives those resources make possible, and the consequences and costs of each alternative. This in turn requires that the decision maker be able to define objectives clearly and rank them in order and degree of importance, so that costs and benefits can be weighed very precisely. From here the decision maker proceeds to a perfect decision – selection of the one best alternative that trades off gains and losses in the most satisfactory way.

As Zagare (1990:239) notes, analysts who describe rationality in this way usually go on to demonstrate how actual human abilities fail to approximate the level of omniscience required by this model (e.g., Verba 1961; Allison 1969). Factors impinging on perfect procedural rationality generally include misperceptions, psychological mechanisms which bias information reception and option selection, emotional responses, and so on. Other analysts (e.g., Snyder, Bruck and Sapin 1962; Braybrooke and Lindblom 1963; Hilsman 1964; Allison 1969) include organizational processes, bureaucratic politics, and domestic political pressures among the elements constraining procedurally rational decisionmaking.

Instrumental rationality

There is a second conception of rationality that is more limited than the image of procedural rationality. This is the concept of "instrumental" rationality. According to Zagare (1990:240–243), a decision-making unit is rational in the instrumentalist sense if it has "connected" and "transitive" preferences across a series of outcomes. Connectivity is defined as the ability to compare outcomes and evaluate them coherently. For example, if a decisionmaker is presented with two outcomes, A or B, connectivity implies that he will either prefer A to B, B to A, or be indifferent toward them (i.e., $A > B$, $B > A$, or $A = B$). An actor whose preferences do not conform to this rule of connectivity is not rational in the instrumentalist sense. The second rule – transitivity – implies that if a decisionmaker prefers outcome A to outcome B, and prefers outcome B to outcome C, he will prefer outcome A to outcome C (i.e., if $A > B$, and $B > C$, then $A > C$). If preferences do not conform to the rule of transitivity, then they are logically incoherent and the actor is not rational in the instrumentalist sense. In essence, these two rules mean that the instrumentally-rational decisionmaker has, at minimum, an ordinal (rank-order) preference function.

It should be noted that the concept of instrumental rationality says nothing about the normative aspect of a decisionmaker's preference function. It merely states that the preferences are logically consistent. As Zagare (1990:242–243) observes:

> the instrumentalist does not presume to offer normative evaluations of an actor's preferences, however bizarre, reprehensible, or ill-founded they may be. For instance, consider a leader who prefers systematic genocide to the benign neglect of a minority population. If his actions are consistent . . . with this obviously repugnant ordering, he is rational by the definition of the instrumentalist. The reason is manifest: as a scientist, the instrumentalist is primarily interested in theory construction, not in judging the ethical, strategic, political, or moral basis of an actor's motivation . . . The question of what preferences and/or perceptions an actor *should* have is considered not particularly relevant for developing explanatory or predictive theories of behavior . . . The individual decision makers analyzed by rational choice theorists can be, at one and the same time, rational in the limited instrumental sense, and irrational in the sense of the proceduralist. Thus, to the extent that subjective interpretations of the world are built into the models of the instrumentalist, such models could also be used to describe the behavior of decision makers suffering from cognitive closure, selective perceptions, misinformation and so on.

Rational choice models of international politics and foreign policy based on game theory and expected-utility theory are grounded in the concept of instrumental rationality.

Rational choice: expected-utility theory

Expected-utility theory has had wide exposure in the field of international politics (e.g, Bueno de Mesquita 1981a; Bueno de Mesquita, Newman and Rabushka 1985; Bueno de Mesquita and Lalman 1992). The foundation of the decision model is located in microeconomic theory which assumes that decisionmakers will attempt to secure through probability calculus the largest net gain available to them, based on a cost/benefit comparison of options, given the levels of risk associated with each outcome.

Bueno de Mesquita (1989:144) describes the core of expected-utility theory in terms of five conditions:

(1) Decisionmakers are rational insofar as they can rank-order preferences (rule of connectivity).

(2) The preference order conforms to the rule of transitivity.

(3) Decisionmakers are aware of the intensity of their preferences (with intensity of preference constituting utility).
(4) Decisionmakers consider options in terms of the probabilities associated with possible outcomes multiplied by the utilities associated with those outcomes.
(5) Decisionmakers choose the option with the highest expected utility.

This model can be placed in the context of a general decision problem of whether or not to challenge an existing policy (Bueno de Mesquita, Newman and Rabushka 1985:22–23).

The equation for the expected utility of a challenge is:

$$E(U)_c = P_s(U_s) + (1 - P_s)(U_f)$$

where

$E(U)_c$ = expected utility of challenging the policy
P_s = probability of successful challenge
U_s = utility of successful challenge
U_f = utility of failed challenge

The equation for the expected utility of not challenging is:

$$E(U)_{nc} = P_q(U_q) + (1 - P_q)[P_b(U_b) + (1 - P_b)(U_w)]$$

where

$E(U)_{nc}$ = expected utility of not challenging the policy
P_q = probability that the policy will not change
U_q = utility of the policy
P_b = probability that the policy will change with positive utility
U_b = utility of a positive policy change
U_w = utility of a negative policy change

The overall expected-utility equation is summarized as:

$$E(U) = E(U)_c - E(U)_{nc}$$

As Bueno de Mesquita, Newman and Rabushka (1985:23) argue, the above equation demonstrates that it is rational to challenge an existing policy when the expected gains from the challenge exceed the expected value of inaction.[10]

[10] For a general mathematical statement of this model, see Lave and March (1975:96) and Olinick (1978:218–219).

The most interesting application of this model is by Bueno de Mesquita (1981a) in an expected-utility theory of war initiation. In this instance, the challenge to an existing policy is military attack (initiation of war). Here, Bueno de Mesquita postulates that a necessary (but not sufficient) condition for war initiation is that the expected utility of victory should be greater than the expected utility of defeat.[11] In short, the overall expected utility of war initiation must be positive. The model is then expanded by incorporating the potential contributions of allies to both the initiator and the target. Lastly, a number of propositions are derived from the theory – some of which are counterintuitive (e.g., war should be more probable between allied states than between enemies). Bueno de Mesquita also provides an empirical test of hypotheses derived from the theory – using Correlates of War Project data from 1816 to 1974 – and reports strong empirical support for the model.

However, expected-utility theory has been criticized both for improper application of rational choice assumptions in foreign policy decisionmaking and for the statistical evidence adduced to support the model.[12] The criticism has been particularly pronounced with regard to some of the operational indicators used to measure elements (such as "utility" by alliance patterns) in the model. Nevertheless, expected-utility theory remains one of the most important constructs in the analysis of war decisions.

Conclusion

It has been argued that both rational and nonrational models of decisionmaking have roles in understanding the causes of war. However, due to extraordinarily high information requirements, nonrational models of war based on psychological principles or organizational interests and routines have primary applicability in detailed explanations of specific events.

---

[11] Also see Bueno de Mesquita and Lalman (1992) where in a game-theoretic framework both necessary and sufficient conditions for a set of foreign policy choices (e.g., negotiation, maintenance of the status quo, acquiescence without violence, capitulation following violence, etc.) are deduced and then tested through statistical and case-history analyses.

[12] For critiques of Bueno de Mesquita's theory of war initiation, see Zagare (1982), Wagner (1984), Majeski and Sylvan (1984), Nicholson (1987), James (1988), and Levy (1989b).

In contradistinction, rational models offer the simplifying assumption that psychological biases or organizational routines have minimal impact and that decisionmakers all calculate in basically the same manner.[13] For example, choice-theoretic models such as those derived from game theory and expected-utility theory both rest on the assumption that decisionmakers will attempt to maximize expected utility in their choices under conditions of risk. Predictions based on game-theoretic and expected-utility analyses have proven accurate in many instances,[14] and empirical tests of expected-utility models of war initiation using historical data have yielded impressive, though controversial, results.

Moreover, the simplifying assumption of rational decisionmaking facilitates examination of other, nondecisional factors among the causes of war located at the analytic levels of the state, dyad, region, or system. In other words, by assuming that all decisionmakers calculate in the same way, factors involving state attributes, dyadic relationships, regional characteristics, or the structure of the international system may be incorporated in a general explanation of war without reference to specific leaders or organizational processes within governments. Chapters 3–6 discuss the evidence of consistent and cumulative patterns of war as they relate to factors at these levels of analysis.

---

[13] One psychological characteristic of decisionmakers that has found its way into rational choice models is risk orientation (i.e., Bueno de Mesquita 1981a, 1989).

[14] Models based on expected-utility theory have been applied in producing forecasts of political events. An example of an expected-utility forecast of the outcome of the Persian Gulf Crisis (1990) is provided in Kugler, Snider and Longwell (1994). A list of published forecasts using this (and related) models can be found in Bueno de Mesquita, Newman and Rabushka (1996:appendix B). For an evaluation of the issue of prediction in foreign affairs, see Ray and Russett (1995).

3 War-prone states

Introduction

This chapter focuses on quantitative empirical research relating to the war-proneness of states at the analytical level of the state. The distinction between the search for causal factors associated with state behavior at the aggregate level of interacting units (dyad/system) or at the level of the acting unit alone (state) was initially described by Waltz (1959) and Singer (1961), and elaborated by Waltz (1979). State- and subnational-level factors presumably associated with foreign policy behavior include governmental variables such as political system-type, the distribution of influence within regimes, bureaucratic characteristics, organizational processes, and electoral cycles. Economic elements postulated to affect the foreign policies of states include the structure of the economic system, business cycles, level of economic development, and the pool of national capabilities that constitute or contribute to military and economic power. The impact of many of these factors on state-level behavior has been explored through the comparative analysis of foreign policy utilizing the Snyder, Bruck and Sapin (1962), Rosenau (1966), and Andriole, Wilkenfeld and Hopple (1975) analytical frameworks.

Issues surrounding rational and nonrational decisionmaking models have been discussed in chapter 2. As noted in that chapter, there is an extensive literature on the impact of psychological characteristics and cognitive processes of decisionmakers on foreign policy choices. In this area, factors such as perception, belief-system, cognitive dissonance, displacement, and the nexus between frustration and aggression are hypothesized to affect patterns of international conflict and war. For example, the impact of situation framing (Pruitt 1965; Kahneman and Tversky 1979), personality (Holsti 1962; de Rivera 1968), small-group behavior under stress (Janis 1972), and hostility spirals (Zinnes 1968; Jervis 1976; Leng 1980, 1983, 1984; Leng and Walker 1982) on interstate conflict all involve individual- or group-level psychological/social–psychological dynamics. The location of the principal explanatory mechanism places these works in the area of decisionmaking theory and their application in accounting for patterns of war depends upon selection between opposing models of rational or nonrational choice in foreign policy decisions. Typical of the early studies produced in the area of nonrational models are those found in the collections by Singer (1965) and Kelman (1965).[1]

This chapter will examine the findings of a range of data-based empirical studies which identify a set of national and subnational factors associated with the war-proneness of states (references listed in appendix 2, table A.1). The research has been classified on the basis of the following principal categories: national attributes, regimes, capabilities, borders, alliances, and status quo orientation. Many of these factors will reappear in studies at higher levels of analysis. However, the compilation, review, and evaluation of evidence in this chapter will be restricted to empirical associations between attribute-based measurements of states (or subnational structures) and state-level patterns of foreign conflict and war.

National attributes

The quantitative cross-national analysis of the effects of national attributes on foreign conflict and war has moved across an extensive range of independent variables. For example, studies have focused on the size and density of populations, levels of economic development, characteristics of national culture, and levels of social cohesion as possible factors associated with conflict and war. However, with few exceptions, the findings do not indicate a substantive association between the attributes of states and their tendencies toward war-proneness.

---

[1] An extensive discussion of the issue of rationality in international politics is found in Nicholson (1992).

Population

Although the size and density of a nation's population – and particularly a growing population that threatens to outstrip available resources – has been used as a political justification for aggressive, expansionist foreign policies, the data do not support such a relationship. Singer (1972) and Bremer, Singer and Luterbacher (1973) examine population, geographic area, and war data (Correlates of War [COW] database) for the European state system from 1816 through 1965 and report that the density of a state's population and changes in its density are unrelated to war.

A broader approach to the question of a linkage between national growth and external expansion is found in the lateral pressure thesis of Choucri and North (1972, 1975), and Choucri, North and Yamakage (1992). "Lateral pressure" is defined as the "extension of a country's behavior and interests outside of its territorial boundaries . . . and, in some circumstances, the extension of the boundaries themselves . . . The theory of lateral pressure is an explanation of the determinants and consequences of extended behavior" (Choucri and North 1989:289). The basic thesis holds that an expanding population and developing technological base create an increasing demand for resources that may not be sustainable without external sources of supply. These resource requirements produce lateral pressure that may manifest itself in an expansionist foreign policy. When multiple states respond to lateral pressure by external expansion, conflicts over territories may develop, leading to increasing military expenditures, alliances, and war. The argument is similar to the Neo-Marxist (e.g., Hobson [1902],1954; Lenin [1916],1939) thesis of war as a result of expansionist (imperialist) requirements of capitalist economies. Choucri and North (1972, 1975) attempt to test their theory using a simultaneous equation model for six European powers (United Kingdom, France, Germany, Prussia, Austria-Hungary, and Italy) over the period between 1870 and 1914. Their findings indicate that national growth was related to external expansion, military expenditures, alliances, and war. However, the strength of the coefficients for the different measures varies substantially among the states in the sample, and the validity of a number of the operational indicators has been questioned (Levy 1989b).

Economic development and business cycles

Levels of economic development have also been used as explanations for war; in this case, in opposing ways. For example, it has been argued that both advanced, capitalist states (e.g., Lenin [1916], 1939) as well as primitive, underdeveloped nations (e.g., Wright [1942], 1964) are expansionist and war-prone. Here, too, the evidence is not supportive of either proposition. Richardson (1960) finds no statistically significant correlation between levels of economic development and 300 deadly quarrels from 1820 to 1945. In two works involving Dimensionality of Nations (DON) data for 82 nations (1955) and 77 nations (1955–1957), respectively, Rummel (1967, 1968) concludes that the level of economic development is unrelated to foreign conflict behavior. The East and Gregg (1967) replication of Rummel's initial study reports the same result. In an analysis of a possible association between phases of the business cycle and war initiation (COW database), Thompson (1982) examines the patterns of four advanced nations between 1792 and 1973 and concludes that expansion and contraction phases of a capitalist economy are unrelated to patterns of war initiation.

War cycles

Singer and Cusack (1981) examine the possibility of "war cycles" in major power behavior. They offer plausible explanations based on economic, psychological, cultural, and demographic factors, but argue that detection of a cyclical pattern of state-level war involvement would be an important social scientific contribution independent of explanation.[2] In their analysis, Singer and Cusack examine the war participation of major powers between the years 1816 and 1965 (COW database). Their variable set includes: war intervals (the years between the termination of one war and the onset of the following war); war outcomes (winner or loser); and war costs (severity, magnitude, and intensity measures based on battle-deaths, war-months, and ratios of battle-deaths to war-months and battle-deaths to total population). The results of the study indicate no substantive evidence in support of the war cycle hypothesis. Other studies that test for

---

[2] Among the explanations for war cycles proffered in Blainey (1973:7–8, 91–93) are Arnold Toynbee's thesis of generational war-weariness and A.L. Macfie's trade cycle argument relating economic upswings to national moods of confidence and mastery over the environment and, hence, to war involvement.

national level war-to-war cycles in terms of either war-weariness or a positive reinforcement process include Singer and Small (1974:283–284), Bremer (1982:48–53), Garnham (1983:11), and Levy and Morgan (1986:46–47). The findings of these studies are consistent with those of Singer and Cusack (1981): there is no evidence of state-level war cycles, war-weariness, or positive reinforcement for war.

National culture

National culture is a factor that has been linked to foreign conflict and war, although the results of analyses in this area are mixed.[3] Three early studies (Cattell 1949; Cattell, Breul and Hartman 1952; Cattell and Gorsuch 1965) report the isolation of a stable factor of national "cultural pressure" that is strongly related to war involvement. The samples for these studies ranged from 40 to 69 nations for the years between 1837 and 1958. Rummel (1968) however, finds no substantive relationship between the psychological character of a population and foreign conflict for the 77 nations in his DON sample over the brief period between 1955 and 1957.

Domestic conflict

The search for an empirical relationship between levels of domestic conflict and foreign conflict or war has produced a sizeable number of quantitative studies. Rummel (1963, 1967) reports no substantive relationship between these variables in his two DON data sets (77 states for 1955–1977 and 82 states for 1955 alone). A similar conclusion is reached by Eberwein, Hubner-Dick, Jagodzinski, Rattinger and Weede (1979) who analyze the foreign conflict behavior (World Event Interaction Survey [WEIS] data) of 125 states for 1966–1967 in terms of factor dimensions of internal protest, violence, and coups. Their results indicate that of the 37 percent variance in total external conflict that is explained by these predictors, approximately 34 percent is accounted for by population size alone when this variable is intro-duced as a control.

However, Feierabend and Feierabend (1969), in a study of 84

---

[3] If religion is included in the category of culture, then it is appropriate to report Richardson's (1960:239) finding that "the C–T–B [Confucianism–Taoism–Buddhism] religion of China stands out conspicuously as being either itself a pacifier, or else associated with one." However, as Wilkinson (1980:119) notes in this example, although it is possible to identify cases of cultural disarmament, a pacifistic culture may invite aggression.

nations for the years between 1955 and 1961, find support for the linkage. Wilkenfeld (1969, 1971) examines evidence for the postulated association using DON data for a sample of 74 nations over the period between 1955 and 1960 and, additionally, subcategorizes his sample by regime-type (personalist, centrist, and polyarchic). His results indicate a set of positive relationships between domestic unrest and forms of foreign conflict behavior for certain types of political structure. Using the same data source (WEIS), Vincent (1981) examines foreign conflict vectors of 128 states over the years 1963 to 1967 for a possible relationship with a factor dimension of domestic turmoil. He reports a statistically significant correlation between these two dimensions and concludes that the level of a state's internal stability may be a useful predictor of its level of foreign conflict behavior. Geller (1985) examines a set of domestic and foreign conflict variables (Comparative Research on the Events of Nations [CREON] data) for 36 states between 1959 and 1968 and concludes that nations exhibiting high levels of internal instability are more likely to engage in conflictual foreign policies than are nations with lower levels of instability. In sum, the evidence for a linkage between domestic and foreign conflict is, at this point, suggestive but not conclusive.

Interactive effects

In studies examining the impact of "sets" of national attributes for interactive effects on foreign conflict and war, the findings generally have not shown a substantive linkage. Using WEIS data, Salmore and Hermann (1969) report negligible interactive effects on foreign conflict behavior for measures of size, economic development, and regime accountability for 76 nations between 1966 and 1967. Similarly, Rummel (1969) notes no statistically significant correlation between size, economic development, population density, political system-type, or Catholic culture, and foreign conflict. East (1973), using CREON data for 32 states between the years 1959 and 1968, reports substantive interactive effects for size and development on foreign conflict: large, developing nations had the highest percentages of conflict behavior, whereas small, developing states had the lowest percentages. However, Vincent, Baker, Gagnon, Hamm and Reilly (1973) report minimal interactive effects for a set of national attributes on foreign conflict. Finally, Duval and Thompson (1980), using WEIS data for 147 states between the years 1966 and 1969, conclude that population size, economic size, geographic size, military size, and economic development are unrelated to proportions of foreign conflict behavior.

Summary

There is little supportive evidence of a connection between these national attributes and foreign conflict behavior or war. With the possible exception of the linkage between internal and external conflict, measures of population size and density, geographic size, economic development, business cycles, and national culture appear to be unrelated to monadic-level foreign conflict. There is also no evidence supporting a national-level war cycle hypothesis. The sole exception in the set of national attributes involves a possible linkage between levels of domestic and foreign conflict. Reasons for such a connection run the gamut from government attempts to divert mass discontent against external targets (e.g., Wright [1942], 1964), foreign intervention or attack on a state undergoing violent formation or transformation (e.g., Denton 1965), domestic violence resulting from an unpopular foreign war (e.g., Denton 1965), to a general systems theory proposition involving system tension and adjustment (e.g., Hazlewood 1973). However, a strong and consistent empirical association between internal and external conflict has not been established.[4]

Regimes

A substantial body of evidence has accumulated on the topic of regime characteristics and war. While most of the research in this area

---

[4] In an essay on the causal connection between internal and external conflict, Starr (1994) lists deficiencies in this area of study in terms of theory, logic, and research design. He proposes a reformulated approach based on what he terms "the common logic" in calculations of decisionmakers who must "simultaneously deal with domestic and foreign threats to security" and suggests that explanations of the linkage must incorporate a decisionmaker's assessment of his "government's capacities and the distribution of capacities across other actors in the system, and how that distribution affects willingness to initiate violence" (Starr 1994:501–502). Starr concludes his essay by noting a study by Wallensteen and Axell (1993) which identifies the occurrence of 82 armed conflicts for the global system in the period between 1989 and 1992, and he argues that a link between revolution and war is evident in 40 of the 82 cases. In a provocative analysis, Gelpi (1996:36) presents evidence that only *democracies* initiate the use of major force in an effort to divert attention away from domestic problems, whereas *authoritarian* states become less likely to initiate the use of force when confronted with domestic unrest "as they turn their assets inward toward the task of forceful repression." Also see Levy (1989a) on this general subject.

has focused on the issue of the war-proneness of democratic and autocratic regimes, other factors that have been explored include the effects of government centralization, bureaucratic attributes, election cycles, and type of regime formation. The following discussion involves the impact of regime characteristics on foreign conflict and war at the level of the monad.

Government centralization

It has been hypothesized that the degree of government centralization will vary positively with foreign conflict and war. Wright ([1942], 1964) reports that highly centralized governments are more likely war participants than are decentralized governments, and that the process of centralizing or decentralizing will also influence war involvement. Similarly, Gregg and Banks (1965), using data from *A Cross-Polity Survey* for 115 states for 1963, report that the stronger the degree of executive leadership the greater the tendency toward both diplomatic and violent foreign conflict.

Bureaucratic attributes

Brady and Kegley (1977), using CREON Project data for 35 nations covering yearly quarters (three-month segments) between 1959 and 1968, examine the state-level hostility/friendliness balance (which they call "affect") in terms of a set of bureaucratic attributes. Their findings suggest that affect varies positively with the age of the bureaucratic organization, the extent of intra-governmental bargaining, and requirements for higher authority policy approval, and negatively with decisionmaking participation by the head of state.

Election cycles

The question of whether war involvement of democratic states is affected by election cycles is examined by Gaubatz (1991). Using COW data for war participations of democratic nations during the period between 1816 and 1980, he concludes that the frequency of war *initiation* by democratic states is unrelated to the phase of the election cycle, but that there is a significant tendency for these nations to *enter* wars during the earlier – rather than later – phases of their election cycles. Gaubatz suggests that the latter finding (lesser war involvement in the final phases of the election cycle) may be due to the leadership's fear of punishment at the polls as an election approaches.

Evidence of a less extensive type – relating only to the United States

– is presented by Stoll (1984), Russett (1990a), and Nincic (1990). Stoll examines the use of military force by the United States in presidential reelection years (i.e., with an incumbent seeking an additional term). The temporal period for the analysis is 1947–1982, and the data sources on the use of military force are a combination of the events reported in Blechman and Kaplan (1978) and in the *Strategic Survey* (International Institute for Strategic Studies). Stoll reports a statistically significant correlation indicating fewer visible uses of force in presidential reelection years (absent an ongoing conflict).

Russett (1990a) explores a possible interaction between elections, economic conditions, and involvement in interstate disputes, with the analysis focusing on the United States for the period 1853–1976 (Militarized Interstate Dispute [MID] database). He reports that participation in an interstate dispute "is more likely in the year of a presidential than a congressional election and more likely in either than in a nonelection year." He also notes that over 85 percent of presidential election years preceded by weak economic performance were accompanied by United States involvement in militarized disputes, whereas only 50 percent of nonelection years preceded by strong economic performance were accompanied by dispute involvement. Russett concludes that a combination of elections and economic performance affects United States dispute involvement.

Nincic (1990) tests the more limited hypothesis that United States policy toward the Soviet Union was largely shaped by electoral considerations rather than by the nature of the Soviet threat. His data cover the years between 1955 and 1988, and he examines policy variables such as strategic spending, arms control agreements, and summit meetings. His conclusions indicate that in periods without impending elections, American presidents were less inclined to adopt confrontational policies toward the Soviet Union.

State formation/transformation

Maoz (1989) poses the question of whether the method of state formation/transformation (i.e., violent or non-violent) affects foreign conflict patterns. Using COW militarized dispute data for the years between 1816 and 1976, he finds a positive association between violent or revolutionary state formation/transformation processes and militarized dispute involvement: states formed through non-violent or "evolutionary" means tend to be less conflict-prone in their international behavior.

Democracy

Of all regime characteristics, the issue of democracy and war has been the most thoroughly researched – at both state and dyadic levels. At the level of the state, the accumulated body of cross-national quantitative evidence suggests that democratic regimes are neither more nor less war-prone than other regime-types. Early studies by Wright ([1942], 1964), Rummel (1968), Weede (1970), Russett and Monsen (1975), and Small and Singer (1976) all report that regime-type is unrelated to violent foreign conflict. However, Rummel (1983) reexamines the question in terms of "libertarianism" and foreign conflict and concludes that the "less free – libertarian – a state, the more violence it engages in" (Rummel 1983:67). This study includes the set of all sovereign and independent states for the half-decade of 1976 through 1980. In a later analysis dealing with the cumulative literature on the subject, Rummel (1985) reports (non-robust) support for this finding. Weede (1984) also reexamines the hypothesis using COW data for the years between 1960 and 1980, and reports that democracy and war involvement are statistically unrelated; moreover, he argues that the association discovered in the Rummel (1983) analysis is unique to that restricted five-year time period. Weede's results are corroborated by Chan (1984), Domke (1988), and Dixon (1989). Finally, Maoz and Abdolali (1989), using COW Militarized Interstate Dispute data for all nations for the years 1816–1976, report the absence of any significant relationship between regime-type and a state's conflict proneness.

Gleditsch (1994) questions this conclusion following an examination of the frequency of democratic war initiations as distinct from war participations. On the basis of his coding of war initiators, Gleditsch (1994:14) argues that democratic states "would appear to *initiate* violence very rarely, if ever, but if violence has started in some form, they are not averse to intervening or [escalating] the dispute." Nevertheless, he concedes that his evidence rests on weaker empirical grounds than that which is supportive of the democratic peace proposition at the dyadic level of analysis. Ray (1995a, 1995b) takes a stronger position on the issue and argues that the evidence supporting the conclusion that democratic states are as war-prone as autocratic states is less convincing than is usually asserted (e.g., Levy 1988, Gleditsch 1992). Ray cites studies by Haas (1965), East and Gregg (1967), Salmore and Hermann (1969), Zinnes and Wilkenfeld (1971),

East and Hermann (1974), and Geller (1985) all of which focus on "foreign policy conflict" and reports "strikingly similar findings, i.e., that democratic states have less conflict-ridden foreign policies than do nondemocratic states" (Ray 1995b:10). However, all of these studies use measures of foreign conflict which include actions other than war or militarized threats (e.g., protests, accusations, economic sanctions, diplomatic hostility, etc.). Nevertheless, Ray's analysis raises questions in the area of the "conflict-proneness" of democratic states (as distinct from patterns of war) that deserve further study. Evidence of a different type has been reported in a recent monadic-level study by Mansfield and Snyder (1995:6) who argue that states undergoing democratization "are more likely to fight wars than are mature democracies or stable autocracies." Their explanation for the statistical evidence suggests that democratizing states are belligerent due to the nature of domestic political competition following the demise of the previous autocratic regime: foreign conflict is used by elites to control the newly mobilized mass public. However, these findings have been questioned on the basis of the interpretation of significance levels (Weede 1996a) and improper research design (Enterline 1996).

Summary

Evidence regarding a connection between regime characteristics and war can be divided into two categories – regime attributes and regime-type. The former (attribute) category consists of factors inclusive of centralization, bureaucracy, election cycle, and formation/ transformation. Results in this area show consistent relationships between regime attributes and foreign conflict behavior. However, the imprecision of some of the concepts and the absence of replications precludes a substantive evaluation based on cumulative evidence. The case is quite different with regard to regime-type and patterns of war. Here, the weight of cumulative evidence reveals the lack of a substantive connection between the form of government and involvement in militarized disputes or wars. At the level of the monad, democracies are as likely to engage in war as are states with other types of regimes.

Capabilities

The power-base of a state as a determinant of its involvement in international conflict is a principal component of realist thought.

Whether conceptualized as military capabilities alone, or as a broader set of military, economic, and demographic capabilities, the power-base of a state has long been considered to be an important factor shaping foreign behavior. While many theories of international conflict and war focus on dyadic- or systemic-level capability distributions, there remains a substantial body of literature dealing with state-level capabilities. Within the area of state-level analyses, studies have coalesced around the factors of power status, militarization, military buildups and the power cycle.[5]

Power status

The earliest cross-national quantitative research on capabilities and conflict attempted to isolate possible differences in behavior between strong and weak states. Hence, the power status of nations was postulated to be a factor influencing conflict patterns. For example, Wright ([1942],1964) reports a positive correlation between state capabilities and belligerency. However, in a subsequent study, Rummel (1968) using the DON database for 77 nations from 1955 to 1957 finds no substantive relationship between national capabilities and foreign conflict. In contradistinction to Rummel, Weede (1970) – also employing the DON data (for a longer time period of 1955–1960) and utilizing different operations in measure construction – reports that state capability is positively related to verbal foreign conflict.

Two definitive studies on the subject of power status and war are by Small and Singer (1970, 1982). Using the original (1816–1965) and expanded (1816–1980) COW database, Small and Singer demonstrate that major powers are much more likely to engage in wars than are minor powers. Köhler (1975) examines the war behavior of 15 "imperial leaders" at different stages of leadership (COW database) to answer the question of whether dominant nations become less war-

---

[5] The terms "power" and "capability" are often employed interchangeably, although they are not synonymous. "Power" includes more than material capabilities, comprising the ability to exercise influence and resist the influence attempts of others. Moreover, different measures tend to produce different estimates of national capability. Some studies use single indicators such as Gross National Product (e.g., Organski and Kugler 1980), whereas others utilize multiple indicators (e.g., Doran and Parsons 1980). Arguments for the use of multiple indicators are presented in Singer, Bremer and Stuckey (1972) and Bremer (1980). Various approaches to capability measurement are discussed in Moul (1989) and Merritt and Zinnes (1989), and a comparison of single and multiple indicator estimates is provided in Kugler and Arbetman (1989).

prone after the loss of hegemony, and he concludes that once-dominant states become more peaceful following the loss of their leadership status. Bremer (1980), also using COW data, contributes to the evidence on power status and conflict by reporting that nations that rank high on a composite index of national capability (CINC) are involved in a greater number of wars and initiate wars with greater frequency than do lower ranked states. Eberwein (1982) in a replication of Bremer's (1980) study adds the finding that more powerful nations tend to use military force more frequently, and that power status alone accounts for over 60 percent of the variance in "joining" ongoing militarized interstate disputes. Lastly, Geller (1988), using the COW database on wars and battle-deaths, reports that major powers are more likely to fight severe wars (more than 15,000 battle-deaths) and less likely to fight moderate wars (between 1,000 and 15,000 battle-deaths) than are minor powers, whereas they are equally likely to engage in small wars (less than 1,000 battle-deaths).

Militarization

Studies dealing with the relationship between the level of militarization of a state and its foreign conflict behavior have also produced consistent findings. For example, Feierabend and Feierabend (1969) report a positive correlation between militarization and foreign conflict for the subset of highly developed states. Similarly, Weede (1970), using the DON database for the period from 1955 to 1960 and defining "militarization" by the twin ratios of military personnel to total population and defense expenditures to GNP, notes a positive association between militarization and both verbal and violent foreign conflict behavior. Kemp (1977), using COW and Stockholm International Peace Research Institute (SIPRI) data for the years between 1925 and 1939, also reports positive and significant links between state-level arms expenditures and international violence.

Military buildups

The evidence regarding military buildups and conflict does not fit this pattern. At the state level of analysis, Diehl and Kingston (1987) examine the rate of change in military expenditures (COW database) for a possible connection to the frequencies of dispute involvement and dispute initiation for a set of major powers. They conclude that military buildups do not affect a state's tendency to initiate or to become involved in militarized international disputes.

Power cycles

A final category relating to the state-level analysis of capabilities and war may be found in the power cycle thesis. Doran and Parsons (1980) posit that certain critical points in a major power's cycle of increasing and decreasing capabilities (relative to the major-power system's capability pool)[6] are likely to be associated with both the onset and the characteristics (i.e., severity, duration, and magnitude) of its wars. They maintain that states move through a general, cyclical pattern of capability growth, maturation, and decline. The pattern itself results from differential rates of comparative economic and political development due to: state variation in size and resource availability; temporal period of industrialization; and differences in productivity/efficiency levels. Four points on the evolutionary curve of a state – termed "critical points" – are important because they present a disjuncture between a "state's interests and aspirations . . . and its actual capability" (Doran 1983:425). Due to the shift in direction or rate of capability growth (lower turning point, rising inflection point, upper turning point, declining inflection point), the state must reevaluate its relative position, capability base, and foreign policy goals. Doran (1985:294) argues that the foreign policy stakes at these critical points are enormous – involving status, security, and power – and are therefore more likely to lead to war involvement. In short, the probability of war involvement increases for states passing through a critical point on the power cycle.

For the initial study (Doran and Parsons 1980), capabilities are measured by an index composed of five material indicators, with the population inclusive of all major powers for the years between 1816 and 1975. War data is drawn from the COW database. Doran and Parsons conclude that a major power's point on the power cycle is an important determinant of its probability of initiating war, involvement in war, and of the characteristics of the wars in which it engages. A subsequent study by Doran (1989) reinforces and elaborates the

---

[6] Doran and Parsons (1980:948, 954) identify critical points in a state's power cycle based on a state's share of the total resource pool available to all major powers at a given point in time. As a consequence, the share is a comparative property of each member of the set of major powers. However, as Houweling and Siccama (1991:643) note: "A critical point on a nation's capability trajectory is an absolute property of the nation concerned." Critical points, therefore, are classified as state-level predictors of warfare.

previous results, noting that 90 percent of major powers passing through a critical point on the power cycle engaged in war.[7]

Summary

At the analytic level of the state, national capabilities – whether measured in terms of military capabilities alone or a combination of military, economic, and demographic variables – reveal strong and consistent linkages to foreign conflict. Most notable are the distinctions among nations in power status and war behavior. Power status has shown a relationship to the frequency of war, the initiation of war, and the severity of war. The level of a state's militarization also reveals consistent positive associations with violent foreign conflict. The exception to these findings involves the rate of military buildups. However, in this area the most relevant results pertain to dyadic-level arms races rather than to state-level increases. Lastly, critical points on a major state's power cycle appear to be strongly associated with both war initiation and war involvement. In sum, the evidence regarding the salience of state capabilities to patterns of conflict stands in stark contrast to the evidence on regime-type: at the level of the monad, the type of regime has little impact on war behavior, whereas the power status, level of militarization, and point on the power cycle all appear to substantially influence the probabilities of a nation's initiation of and involvement in foreign conflict.

Borders

Two basic arguments pervade the literature of international politics on the subject of geography as a facilitating condition of war. One thesis holds that proximity provides the physical opportunity for war: wars occur between bordering or proximate states because short distances provide the opportunity for violent conflict (i.e., proximity decreases the requirement of military reach). The second argument is more complex, suggesting that proximity structures the "context of interaction" in such a way as to increase the probability of conflictual relations. In other words, proximity generates security problems and influences the perception of threats which may then lead to conflict. A

---

[7] For an application of power cycle theory to subwar crisis involvement, see James and Hebron (1993). See Vasquez (1993:118–119) for a discussion of the importance of leaders' perceptions in power cycle theory.

number of quantitative empirical studies have looked at these issues at the level of the monad.

Opportunity

The first perspective – that geographic opportunity (i.e., contact) tends to increase a nation's involvement in foreign conflict – is exemplified by Richardson's (1960) analysis. He concludes that there is a tendency for states to engage in wars in proportion to their number of borders. Similarly, Wright ([1942],1964) notes that "geographic frontiers" are often the location of conflict, and that peace may be promoted by the creation of buffer zones. Weede (1970) reports that his analysis, using the DON database of 59 nations for the years between 1955 and 1960, indicates a positive correlation for contiguity (number of borders) and violent foreign conflict. However, Rummel's (1972) 236-variable factor analysis for the years 1955 to 1957 produces ambiguous results for the contiguity hypothesis. The loading for number of borders on the foreign conflict factor is positive but extremely low.

Context of interaction

The second perspective – that proximity establishes a context of interaction which enhances the motivations for war – is exemplified by the work of Starr and Most (1976, 1978, 1983). They argue that proximity increases the perception of threat (e.g., Herz's [1959] security dilemma; Boulding's [1962] loss-of-strength gradient) and that the security context of such interactions is more likely to lead to conflict. In their first study, Starr and Most (1976) analyze war participations over the years 1946 through 1965 and find a moderate positive correlation between contiguous land/water colonial borders and new war participations. Starr and Most (1978) provide additional evidence in support of the hypothesis in their analysis of 34 states over the same period using a different set of statistical techniques. They report that the average number of borders is significantly higher for countries which exhibit a "high" war-count than for "low" war-count states. In a similar analysis conducted for the African sub-system, Starr and Most (1983) note statistically significant results indicating that African nations with a "low" border-count were less likely to engage in war than African states with a "high" count. A study by Midlarsky (1975) is also supportive of this hypothesis. He argues that there exists a direct relationship between the number of borders for a state and its decisionmaker's level of uncertainty, and that uncertainty is associated with war. In his analysis of wars for the years 1815–1945 for COW Project central-system states, Midlarsky reports an extremely high correlation between the number of borders and the frequency of war. He concludes that – with a small number of exceptions principally involving common sea borders – almost all wars have begun across contiguous land borders or contiguous colonial extensions.

In the most extensive study on a related subject, Siverson and Starr (1990) explore changes in the probability that nations will enter an ongoing war if they have a warring state on their border. Employing COW data for 1816 through 1965 (and with the nation-year as the basic unit of analysis), Siverson and Starr analyze 3,749 cases – of which 94 involve war diffusion. Their findings indicate that the presence of a warring border nation significantly increases the probability of a nation's subsequent war involvement. Siverson and Starr interpret these results as supportive of the border/war-diffusion hypothesis by means of interaction context (i.e., alterations in environment [violence] affecting the decision calculus).

Summary

The evidence on the issue of borders and war is consistent.[8] Irrespective of explanatory model – physical opportunity or the context of interactions – there appears to be a substantive linkage between the number of borders and frequency of war at the level of the monad. However, as Bremer (1992:313) notes, these studies do not permit the conclusion that contiguity increases the probability of war between "a given pair of states [states that share a common border] because they do not demonstrate that the increased conflict involvement of states with many neighbors is directed toward those neighbors." This question will be examined in chapter 4 on war-prone dyads. The additional evidence relating to the presence of warring border states and subsequent war diffusion (involvement) conforms with the general findings on borders.

Alliances

States enter alliances for many reasons, both defensive and offensive. However, in general, alliances are engaged as a means of increasing a

---

[8] For a summary of the literature on geography and war, see Diehl (1991).

state's capabilities through external ties. Questions dealing with the conflict effects of opposing alliance systems, characteristics of alliances, and the extent of alliance in the international system will be discussed in chapters dealing with higher levels of analysis. In this chapter, the issue concerns the effects of alliance membership on a state's foreign conflict and war probabilities.

Alliances

Six analyses provide evidence of alliance effects on state-level conflict. In one of the first quantitative state-level examinations of the relationship between alliances and war, Singer and Small (1966) report that the greater the number of a state's alliance commitments, the greater and more severe its subsequent war involvement (COW database, 1815–1945). Weede (1970) examines the relationship between the number of military treaties in which a state is engaged and its foreign conflict behavior. His analysis employs the DON database of 59 nations for the years 1955 through 1960, and he reports a moderate negative association between the number of a state's military treaties and its verbal foreign conflict behavior. Kemp (1977) analyzes the possible association between state-level alliance patterns and international violence (deaths resulting from violent activity). Using COW data for the years 1925–1939, Kemp reports a positive and statistically significant link between state-level military alliance and international violence. Siverson and Sullivan (1984) produce an extensive study including all war participations in the international system from 1815 through 1965 (COW database) and their findings indicate no substantive connection between the number of a state's military alliances and its probability of war initiation, but do show a positive and significant linkage between the number of alliance ties and the probability of war involvement. Levy (1981) examines evidence regarding a possible connection between great power alliance membership and war over a period that covers five centuries and provides an interesting evaluation. From the sixteenth through the eighteenth centuries, over two-thirds of major power alliance engagements were followed by war, but in the nineteenth century, very few alliance memberships preceded war involvement. In the twentieth century the earlier pattern is repeated: six of the seven major powers end up in war following alliance engagement. However, Levy regards any strong inference from this association as spurious, and argues that alliance engagement was only a response to the anticipation of impending war. Hence, he concludes that alliance formation was not a principal causal factor in the onset of war.

In a study dealing directly with the war-diffusion effects of alliances, Siverson and Starr (1990) examine whether the presence of a warring alliance partner substantially increases the probability of a nation's joining an ongoing war. Drawing on the COW database (1816–1965), Siverson and Starr analyze 94 cases of war diffusion and conclude that a state with a warring alliance partner has a significantly higher probability of subsequent war involvement than does a state lacking such an external commitment. They note that this diffusion effect of alliances (unlike the presence of warring border states) is most likely due to a deliberate process of policy choice.

Summary

At the analytic level of the state, there appears to be a strong connection between the number of alliances and involvement in war. Although Levy (1981:611) notes that alliances are frequently formed in anticipation of war and that, as a result the statistical association may be noncausal, the pattern is nevertheless consistent and cumulative and may be considered substantive.

Status quo orientation

The orientation of a state's decisionmakers toward the status quo might be expected to have a critical impact on the probability of its initiation of, or engagement in, foreign conflict and war. Specifically, a nation that is satisfied with the status quo would be expected to engage in war only if attacked, and to initiate war solely under preemptive or preventive circumstances. In contradistinction, a state which is dissatisfied with the status quo might be expected to initiate the use of force whenever circumstances are favorable and nonviolent means for change prove inadequate. This logic is found in various studies focusing on the behavior of major powers (e.g., Organski 1958; Organski and Kugler 1980; Gilpin 1981; Modelski 1983), but it applies to minor powers as well.

Status quo orientation

Two quantitative analyses provide some preliminary information on the effect of status quo orientation on foreign conflict behavior. Wish (1980), using CREON data for 17 nations over selected quarter-year periods between 1959 and 1968, reports that a state's level of foreign policy hostility varies positively with the leader's desire to expand the state's territory (i.e., dissatisfaction with the status quo). Geller (1994) examines 43 rival wars which occurred between 1816 and 1986 using COW data, and notes that challengers to the status quo initiate 30 of these wars. Defenders of the status quo initiate 13 wars of the preemptive or preventive type.

Summary

Although little data-based evidence exists to date, the preliminary findings indicate that dissatisfaction with the status quo may be an important factor in patterns of war initiation and in levels of foreign policy hostility. Most explanations of war that incorporate status quo orientation relate the factor to the capability balance between challengers and defenders (e.g., Organski 1958; Modelski 1983). However, to examine the interaction of capability balances and status quo orientation requires a shift to a higher level of analysis. This issue will be discussed in chapter 4 on war-prone dyads.

Evaluation

Many of the state-level findings examined in this chapter are based on comparative foreign policy studies. However, serious methodological problems tend to inhibit the substantive interpretation of the findings of this research orientation. Specifically, the CREON, WEIS, COPDAB, and DON databases utilize highly restricted temporal periods – ranging from one or two years in the 1950s to approximately 30 years in the post-World War II era. Restricted time periods may produce unrepresentative results, as is indicated by the profusion of contradictory findings. Moreover, many of these event-data studies employ "dimensions" of foreign behavior as their dependent variables. Multiple ad hoc behavior categories are collapsed into dimensions indicating verbal conflict or cooperation and physical conflict or cooperation. As a result, the conceptualization of foreign behavior tends to be amorphous (e.g., large wars and small military demonstrations combined in a "physical conflict" dimension) and to lack comparability across studies utilizing different databases with different coding schemes.

For example, the initial WEIS database (McClelland and Hoggard 1969) was composed of 63 ad hoc categories of actions and responses (e.g., praise, assure, express regret, demand, warn, break relations, destructive act, etc.). These categories were subclassified into 22 more general behavior groups (e.g., approve, promise, agree, reject, accuse, seize, expel, etc.). Lastly, the behaviors were grouped into six broad categories of verbal cooperation, cooperative action, participation, verbal conflict–defensive, verbal conflict–offensive, and conflict action. The category of "conflict action" included, among others, these specific behaviors: nonmilitary demonstration, military mobilization, cancel planned event, reduce international activity, destructive act, nonmilitary injury, and military engagement. The initial CREON database (Hermann, East, Hermann, Salmore and Salmore 1973) contained 35 ad hoc behavior categories that were collapsed similarly into broad measures of verbal cooperation, physical cooperation, verbal conflict, and physical conflict. The "physical conflict" category included such behaviors as force, demonstrate, reduce relationship, seize, aid opponent, and subvert. The initial DON database (Rummel 1963) included 13 measures of foreign conflict. A factor matrix based on orthogonal rotation (producing uncorrelated factor dimensions) has the following measures loading highly on the "war" dimension: protests, threats, military action, wars, mobilizations, accusations, and number killed. Although the range of behaviors included in general categories such as "physical conflict" is immense, and the lack of correspondence between different data sets dealing with the same events is documented,[9] the careful utilization of the behavior categories with foreign policy events data can produce conceptually meaningful results.[10] Nevertheless, substantive interpretation of consistency and cumulation in findings on war and militarized conflict drawn from studies using these measures is seriously hampered by

[9] A brief list of works dealing with the validity, reliability, and comparability of the principal foreign policy events databases includes Burgess and Lawton (1972), Burrowes (1974), Hoggard (1974), Howell (1983), McClelland (1983), Merritt (1994), Peterson (1975), Rosenau and Ramsey (1975), and Vincent (1983). Recent studies discussing statistical methods to compensate for misclassification and censoring errors in the construction of foreign policy events databases (Schrodt 1994), the use of artificial intelligence programs for events datamaking and analysis (Mallery 1994), and deconstructionist/hermeneutic analysis of events-data descriptions of international interactions (Duffy 1994) have been funded through Data Development in International Relations (DDIR). For discussions of evolution in foreign policy analysis, see Neack, Hey and Haney (1995) and Hudson (1995).

[10] For example, see Goldstein (1991) on the subject of superpower reciprocity; Rousseau, Gelpi, Reiter and Huth (1996) on crises and the democratic peace; and Hensel and Sommer (1996) on rivalries and nonmilitarized conflict.

both the limited temporal periods of the databases and by the amorphous composition of the dependent variables.

There is little evidence reviewed here that suggests a broadly-based link between national attributes and militarized conflict or war. Population pressure, geographic size, economic development, business cycles, national culture, and political system-type appear to be unrelated to state-level involvement in militarized conflict or war. Perhaps the strongest findings relate to capabilities and war – specifically power status, level of militarization, and position on the power cycle all appear to affect a nation's probability of involvement in interstate disputes and wars: major powers are much more likely to engage in war than are minor powers, and they are more likely to fight severe (high battle-death) wars than are minor powers; high levels of militarization are also positively associated with violent foreign conflict; and major powers passing through critical points on the power cycle have an increased probability of war initiation and war involvement. Although methodological difficulties also impair state-level studies of the effects of borders as well as alliances on foreign conflict, the cumulative evidence points toward a positive association between both the number of borders, the number of alliances, and the frequency of war involvement. Reinforcement of these general patterns can be found in the results on the war-diffusion effects of both warring border states and warring alliance partners on the probability of a nation's joining an ongoing war. Preliminary findings also indicate that dissatisfaction with the status quo may be an important factor in patterns of war initiation and in levels of foreign policy hostility.

4 War-prone dyads

Introduction

This chapter examines quantitative empirical research that relates to patterns of foreign conflict and war at the level of the dyad (references listed in appendix 2, table A.2). Seven general categories of predictors are discussed in terms of the war-proneness of nation-pairs. Some of these factors have a substantial history in realist explanations on the causes of war (e.g., capability differentials, alliances, and arms races), while others have constituted cornerstones of liberal philosophy as elements associated with peaceful interstate relations (e.g., economic development, free trade, and democracy). Dyadic-level theory is more fully specified and elaborate than theory at the state level and as a result much of the current research in international politics is conducted at this level of analysis. In addition to the factors mentioned above, other elements included in this chapter that are postulated to affect the conflict patterns of nation-dyads include the proximity or actual contiguity of states, and the basic orientation toward the status quo as either challenger or defender. It should be noted that explanations regarding the effects of many of these factors utilize some form of decisionmaking theory (e.g., expected-utility theory) as discussed in chapter 2. However, as in chapter 3, the compilation and review of evidence will be limited to empirical associations between characteristics of dyads and their patterns of foreign conflict and war.

Capability balance

The relationship between capability distributions and war is a recurring theme in the literature on international relations.[1] Balance-of-

---

[1] Holsti (1991:158, 171–172) discusses changes in the conceptions of power over time

power, long cycle, power transition, hegemonic decline, and world economy theories all focus on the distribution of capabilities and shifts in these distributions as a principal factor associated with interstate conflict. At the level of the dyad, static (stable) and dynamic (unstable) capability balances can be analyzed in terms of static parity and preponderance, or dynamic shifts and transitions.

There is an extensive body of work in international politics involving the connection between static capability balances and war. At the dyadic level of analysis, two opposing theoretical positions have been articulated: "balance of power" and "power preponderance." Balance-of-power theory maintains that an approximately equal distribution of capabilities *reduces* the likelihood of war. This thesis rests on the logic that victory becomes problematic under a condition of relative parity and that the resulting uncertainty enhances deterrence and discourages aggression. A capability imbalance (i.e., preponderance) will tend to support aggression and weaken deterrence by increasing the probability for the successful use of force by the stronger state (e.g., Wright [1942], 1964; Waltz 1979).

This logic is rejected by the power preponderance theorists. Their thesis holds that the probability of war *increases* under a condition of relative parity. The logic of this position is that the likelihood of war is greatest when *both* sides see a prospect for victory, and that this condition is met when parity characterizes the balance. With the alternative capability distribution – preponderance – the weaker cannot afford to fight and the stronger usually does not have to in order to achieve its goals (e.g., Blainey 1973).[2]

An interesting corollary to the basic preponderance logic is offered by the power transition theorists who maintain that dynamic as well as static capability distributions are related to war. For example, Organski (1958), Organski and Kugler (1980), Gilpin (1981), Modelski (1983), and Thompson (1988) all focus on shifting capability distributions as a principal factor in the wars which shape the hierarchy of the international system. The general thesis suggests that great power wars are the result of unstable capability balances: the erosion of a dominant nation's relative capability advantage as a consequence of a

and how, from the nineteenth century on, power calculations increasingly concentrated on relative military capabilities.
[2] Wagner (1994), in a formal mathematical analysis, notes that each of these contradictory propositions (i.e., war is less likely if power is distributed equally / war is less likely if power is distributed unequally) is derivable from a plausible set of premises.

challenger's rising power trajectory increases the probability of conflict. This logic appears in the configuration of hegemonic decline
(Gilpin), long cycle (Modelski), and power transition (Organski)
theories. All of these formulations focus on a mechanism for war in
the operation of dynamic capability distributions which lead away
from preponderance and toward equality.

The basic arguments of Organski, Gilpin, and Modelski have been
supplemented by studies by Levy (1987) on preventive war, Wayman
(1996) on power shifts, and Gochman (1990a) on rapid capability
convergence and divergence. Conceptually, dynamic capability balances can be divided into two categories: shifts (capability convergence or divergence) or transitions (a reversal of relative capability
position). At the level of the dyad, factors internal to nations which
lead to changes in capability balances include those associated with
development (e.g., industrialization, urbanization, technological
advance, resource reallocation) and those associated with decay (e.g.,
decreasing investment, lower productivity, corruption). These processes influence the differential capability growth rates between
rising and declining nations and result in capability shifts and
transitions. Intricate explanations as to why dyadic capability shifts
may produce conflict can be found in Levy (1987) and Wayman
(1996). Most simply, however, either the possibility of advancing
national interests or a growing perception of threat to those interests
may be generated by closure or transition in relative capabilities
among nations.[3]

Most theories of international conflict and strategic interaction are
based on assumptions of rationality. Typically these explanations also
incorporate decisionmaker estimates of the relative capability balance
between belligerents. Indeed, many studies demonstrating an empirical connection between war initiation and subsequent victory
interpret the association as evidence reinforcing the rationality assumption: war initiators calculated the capability differentials and
expected to win (e.g., Singer 1972; Bueno de Mesquita 1978, 1981a;
Small and Singer 1982; Wang and Ray 1994).

For example, if weaker states initiate wars against stronger states, it
should be under conditions of relative parity (where contextual battle-

---

[3] Summaries of theoretical and empirical issues involving the effects of static and
dynamic capability balances on dyadic-level patterns of dispute initiation/escalation
and war can be found in Maoz (1993) and Siverson and Miller (1993). Also see Kugler
and Lemke (1996 *passim*).

field factors or first-strike advantages might seem to provide a decisive edge) or in response to a shift or transition (where capability closure [shift] or loss of position [transition] provide either a new option resulting from convergence or increasing pressure to preempt before further loss of position is sustained). In sum, these arguments suggest that static and dynamic capability differentials may evidence not only empirical association with the *occurrence* of war but with the *identity* of the war initiator as well.[4]

Preponderance and war

Balance-of-power theory (e.g., Claude 1962; Wright [1942], 1964; Waltz 1979) posits that the likelihood of war increases among disputants if one side possesses preponderant capabilities. Moreover, it is suggested (implicitly or explicitly) that the more powerful state will be the war initiator. At least partial evidence in support of the initiation hypothesis is found in Bueno de Mesquita (1980), who reports that initiators of interstate wars (COW data 1816–1974) are approximately twice as likely to be stronger than their targets. Although Bueno de Mesquita notes that expected-utility theory produces even more impressive results than a simple comparison of capabilities, he records that the capability-balance results are statistically significant. Siverson and Tennefoss (1984) also provide evidence in support of the basic hypothesis. Using data for the years 1815 through 1965, they examine both the initiation and escalation of international conflicts. Their dyadic-level findings suggest support for balance-of-power theory: few disputes among major powers (presumably equal in

---

[4] The risk orientation of decisionmakers is an element that logically impacts on the relationship between power distributions and war (Bueno de Mesquita 1981a, 1989). When dealing with conflicts between major powers, for example, Bueno de Mesquita (1981a:124–125) assumes decisionmaking risk neutrality or risk acceptance. Prospect theory (Kahneman and Tversky 1979) has been proposed as an alternative to expected utility as a theory of foreign policy decisionmaking under conditions of risk (Levy 1992a, 1992b). Prospect theory differs from expected-utility theory in positing that risk orientations vary according to estimates of outcomes as deviations (gains or losses) from a reference point. Specifically, it is hypothesized that individuals tend to be risk acceptant with respect to losses and risk averse with respect to gains. Regarding both theories, the introduction of the risk-orientation variable creates extraordinary measurement problems (Levy 1989b:234), especially in studies dealing with large populations over extended temporal periods. Within the expected-utility context, a simplifying assumption for large population studies is to posit that risk orientation at the margins conforms to a normal distribution, with risk-neutrality as the central tendency. See chapter 2, pp. 36–39, on this subject.

capabilities) escalated to mutual military action, whereas a much higher proportion of conflicts initiated by major powers against minor powers escalated to reciprocated military action. However, they also note that approximately 19 percent of the total conflicts involved minor power initiation against stronger states, and that over 25 percent of these escalated to the mutual use of force.

Equality and war

A greater number of empirical research studies provide evidence supportive of the parity and war hypothesis. An early study by Mihalka (1976), using COW data for the years between 1816 and 1970, indicates that the probability of a confrontation escalating to the level of military violence was significantly lower when the capability differentials between the disputants was high. More evidence supportive of the parity and war hypothesis is provided in a study by Garnham (1976a). Comparing "lethal" with "non-lethal" dyads for the years 1969–1973, Garnham reports that relative parity is associated with violence irrespective of whether power is measured by a composite capability index or by separate indicators. Weede (1976), employing COW and SIPRI data on contiguous Asian dyads for the years 1950–1969, concludes that war was much less frequent under a condition of overwhelming preponderance than in its absence. Mandel (1980) examines interstate border disputes for the years between 1945 and 1974 with Managing Interstate Conflict (MIC) data and reaches a conclusion consistent with that of Mihalka, Garnham, and Weede: violent border disputes were more likely to occur under a condition of relative parity in capabilities. Moul (1988), focusing on patterns of dispute escalation among the European great powers (COW database 1816–1939), reports that over 50 percent of the disputes under a condition of relative parity escalated to war, as opposed to a less than 3 percent escalation rate under an unequal distribution of capabilities. Kim (1991) also examines great power wars (COW database 1816–1975) and reports that the probability of war for major power dyads whose capabilities (including alliances) were equal is more than double the probability for dyads whose capabilities were unequal.

In an expanded analysis, Kim (1996) examines the interaction of dyadic capability balances, status quo orientation, and alliance relationships among great powers for the period from the Peace of Westphalia in 1648 to 1975. His findings indicate that basic equality in capabilities between great powers and dissatisfied challengers increases the probability of the onset of war. In the most comprehensive study to date, Bremer (1992) analyzes all dyads in the interstate system present in the COW database (202,778 nondirectional dyad-years) for the period between 1816 and 1965. Relative capability was determined by CINC (composite index of national capability) scores using the COW material capabilities data set. Bremer concludes that war is about 33 percent more likely in dyads with small or medium differences in relative capabilities than in dyads with large capability differentials. Lastly, Geller (1993) examines dispute-to-dispute war probabilities for a set of 29 enduring dyadic rivalries (COW database 1816–1986) inclusive of 456 militarized conflicts. This subset of all interstate dyads is the most violence-prone group of nation-dyads in the interstate system, and is responsible for almost 40 percent of all militarized disputes which occur during the period under examination. Geller concludes that static parity (measured by composite military capability) is roughly twice as likely to be associated with war in these dyads as is static preponderance.

Shift/transition

The corollary to the basic parity and war hypothesis involves dynamic capability shifts and transitions as a source of conflict (e.g., Organski 1958; Gilpin 1981; Modelski 1983; Wallerstein 1984). Organski and Kugler (1980) provide evidence in support of Organski's original power transition theory based on an analysis of dynamic capability balances. They report that differential capability growth rates (measured by GNP) that produce transitions in relative position within "contender" dyads are associated with war. In a more comprehensive study, Anderson and McKeown (1987) examine 77 wars (COW database 1816–1980) in terms of capability balances and report that an unstable military balance is associated with war. Houweling and Siccama (1988) provide a re-analysis of the Organski and Kugler power transition test using a more extensive set of nations (all major powers) and a composite indicator of national capabilities (instead of GNP). They conclude that differential growth rates that result in capability transitions are strongly associated with the occurrence of dyadic-level major power war.

The rate of capability convergence has been postulated in some studies (e.g., Levy 1987:97–98; Schampel 1993:397–399) as a key factor in the occurrence of war. Rapid approaches (Wayman 1996) and rapid convergence/divergence (Gochman 1990a) have been posited as exacerbating the conflict potential in rival dyads. It is argued that a rapid shift in relative capabilities provides little time for peaceful adjustment and may increase the sense of both threat and opportunity. Alternatively, a gradual change in relative capabilities allows more time for nonviolent adjustment to the shifting power balance. The evidence on the salience of rate of change is mixed: Schampel (1993:405) and Gochman (1990a:154–155) report results indicating substantive effects for rapid approaches on the probability of war, whereas Kim (1992:171) and Kim and Morrow (1992:917) report the absence of any statistically discernable association between war occurrence and the rate of capability change among major power rivals.

Focusing on conflict initiation (rather than occurrence) in militarized disputes, Huth, Bennett and Gelpi (1992) report significant effects for capability transitions on dispute initiation patterns (MID database) among a set of 18 great power rivalries for the period from 1816–1975. The findings indicate that the presence of a capability "transition" (defined as a military expenditure growth rate differential of 10 percent or more) has a significant impact on the initiation of militarized conflict among great power rivals. In a similar study, Huth and Russett (1993) analyze dispute initiation patterns (MID database) for 10 nondirectional enduring rivalries which appear in the post-1945 period. The study reports the substantively important effects of shifts in the military balance on the probability of militarized dispute initiation. Geller (1992a) analyzes the relationship between capability differentials and dispute/war initiation among the set of strongest nations for the period between 1816 and 1976 (COW database). The population consists of a restricted group of great power "contenders" with inclusion based on the possession of 10 percent or more of the capability pool available to the larger set of all major powers. The study examines 13 war dyads and 71 subwar dispute dyads and reports that a shifting capability balance within contender-pairs is substantively associated with patterns of militarized dispute initiation.

In an analysis of differences within dynamic balances for 29 enduring rivalries (COW database 1816–1986), Geller (1993) notes that capability shifts – and particularly shifts toward parity – are associated with higher probabilities of war than are actual transitions. These results are consistent for both composite capability and military capability indices. Lastly, Wayman (1996) analyzes a set of major power rivalries (COW database) and compares their capability and war patterns with nonrival dyads. He reports that the statistical association between capability shifts and war is stronger among rival states than for nonrivals, and that a capability shift within a rival dyad approximately doubles its probability of war – from 14 percent to 31 percent.

Nuclear weapons

As Siverson and Miller (1993) note, little systematic quantitative research has been conducted on the effects of nuclear weapons possession on dyadic-level conflict interaction. Organski and Kugler (1980) discuss 14 conflict cases where nuclear weapons were available to at least one of the belligerents. Their analysis suggests that non-nuclear opponents of nuclear powers do not appear cautious or restrained in their hostile activity. Bueno de Mesquita and Riker (1982), using COW data for 1945–1976, report that disputes involving both nuclear and nonnuclear powers were more likely to escalate to the "intervention" level than disputes between nuclear-armed states. They conclude that a system where all states possess nuclear weapons may be less dangerous than a system with partial possession. Geller (1990) analyzes the 393 militarized disputes that occurred between 1946 and 1976 (COW database) and concludes that dispute escalation probabilities are significantly affected by the distribution of nuclear capabilities. Moreover, the possession of nuclear weapons does not appear to impede escalatory behavior by nonnuclear opponents. This last finding is reinforced by three of Paul's (1994) case studies (i.e., China/United States 1950; Egypt/Israel 1973; and Argentina/Britain 1982). Paul concludes that nuclear weapons appear to have limited utility in averting conflict between nuclear and nonnuclear states.

Summary

The review of quantitative empirical research on the possible relationship between dyadic-level capability balances and conflict has focused on patterns of dispute/war initiation and dispute/war occurrence for populations of all interstate dyads, major power dyads, and enduring dyadic rivalries. The analysis suggests a growing and cumulative body of evidence pointing to the salience of both static and dynamic capability balances for the occurrence and initiation of militarized disputes and warfare. Specifically, conditions of approximate parity and shifts toward parity are consistently and significantly associated with conflict and war irrespective of population. Although broadly-based composite indicators of relative capability evidence these relationships, the most recent research is beginning to suggest the greater importance of narrowly defined military capabilities (e.g., Anderson and McKeown 1987; Geller 1994, 1998). The limited evidence to date regarding the possession of nuclear weapons suggests that conflict patterns between nuclear-armed dyads are different from those of nonnuclear dyads (no escalation to war), but that in nuclear/non-nuclear confrontations this type of technological superiority does not appear to accrue a bargaining advantage.[5]

Contiguity

Research at the monadic level regarding the positive association between the number of state borders and foreign conflict and war was discussed in chapter 3. However, as Bremer (1992) notes, these studies permit no strong inference about contiguity and war because they do not examine the identity of the opposing conflict-partner. Hence, their evidence on the issue of geographic contiguity and war must be considered, at best, indirect. This section will focus on the results of quantitative empirical studies of both proximity/contiguity and war at the analytic level of the dyad.

Proximity

The initial dyadic studies of geography and war examine differences in proximity of warring and non-warring nations. Using the COW database (1816–1965) Gleditsch and Singer (1975) report that the average distance between the capitals of warring states was significantly less than the average intercapital distance of all state-dyads for the period under analysis. Garnham (1976b) examines all dyadic international wars between 1816 and 1965 (COW database) using the distance between state capitals (proximity) as a predictor. His finding coincides with that of Gleditsch and Singer: warring dyads were geographically more proximate than nonwarring dyads.

---

[5] However, most nuclear/nonnuclear conflicts have not involved the survival of the nuclear-armed state. As Kissinger (1957:167) argued, a nuclear-capable power is unlikely to accept unconditional surrender or annihilation without using all types of weapons in its possession.

Contiguity

Weede (1975) examines the question of contiguity and the frequency of military conflict for a population of 3,321 dyads over the period 1950–1969. He reports that contiguous dyads with at least one major power and which had a latent territorial conflict were statistically more war-prone than dyads with other characteristics. Mihalka (1976) focuses on military disputes of the European state system for the period between 1816 and 1970 (COW database) and reports that the likelihood of a confrontation escalating to the level of military violence is significantly higher between contiguous nations. Moul (1988) also examines the dispute patterns of European states – however, he limits his analysis to conflicts among great powers. His temporal period covers the years 1815 through 1939 and he uses militarized interstate dispute data (COW database). In an unusual addition, Moul expands the concept of contiguity to include the borders of an alliance partner. Hence, "nonseparated" European great powers are either contiguous or tied to an ally contiguous to another great power (Moul 1985:252). He reports that of the 22 disputes which occurred between separated European great powers, none escalated to war; however, over 10 percent (6 out of 56) of the disputes between nonseparated great powers escalated to warfare. Moul concludes that contiguity (nonseparation) appears to be a necessary condition for the escalation of disputes to the level of war. Gochman (1990b) adheres to a more conventional definition of contiguity in his study of all interstate disputes occurring between 1816 and 1976. He reports that approximately 65 percent of the militarized conflicts during that period were between contiguous states or between states separated by 150 miles or less of water. Lastly, Bremer's (1992) study of all 202,778 nondirectional dyad-years for the period between 1816 and 1965 provides evidence fully consistent with the previous analyses. Bremer classifies dyads as either land contiguous, sea contiguous (separated by 150 miles or less of water), or noncontiguous. Bremer concludes that the probability of war increases significantly with the presence of either land or sea contiguity. If the categories of land and sea contiguity are combined, then the probability of war between contiguous states is approximately 35 times greater than the likelihood of war between noncontiguous nations.

Summary

The findings of research on proximity/contiguity and war are cumulative and consistent. At the level of the dyad, the distance between states is inversely related to warfare.[6] Proximate dyads are more likely to engage in war than are nonproximate states. The results on contiguity are even more compelling. War within dyads with a land or (narrow) water border is much more likely than between noncontiguous states. Explanations for this relationship vary. For example, Wesley (1962) argues that proximity/contiguity provides opportunities for conflict. Starr and Most (1976, 1978) suggest that proximity/contiguity structures the context of interactions (e.g., threat perception) and may promote hostile behavior. Vasquez (1993, 1995) argues that these findings are consistent with an explanation of conflict based on human territoriality.[7] Which explanation best accounts for the relationship remains to be established.

[6] See Gleditsch (1995) for a review of both the theoretical arguments and empirical findings on proximity/contiguity and war. Also see Lemke (1995), who provides an interesting approach to the identification of a population of dyads which are proximate enough in terms of distance and terrain to be potential war-fighters. He adapts the loss-of-strength gradient concepts of Boulding (1962) and Bueno de Mesquita (1981a) and defines an area in which each state can engage in military action. Lemke argues that potential war dyads are those in which the defined areas overlap.

[7] Rummel (1979:177) asserts unequivocally that: *"It is only attempts to change the territorial status quo by hostile states that risks violence and war"* (italics in the original). However, according to Vasquez (1993:124–125), the issue is less absolute: "a dispute over territorial contiguity is of *causal* significance in that its presence makes war possible and its absence makes war highly unlikely . . . [O]f all the possible issues that could end in war, issues involving territorial contiguity are indeed the most war-prone."

More precisely, the framework Vasquez (1993) utilizes to explain the onset and expansion of war involves a "process" or "steps to war" model. In identifying the causal sequences that precede wars, he begins by distinguishing between "underlying" and "proximate" causes. Underlying causes are fundamental causes that trigger a chain of events (the proximate causes) that results in war. He identifies territorial disputes between contiguous states to be the principal source of conflict that sets off the chain of events. The proximate causes involve foreign policy actions that escalate the conflict. Specifically, Vasquez argues that given a territorial dispute among states with approximately equal capabilities, the use of the methods of "power politics" (drawn from the realist tradition) increases the probability of war. Such practices include military buildups, coercive tactics, and alliance.

Hence, the probable escalation of territorial disputes to war depends on whether or not realist foreign policy practices are employed. Moreover, the tendency to use the foreign policy practices of power politics is affected, at least in part, by the nature of

Arms race

The study of arms races and their relationship to the outbreak of war revolves around the fundamental question of whether military competition serves as a deterrent or as a contributing factor to the onset of war. Definitions of arms races vary, but at base they must possess at least two general characteristics: unusually high growth rates in military spending or military procurements for at least two nations; and the existence of a competitive rivalry between the two states. Specifically, two hypotheses exist with regard to competitive military buildups and war. One proposition suggests that well armed states should enjoy deterrence against all but the most committed opponents, and that dyads characterized by military preparedness should be nonviolent under the deterrent relationship. However, an alternative hypothesis suggests that dyads characterized by joint military buildups suffer from perceived security threats. Minor disputes may easily escalate to major confrontations or even to violence when pressures to preempt are powerful. Hence, heavily armed dyads reflect a precarious stability that may be easily toppled. The following section will focus on the results of quantitative empirical studies of arms races and war at the analytic level of the dyad.[8]

Arms race

The principal empirical evidence in support of a positive relationship between arms races and war is found in the work of Wallace (1979,

the global political system. For example, Vasquez argues that if global institutions provide norms and rules for resolving conflicts peacefully, this will have a major effect on whether or not states resort to power politics. In short, preventing war depends on the presence (or construction) of mechanisms and institutions for settling disputes through diplomatic means rather than through the use of violence. In sum, Vasquez attempts to provide an explanation for the onset and expansion of war based on the combined causal effects of territoriality and the foreign policy practices of power politics (military buildups, coercive tactics, and alliance). The explanation is limited to a specific class of wars – between relative equals – which he calls "wars of rivalry" (see chapter 8, n. 1 for a discussion of this war typology). See Starr (1991) and Diehl (1991) for a review of the literature on geography and war.

[8] Richardson's (1939) formal mathematical model of an arms race between two hypothetical states (Jedesland and Andersland) is considered the classic work on the subject in the area of deductive modeling. See Intriligator ([1964],1969) for a discussion of the limitations of such reaction-curve analyses. Other examples of formal deductive arms race models are Intriligator and Brito (1984) and Majeski (1986). See Nicholson (1989) for a discussion of formal arms race models in international politics.

1980, 1981, 1982, 1983, 1990). Empirical evidence disputing this connection comes primarily from the research of Weede (1980), Altfeld (1983), Diehl (1983, 1985), and Diehl and Kingston (1987).

An early study by Huntington ([1958], 1969) focuses on 13 arms race cases that occurred during the nineteenth and twentieth centuries. As Huntington notes, these arms races did not always end in war. He argues that the competitive military relationship is a complex one and draws two conclusions from his analysis: (1) war is less likely to follow arms races which are qualitative rather than quantitative in character; and (2) war is more likely to occur in the early stages of an arms race rather than in its later stages. However, Huntington's study has been criticized for its limited case set (Joynt 1964) and for its misspecification of the causal sequence – some of the cases appear to include instances where the belligerents anticipated war and moved to prepare for it rather than where the race itself provoked the war (Mueller 1969).

The initial study by Wallace (1979) provides the first extensive empirical analysis of the relationship between arms races and the outbreak of war. He establishes two competing hypotheses based on military competition: (1) arms races increase tension, and tension leads to war; and (2) failure to match a rival's military capability creates opportunities for war initiation. Wallace uses a list of 99 militarized disputes between major powers for the years 1833 through 1965, and employs military expenditure data to identify nation-dyads with high-rate increases prior to disputes (COW database). He also creates an arms race index and divides the dyads into two categories – those engaged in a race, and those not engaged. Of the 99 dispute dyads, 23 of 28 arms races preceded wars, whereas only three wars occurred without arms races. Wallace interprets this evidence as supportive of the first hypothesis (arms races contribute to war) and unsupportive of the second hypothesis (arms races deter war). In subsequent works, Weede (1980), Diehl (1983), and Altfeld (1983) criticized Wallace's study. Weede notes that many of the dyadic escalations were associated with two wars (World Wars I and II) and were therefore not independent but rather the result of a diffusion process. Both Weede (1980) and Diehl (1983) analyze the same data treating multiparty disputes as single (combined) cases rather than disaggregating them, and conclude that arms races have only a weak relationship to war (Weede), or no relationship to war (Diehl). Altfeld's (1983) criticism of Wallace's study also notes the influence of alliances in diffusing races and distorting the results, and he adds a critique on the validity of Wallace's definition of arms races and their measurement. Altfeld reanalyzes Wallace's data with a higher threshold level for what constitutes a "race" and reports that due to problems in measurement, data, and interpretation, Wallace's conclusion that an arms race increases the probability of the onset of war is unsubstantiated. Diehl (1985) furnishes a subsequent study with a population of major power rival dyads and concludes that war occurs in the late stages of enduring rivalries irrespective of whether an arms race was present or not. Wallace (1980, 1981, 1982, 1983, 1990) produced additional studies which address the critiques of his previous work, and he continues to report findings supportive of the arms race and war hypothesis.

Summary

As Siverson and Diehl (1989:214) note, "If there is any consensus among arms race studies, it is that some arms races lead to war and some do not." Given the lack of consistent and cumulative findings in this area, it would appear that an additional factor (or factors) must be included in the model which will account for the incongruent results and permit the integration of arms race dynamics in an explanation of war.[9] Morrow (1989) attempts to solve this problem by developing a formal (expected-utility) model of an arms race and testing it empirically. He argues that arms races create transitory advantages that may be exploited; however, the risk orientation of decisionmakers on both sides will determine whether or not the temporary vulnerabilities will be challenged or resisted, with risk-acceptant actors more likely to initiate arms race wars. The data-based test involves 35 dispute cases and 17 core cases in which major power disputes were preceded by arms races. However, Morrow notes that the tested propositions are supported robustly but not strongly by the data.

---

[9] As a case in point, Vasquez (1993) proposes the additional factor of a territorial dispute. Vasquez argues that "rivalry wars" (i.e., wars between equals) begin over territorial disputes, with each side taking a series of steps that increases hostility and threat. He suggests that a military buildup (resulting in an arms race) is a tactic that fuels the dispute and increases the probability of war. Also see Vasquez and Henehan (1992:103–108) on the arms race debate.

Alliances

At the level of the dyad, research regarding a possible relationship between alliance and war has coalesced in two areas: (1) alliance within dyads; and (2) alliance external to dyads. With regard to the first area, conventional wisdom has held that alliance between nations reduces mutual conflict (e.g., Brzezinski and Huntington 1963:406). Whether based on common or complementary interests and objectives, it has been customarily assumed that allied nations might disagree on joint policy but will rarely engage each other in war, at least for the duration of the alliance. However, using expected-utility theory, Bueno de Mesquita (1981a) deduces the counter-intuitive proposition that war is *more likely* between allies than between enemies.

The second area of research has involved the impact on war of alliance external to dyads. Here, the issues focus on the number of ties to external blocs and their effects on dyadic conflict. For example, if one member of a dyad is allied with a bloc while the other member is unaligned, is war more or less likely than if both members of the dyad possessed external ties? These types of questions generally involve the viability of extended deterrence by superpowers, although some analyses deal explicitly with the aggregate effects of alliance on relative military capabilities for members of a dyad.

Alliance within dyads

Bueno de Mesquita (1981a:76–78) derives from his expected-utility theory the unsettling hypothesis that allied nations are more likely to engage in war with one another than unallied states and presents evidence (1981a:159–164) in support of this deduction (COW database). He reports that of the 76 war initiations that occurred between 1816 and 1974, 15 were among nations that had a formal, standing military agreement between them. These 15 wars between allies constitute approximately 20 percent of all wars in his data set, whereas allied dyads represent only about 7 percent of all annual dyads in the data. Bueno de Mesquita concludes that wars between allies are approximately three times more likely than would be expected by chance. Additional evidence in support of this proposition is provided by Ray (1990). Ray tests the hypothesis with more stringent coding rules and a refined COW database and reports that there is evidence of a positive association between allied dyads and conflict-proneness for the years 1816–1974: allied nations have been more likely to engage in both militarized disputes and war among themselves than unallied nations.

However, two studies (Weede 1975, Bremer 1992) report contrary results. Weede's (1975) analysis of military conflict among 3,321 dyads for 1950 through 1969 shows that common bloc membership (alliance) was negatively associated with war between members of a dyad. In a subsequent analysis, Bremer (1992) codes all dyad-years between 1816 and 1965 into four categories: defense pact, neutrality pact, entente, and no alliance. His bivariate results are similar to those of both Bueno de Mesquita and Ray: the conditional probability of war with the three types of pacts combined compared to no alliance is approximately 4.5:1. However, Bremer's multivariate analysis of the data indicates an interaction effect with the level of militarization in the dyad. Specifically, if the dyad is highly militarized, then the alliance coefficient indicates a significant, negative relationship between alliance and war probability. Bremer concludes that the absence of an alliance (in conjunction with other factors) increases the war-proneness of a dyad.

Alliance external to dyads

Alliance ties that are external to the dyad present a different though related research problem. Kim (1991) examines great power wars from 1816 to 1976 in terms of the relative capabilities of the dyads (COW database) and reports that war occurrence is related to the capability balance of major power dyads (i.e., parity) when alliance capabilities are included in the measurement.[10] The question of one alliance-tie external to a dyad is examined by Mihalka (1976) and Siverson and Tennefoss (1984). Mihalka employs the COW database covering the years between 1816 and 1970 for European state-system dyads. He reports that dyads with only one member in an external alliance were most likely to experience dispute escalation to the level of war and dyads with both members tied to external alliances least likely to escalate to war. He concludes that the probability of a confrontation ending in military hostilities is significantly higher if only a single dyad-member has external alliance-ties. Siverson and Tennefoss (1984) report a similar finding for dyads in the interstate system over the period between 1815 and 1965. Specifically, they report that disputes were most likely to escalate to war if one dyad-member

---

[10] Similar findings are presented in Kim (1992, 1996) and Kim and Morrow (1992).

possessed a major power ally while the other did not. In sum, a dyad with one external alliance-tie has a higher war probability than one in which neither party has any external ties.

The issue of two external alliance-ties offers some interesting contrasts. Weede (1975) reports that during the period between 1950 and 1969, dyads composed of a United States bloc member and Soviet bloc member were less war-prone than other dyads. This may be interpreted as reflecting successful mutual extended deterrence. Weede's (1989) results for subwar disputes also indicate conflict reduction for two-alliance dyads. Mihalka (1976), using COW data for the period 1816–1970 reports that confrontations between dyad-members where each possessed an external alliance were the least likely to escalate to military hostilities. Finally, Siverson and Tennefoss (1984) report that, for the period between 1815 and 1965, conflicts were least likely to escalate to the level of war where both dyad-members had external alliances with major powers.

Summary

The evidence regarding alliance within dyads and the onset of war is intriguing. Bueno de Mesquita, Ray, and Bremer all produce bivariate results indicating a positive connection. However, Weede reports that common bloc membership was associated with a lower incidence of dyadic war for the post-1945 period, and Bremer provides multivariate evidence which suggests that the direction of the relationship between in-dyad alliance and war varies according to the level of militarization of the dyad. Perhaps Ray (1990:89) places the issue in the proper perspective when he notes that this specific hypothesis is not terribly important in isolation. Intra-dyad alliance is not a major cause of war, even if the correlation exists. Rather, the importance of this empirical association relates to the validity of the theory from which it is derived (i.e., expected utility). To the extent that the counter-intuitive proposition receives empirical support, it increases confidence in the theory of which it is a part. In contradistinction, the evidence regarding alliance external to dyads and the probabilities of war or dispute escalation has more extrinsic meaning. The results here appear to be consistent and cumulative. Dyads where only one member has an external alliance-tie are more likely to experience war than are dyads where both members have external ties. Explanations for these different relationships may involve military balances as they are affected by the capability additions of allies, estimates of reliability of allies, extended deterrence by nuclear-armed superpowers, or a greater caution on the part of decisionmakers induced by the potential for a wider war. Additional research is required to choose among these alternatives, but whatever the explanation, dyads with one external alliance are more war-prone than dyads where both parties have external ties.

Regimes

A consistent theme in classical liberal political thought holds that democratic institutions reduce the likelihood of violent conflict, both in the domestic and international realms. For example, Kant ([1795], 1939) in *Perpetual Peace* argues that in democratic states the general public and public opinion will oppose war due to the costs the mass population would be compelled to bear. Hence, leaders who make decisions for war will be removed and replaced with more pacifistic individuals. Autocratic leaders, Kant reasons, do not hold power on the basis of elections and therefore are unconstrained in pursuing a belligerent or violent foreign policy. Waltz (1959) and Ray (1995a) note that similar arguments have been made by such diverse theorists as Jeremy Bentham, Thomas Paine, Georg Wilhelm Friederich Hegel, and Woodrow Wilson.

As discussed in chapter 3, the accumulated body of cross-national quantitative evidence at the level of the state suggests that democratic regimes are neither more nor less war-prone than are other regime-types. Studies by Wright ([1942], 1964), Rummel (1968), Weede (1970, 1984), Chan (1984), Domke (1988), Dixon (1989), and Maoz and Abdolali (1989) all indicate that the proportional frequencies of militarized conflict and war involvement of democracies are approximately the same as for nondemocratic states. However, despite the fact that democracies appear no less war-prone than nondemocratic states, recent dyadic-level analyses suggest that democratic nations rarely fight each other. Ray (1995a) demonstrates that large numbers of "exceptions" to this statement may be found, depending on the definition of "democracy" that is applied, but the strength and consistency of the dyadic-level findings has led both Levy (1988:662) and Russett (1990b:123) to assert that the absence of war between democratic nations is one of the strongest empirically-based generalizations that exists in the field of international politics.

Democratic dyads

Two early quantitative empirical studies by Babst (1972) and Small and Singer (1976) dealing with the question of democracy and war at the level of the dyad report results strongly supportive of the democratic peace generalization. Six (more recent) studies provide confirmatory evidence. The first, by Rummel (1979), established the "joint-freedom proposition." Specifically, Rummel hypothesizes that "libertarian systems" will not engage in violence with each other. Examining 50 interstate wars from 1816 to 1965 (COW database) across political system categories of libertarian, authoritarian, and totalitarian, Rummel notes that there were no wars between libertarian states, 14 wars between libertarian and authoritarian states, and 36 wars between nonlibertarian states. He concludes that war does not occur between free societies. In a second study, Rummel (1983) examines both wars and "campaigns of violence" (i.e., patterns of discrete and continuous military actions) and draws his data from multiple sources – primarily from newspapers and magazines for the years 1976 through 1980. Rummel reports that his findings indicate that violence does not occur within libertarian dyads, and that a necessary condition for interstate conflict between two nations is for one of them to be partially or completely nonlibertarian. Maoz and Abdolali (1989) examine all nation-dyads in the international system for the years between 1816 and 1976 (COW database). Here they include subwar militarized disputes as well as wars, and report that democratic states are significantly less likely to engage in militarized conflict or war with each other than are dyads with other regime-types. They conclude that the joint-freedom proposition is supported by their results.

Bremer (1992) produces the most extensive evidence on this question. Utilizing the COW database and two collections of regime classifications (Chan 1984 and Polity II [Gurr, Jaggers and Moore 1989]), Bremer examines all dyad-years between 1816 and 1965. With Chan's data, he reports bivariate findings that the occurrence of war for undemocratic dyads (neither state democratic) is approximately 14 times more likely than for democratic dyads. The results with the Polity II data are similar. Bremer also examines six other factors that might impact on this relationship (proximity, power status, alliance, militarization, economic development, and capability differential). Here he reports multivariate findings which indicate that even after the effects of the other factors have been removed, the negative relationship between democracy and war remains. Although proximity is the strongest predictor of war probability, the absence of democracy (one or both states nondemocratic) in a dyad is second in salience. Bremer (1993a) furnishes a second study with the COW database (this time with seven control factors) and reports findings consistent with his earlier analysis. Specifically, the bivariate coefficients indicate that nondemocratic dyads (one or both states nondemocratic) are almost 50 times more likely to engage in war than are democratic pairs. The multivariate results show a 40 fold increase in the probability of war for nondemocratic as opposed to democratic dyads. Lastly, Bremer notes that in a comparison of subwar disputes with wars, democracy is 10 times more potent in suppressing war than in suppressing disputes, and he concludes that this is indicative of a tendency for democratic dyads to contain conflict at lower levels of intensity rather than to avoid conflict entirely.

In a recent study, Gleditsch (1995) tests the hypothesis that the absence of wars between democratic states might be due to geographical distance between them (i.e., lack of proximity). Using the COW database for the years 1816–1986, Gleditsch produces evidence for rejecting the hypothesis, and he concludes that "double democracy is a near-perfect *sufficient condition* for peace" (Gleditsch 1995:318).

Summary

The evidence in the area of the joint-freedom proposition is consistent and cumulative.[11] Democratic dyads are less likely to engage in war

[11] Although not indisputable (e.g., Waltz 1993). Ray (1993) demonstrates how definitions of democracy affect the case set of warring democratic dyads. Spiro (1994) further shows how statistical findings based on this small case set are sensitive to extremely minor variations in the hypergeometric distributions of all wars and democratic wars (1816–1980) that are produced by different definitions of either democracy or war. Spiro's analysis indicates that the absence of wars between democratic states over the last two centuries is not a statistically significant pattern and can be explained on the basis of random chance. In another quantitatively-grounded study, Farber and Gowa (1995) report no statistically significant relationship between democracy and war before 1914, and argue that it is only after 1945 that the probability of war is lower between democratic states than between other dyads. They posit that the Cold War created a strong set of common interests among democracies, and that therefore the post-1945 democratic peace may be more the result of common interests than of common political systems. Using a different method, Layne (1994) attacks the democratic peace thesis by examining four historical cases of confrontations between democracies which failed to escalate to

than are nondemocratic pairs. However, there are two competing explanations for this phenomenon. One explanation focuses on the political culture of democratic states (i.e., nonviolent norms), whereas the other explanation involves democratic political structure (i.e., decisionmaking constraints). According to the normative or cultural school (e.g., Doyle 1986; Dixon 1993, 1994; Russett 1993), liberal democracies tend to be less violent than autocratic states because democratic societies value and inculcate nonviolent methods of conflict resolution. These preferences for the peaceful resolution of disputes shape policy decisions, and particularly impact on relations with other democratic states which are believed to share the same norms. As a result of these common values, disputes between democracies tend to be settled in a nonviolent manner. Maoz and Russett (1993) attempt to test models representing both the normative and structural explanations for the democratic peace. Although they find that both models are supported by the data, they report that support for the normative model is more robust and consistent.

The alternative explanation rests on structural or institutional factors (e.g., Bueno de Mesquita and Lalman 1992). This thesis holds that the decisionmaking structures of democracies operate in an environment of divided political power and must gain support or at least acquiescence from legislatures, bureaucracies, interest groups, and public opinion before engagement in war. Creating this consensus is often a long and difficult process. Therefore, the structural explanation posits that democratic dyads tend not to engage in violent conflict due to these double constraints on war decisions.[12] Works by Morgan and Campbell (1991) and Morgan and Schwebach (1992) attempt to

war. He concludes that none of the postulated conflict-dampening factors of democratic peace theory appears to have played any role in the outcomes of the crises. James and Mitchell (1995) take a different tack. They argue that while war between democratic states may be rare, these dyads do still engage in coercive behavior. James and Mitchell specify a formal model that demonstrates an incentive for powerful democracies to undermine (through covert pressure and subversion) the efforts of weak democratic states to restructure dependent relationships, and they provide a list of cases – all of which involve the United States as one of the participants – that is consistent with their model.

[12] Layne (1994) argues that the structural/institutional explanation is logically inconsistent with the evidence. Democratic monads are as war-prone as autocratic monads (e.g., Small and Singer 1976; Chan 1984; Weede 1984; Domke 1988; Dixon 1989). If structural constraints had the effects ascribed to them, democratic states "would be peaceful in their relations with all states, whether democratic or not" (Layne 1994:12). Also see Gates, Knutsen and Moses (1996) on this and related points.

produce evidence on this issue. Their findings are supportive of the political constraint explanation; however they suggest that *all* constraining institutional structures – and not just those associated with democracy – may inhibit war.[13]

Status quo orientation

One of the principal insights provided by Organski's (1958) original thesis on power transition involves the interaction of capability distributions and status quo orientation (Vasquez 1996a:35–36). Specifically, it has been argued that whether the status quo challenger or defender has the advantage in relative capabilities may affect the probability of war. For example, a status quo defender with a relative capability advantage over a challenger may have no incentive to attempt to utilize that superiority and be satisfied with a posture of deterrence, whereas a status quo challenger possessing a capability advantage over a defender may have a strong incentive to attempt to exploit its superiority through war. Even states committed to defending the status quo may experience pressure for the initiation of preventive war if the balance of capabilities appears to be shifting in favor of the opponent and future war is anticipated (e.g., Levy 1987; Morrow 1996).

Status quo orientation

Early work in this area may be found in Organski's (1958:330–333) power transition theory which focuses on the distinction between the dominant nation satisfied with the status quo and a dissatisfied challenger. He argues that as the capability trajectories of these states converge, war becomes increasingly probable. Rummel (1979:264) also hypothesizes that an actual or growing weakness of the party favoring the status quo compared to the anti-status quo party will be positively correlated with violence. A similar thesis is put forward by Anderson and McKeown (1987:4) who suggest that a discrepancy between national aspirations and national achievements may lead governments to attempt to alter their external environments. The status-inconsistency theories of war by Galtung (1964), Wallace (1971), and

---

[13] An analytic framework on political constraints is found in Salmore and Salmore (1978). For early empirical studies on political constraints and foreign conflict, see Geller (1985) and Hagan (1987).

Midlarsky (1975) explore a related logic. Maoz (1982:203), too, notes that crisis initiation is likely to be tied to national dissatisfaction and a commitment to revise the status quo, particularly when this is coupled with a rapid capability growth rate relative to an opponent.

Ray's (1995a) comparative case study of the Fashoda Crisis and the Spanish–American War suggests that the distribution of capabilities between status quo challengers and defenders may have had a critical impact on the outcomes of these two confrontations. Specifically, Ray argues that war was avoided in the Fashoda Crisis due to British (status quo defender) military superiority over France; whereas in the Spanish–American confrontation of 1898, the United States (status quo challenger) possessed military superiority over Spain and therefore that crisis ended in war. The logic that war initiation is likely when the balance of military capabilities favors the status quo challenger rather than the defender is also found in Huth, Bennett and Gelpi (1992:489).

However, Maoz (1982:74–75) takes the reasoning further and notes that "crisis initiation is not only an option open to revisionist states; it could be and has been utilized historically by strategic defenders of the status quo." It is reasonable to expect that under certain dynamic capability balances war initiation by status quo defenders would be a highly probable outcome. For example, Gilpin (1981:191, 201) and Levy (1987:83–84) provide explanations for why capability convergence may trigger defender-initiated wars: confronted with a faster-growing challenger, preventive military action by the status quo defender would appear to be a rational foreign policy choice. In sum, there are substantial theoretical reasons for expecting patterns of war initiation to be influenced by the power balance between status quo challengers and defenders.[14]

There is little systematically derived statistical evidence on the effects of status quo orientation on war initiation. Huth, Gelpi and Bennett (1993:617–618) report findings for a set of nine major powers (MID database 1816–1984) in "extended and direct immediate deterrence encounters" which suggest the salience of the conventional

---

[14] Schweller (1992) addresses the question of war initiation and shifting capability distributions from the perspective of democratic and authoritarian regime-types rather than status quo orientation. He argues that preventive war is the preferred response of declining authoritarian states, whereas declining democratic states avoid war and choose accommodation, defensive alliances, or internal balancing as response measures to relative capability loss.

military balance between challengers and defenders for probabilities of conflict escalation. They conclude that a shift in the military balance "from a three-to-one defender advantage to a three-to-one challenger advantage increases the probability of escalation by approximately 33%." In other words, a conventional military power transition providing the challenger with a substantial advantage is associated with dispute escalation.

Anderson and McKeown (1987) analyze 77 wars (COW database 1816–1980) in terms of capability balances and the degree to which belligerents' "aspirations diverge from actual or expected achievements" (status quo orientation). Their model also allows for preemptive war initiated by a status quo defender. The basic hypothesis is that dissatisfied nations examine the power balance and initiate war when the military capability ratio is favorable. The findings of Anderson and McKeown (1987:19) indicate that:

> the supersatisfied model [with defender preemption] performed better than the others . . . [providing] empirical support for Lebow's [1984] contention that perceptions of "falling behind" and of possessing large advantages can *both* lead to aggression. It is important to note, however, that the less complicated model performed only slightly less well . . ., suggesting that the more prevalent dynamic is that of aggression being triggered by perceptions of falling behind.

In short, an unstable military balance is associated with war initiation by both challengers and defenders of the status quo.

Geller (1994) examines the question of the identity of the war initiator as it relates to both military balances and status quo orientation for a set of 20 nation-dyads that formed long-term rivalries during the period 1816–1986 (COW database). The study analyzes the 43 wars which occurred between these "enduring rivals" and concludes that status quo challengers are the most probable war initiators and are likely to initiate under any capability distribution,[15] whereas

---

[15] This conclusion is consistent with Paul's (1994:173) analysis of six cases of asymmetrical war initiations by weaker states. He notes that militarily inferior states may use force to reduce uncertainty, alter an unacceptable status quo, or gain sympathy from other parties. Paul concludes that a significant capability advantage may be insufficient "to deter an adversary who is highly motivated to change the status quo." The conclusion also is reinforced by the findings of Huth (1996:85) as reported in his analysis of relative military strength between challengers and targets engaged in territorial disputes (1950–1990; 129 dispute cases). Specifically, Huth notes that "the

status quo defenders initiate wars almost solely under unstable military balances.

Summary

Based on a small number of recent studies, patterns of both conflict escalation and war initiation appear to be affected by the distribution of military capabilities between status quo defenders and challengers. Two implications of these findings bear heavily on explanations of war decisions. First, the finding that the pattern of defender war initiations emerges only when relative capabilities are measured by military criteria rather than by a more broadly-based composite index of power suggests that war decisions tend to focus on those factors that will have an immediate bearing on military success (e.g., Anderson and McKeown 1987; Geller 1994). Advantages or disadvantages in relative industrial or demographic strength may appear less relevant in such circumstances than existing military capabilities.

A second implication of these results involves the initiation of preemptive or preventive war by status quo defenders. Almost every case of defender initiated war occurred under an unstable military balance (Geller 1994). This pattern suggests that stable military balances of either preponderance or parity are generally interpreted by status quo defenders as supportive of deterrence, whereas unstable balances producing capability shifts or transitions are deemed dangerous enough to provoke preventive military action.

Economic factors

There exists a long history in liberal economic thought suggesting a relationship between free trade, market economies, and international peace. For example, the theories of Adam Smith and David Ricardo hold that interference with the natural functioning of the market mechanism – such as through trade restrictions that protect specific domestic economic interests – impacts negatively on the wealth of society as a whole. Theorists as diverse as Richard Cobden, John Stuart Mill, and Henry Thomas Buckle all argued that unfettered free trade and economic development would promote world peace. A corollary to this logic maintains that wealth and territorial acquisition

balance of conventional military forces between challenger and target *did not* have a powerful effect on the decisions of the challenger to dispute territory."

92

are unrelated in an international economic system based on trade and development; hence the need to gain additional territory through war as a means of generating new wealth disappears (Buzan 1984). Moreover, it is argued that as free trade creates greater prosperity for all states, growing economic interdependence will increase the costs of war for the entire system. In short, because war would disrupt a market-based international economic system that serves the interests of all states, force as an instrument of foreign policy should decline in utility as free trade and economic development increasingly come to characterize the international economy. This thesis has produced two areas of dyadic-level research – one dealing with trade and the other with economic development – and will be discussed in the context of international conflict and war.

Trade

Sullivan (1974) examines the dyadic trade flow of states for evidence of conflict patterns over the brief period 1955–1957. Employing trade data generated by the United Nations, he reports that trade flows are negatively correlated with dyadic-level verbal conflict and are positively correlated with the percentage of cooperative interactions. As an indicator of the "social distance" within dyads, Sullivan concludes that trade flows are an important factor in predicting levels of dyadic conflict. Similar results are reported by Gasiorowski and Polachek (1982), who examine the interaction patterns of the United States and Warsaw Pact states for the period between 1967 and 1978 (Conflict and Peace Data Bank [COPDAB] and International Monetary Fund [IMF] data sources). As did Sullivan, Gasiorowski and Polachek also report an inverse relationship between trade (imports, exports, total trade) and dyadic-level conflict behavior and note that the results of Granger causality tests indicate that trade affects conflict, rather than conflict levels determining trade patterns.

Oneal, Oneal, Maoz and Russett (1996) examine the interaction effects of bilateral trade and regime type on interstate conflict. Using the period 1950 through 1984, Oneal *et al.* focus their study on dyads composed of contiguous states and dyads containing at least one major power, and they introduce controls for income growth rates, alliances, and relative power. Their results indicate that trade is positively associated with peace, and that conflict becomes even less likely when external economic relations are important and the dyad is composed of democratic regimes.

A different finding is reported by Barbieri (1996). Her analysis entails 14,341 dyad-years for the period 1870–1938 and includes 270 militarized disputes and 14 wars. Barbieri concludes that economic linkages have a substantive effect on whether or not dyads engage in militarized disputes, but no effect on the occurrence of wars. However, rather than *inhibiting* militarized conflict, extensive trade interdependence *increases* the probability that dyads will experience militarized disputes. Barbieri notes that the relationship holds for both symmetrical and asymmetrical interdependencies.

Development

Bremer (1992) provides evidence regarding dyadic economic development levels and war. Using four variables from the COW material capabilities data set, he constructs two indices reflecting the demographic and economic dimensions of development and then classifies the dyads as symmetrically developed, asymmetrically developed, or symmetrically underdeveloped. The multivariate results (for the years between 1816 and 1965) with six additional predictor variables indicate a negative relationship between economic development and war. This association is the third strongest among the set of seven predictors, and Bremer concludes that dyads characterized by the absence of advanced economies or dyads with one advanced and one underdeveloped economy are more war-prone than highly developed dyads.

Summary

The evidence in the area of economic factors and patterns of war is suggestive but limited. The most compelling finding on the basis of research design and execution reveals the relative absence of war within dyads characterized by a high level of economic development. Some studies report that dyadic-level trade is associated with less conflict and war, but these analyses do not approach the requisite for a test of liberal economic theory.[16] Buzan (1984) argues that some elements of the evolving, interdependent world economy are stabilizing and may reduce conflict, whereas other aspects of the market economy are destabilizing and may increase conflict among states.

[16] For example, Weede (1995) suggests that although free trade may be associated with less war, the relationship may be indirect. He argues that free trade promotes prosperity, prosperity promotes democracy, and democratic dyads do not fight wars.

Preliminary empirical evidence exists for both patterns. Analyses by liberal theorists such as Hoffmann (1978) and Nye (1990) also reflect this ambivalent view.

Evaluation

Research based at the analytic level of the dyad has produced some of the most interesting, consistent, and cumulative findings in the area of international conflict and war. For example, a general body of research indicates that static and dynamic capability balances are associated with both the occurrence of war and the identity of the war initiator. Specifically, conditions of dyadic military parity and shifts toward parity are consistently and significantly related to the outbreak of war. As Maoz (1993:37) notes:

> the likelihood of conflict in a dyad is significantly affected by the degree of parity in military capability . . . This suggests that as states grow more equal in military capabilities, they are more likely to be subject to the kind of calculations that are consistent with the power transition theory (Organski and Kugler 1980) . . . The state losing in relative capabilities invokes the declining power logic (Levy 1987), while the state gaining in capabilities invokes the status inconsistency logic described by East (1972).

This conclusion is reaffirmed by Lemke and Kugler (1996:14) who note that "a large number of studies linking parity and war at the dyadic level suggest that parity increases the probability of war, and consistently confirm the claim that parity and transitions increase the probability of war." In sum, cumulative evidence has developed which indicates that parity in military capabilities and convergence toward military parity within dyads are associated with the onset of militarized conflict and war.

Consistency and cumulation also characterize the findings on proximity/contiguity and conflict. At the level of the dyad, the distance between states is negatively related to warfare. Proximate states are more likely to engage in war than are nonproximate states, and war within dyads having a land or narrow water border is much more probable than between noncontiguous states.

In contradistinction, the evidence on the effects of arms races on the outbreak of war is disputed and inconclusive, and the results of analyses on alliance and war also are mixed. In the area of alliance within dyads, the findings are inconsistent. However, the results of studies focusing on alliance-ties that are external to the dyad present a different picture. Dyads in which only one member has an external alliance-tie are more likely to experience war than are dyads where both members have external ties.

The findings on the democratic peace proposition are both strong and cumulative. Despite questions regarding the logical consistency of the structural/institutional explanation of constraints on war decisions with monadic-level evidence on the equivalent war-proneness of democratic and nondemocratic states (Layne 1994) and statistical problems associated with definitions in small-case hyper-geometric distributions (Spiro 1994), the weight of the findings indicates that democratic dyads are less likely to engage in war than are nondemocratic pairs (one or both states nondemocratic).

Evidence on a relationship between dyadic trade patterns and conflict is mixed, but an exhaustive analysis by Bremer (1992) of 197,922 dyad-years between 1816 and 1965 indicates a strong association for dyads characterized by highly advanced economies and the absence of war. Preliminary findings for sets of rivals also indicate that both the status quo orientation and the relative capability balance within the dyad affect patterns of war initiation.

In sum, data-based research on conflict and war at the level of the nation-dyad has produced some impressive results. Geographic proximity/contiguity, static parity in capabilities and shifts toward parity, unbalanced external alliance-ties, the absence of paired democratic regimes, and the absence of joint advanced economies are factors substantively and positively associated with the occurrence and initiation of both militarized disputes and war. These findings are drawn from studies that represent improvements over the earlier state-level foreign policy analyses in terms of population size, temporal span, and the conceptualization, operationalization, and measurement of variables.

5 War-prone regions

Introduction

While the analysis of political patterns as they appear within geographical regions is well established in the fields of comparative and international politics, the majority of these area studies tend to be methodologically subjective and impressionistic. Relatively little quantitative empirical research has been conducted with the purpose of exploring cross-regional variation in patterns of conflict and war.

This chapter examines data-based research on war-prone regions (references listed in appendix 2, table A.3). The initial section of the chapter focuses on simple comparisons *between* geographic regions in terms of the frequency of crises, subwar disputes, and wars, as well as inter-regional comparisons of processes of militarized dispute contagion. The second section explores evidence relating to *intra*-regional patterns of conflict and war that may be dependent upon spatial heterogeneity, population pressure, polarity, and normative constraints. The third section of the chapter examines evidence of war contagion as it pertains to patterns of intra-regional conflict behavior. Both spatial and temporal distances are incorporated as factors in a possible contagion process. The final section examines evidence of intra-regional cycles of war. Although there is some overlap with Europe-centered theories of cycles in global warfare, evidence relating specifically to more narrowly defined regional conflicts is the primary focus here. The majority of data-based studies on war cycles, contagion/diffusion processes, polarity, and norms is conducted at the systemic level of analysis and will be discussed in chapter 6.

Comparisons

Quantitative empirical studies of the frequencies of wars, crises, and militarized disputes have provided a simple means of comparing the conflict tendencies of different geographical regions. While many of these studies focus on the post-World War II period, a small number of data sets (Correlates of War [COW]/Militarized Interstate Dispute [MID]) permit comparisons reaching back to the beginning of the nineteenth century. A brief review of the findings identifies the regions that have suffered the highest frequencies of conflicts and wars.

Comparisons

Kende (1978) examines the set of all wars occurring in the international system between 1945 and 1976. The category of "war" includes international, intra-national, and tribal conflicts. For the 120 wars in Kende's data set during the 1945–1976 period, the most war-prone regions were the Middle East and Asia (each with approximately 29 percent of the total wars), followed by Latin America (approximately 19 percent), Africa (approximately 17 percent), and Europe (approximately 5 percent). Kende also examines the 49 wars that occurred between 1967 and 1976 – the latest period in his data set – and reports that the Middle East was the most war-prone region (with approximately 35 percent of the total number of conflicts), followed by Africa (approximately 29 percent), Asia (approximately 25 percent), Latin America (approximately 10 percent), and Europe (approximately 2 percent).

Eckhardt and Azar (1978a, 1978b) examine the distributions of conflictual and cooperative interstate events, rather than inter- and intra-national wars, for the period between 1945 and 1975 using information from the Conflict and Peace Data Bank (COPDAB). They report that on a per-nation basis, the number of conflict-years is lower than expected in both Europe and Latin America, and higher than expected in the Middle East and Asia. These conflict rankings are similar to Kende's war rankings for the same temporal period. With regard to cooperative events, Eckhardt and Azar note that on a per-nation basis, there was proportionately more cooperation in North America, West Europe, and East Europe, whereas less cooperation on a proportionate basis was manifest in Asia, Southeast Asia, and sub-Saharan Africa.

Brecher and Wilkenfeld (1982) and Brecher (1984), using data from the International Crisis Behavior (ICB) Project, provide comparative information on the characteristics of regional crises, as well as their distributional frequencies for the period between 1945 and 1975. Brecher and Wilkenfeld (1982:383) define an "international crisis" as a situation developing either internal or external to the state that: (1) creates perceptions in decisionmakers of threat to basic values; (2) provides limited decision-time; and (3) has a high probability of military hostilities. With these criteria, they identify 90 crises for the temporal period. As with Kende, and with Eckhardt and Azar, the highest frequency in the Brecher and Wilkenfeld study was noted for the Middle East (26 crises), followed by Southern Asia (15), Africa (13), and Central and South America (13). Less than 10 crises each were recorded for East Asia (8), Central and Eastern Europe (7), Southern Europe (5), and Western and Northern Europe (3). Brecher (1984) reports on the characteristics of these interstate conflicts and notes that East–West crises were usually triggered verbally or by nonviolent events, were dealt with by verbal negotiations, and were terminated informally. In contrast, Middle Eastern and South Asian crises were triggered by violent events that threatened the territory of participants, involved the use of violence or war, and were terminated by formal agreements. In sum, the Brecher study points toward the relative conflict-proneness of the Middle East and Asia for the post-World War II period.

Bremer (1982), using COW data, extends the temporal period of analysis to the beginning of the twentieth century (1900–1976) while raising the issue of conflict contagion. His examination includes all militarized interstate disputes ("coercive behavior" disputes) and compares regional disputes-per-month with a Poisson distribution in order to determine if intra-regional conflict is contagious. He concludes that all regions, with the exception of South America, show evidence of internal contagion in the use of coercive behavior. Houweling and Kuné (1984) also examine contagion – but in this case for wars. Using the COW database for the period between 1816 and 1980, they report that the number of war outbreaks for every geographical region, except the Western Hemisphere, is not random over time. In a related study (COW database 1816–1980), Houweling and Siccama (1985) report that the outbreak of war in both Europe and Asia shows significant space–time interaction (contagiousness), whereas this process appears absent in the Western Hemisphere and Middle East.

The most extensive study of the comparative conflict-proneness of regions over time is by Gochman and Maoz (1984). As a component of their report on the distributions within the MID database, they provide inter-regional comparisons for the period between 1816 and 1976. Gochman and Maoz (1984:604) note that from 1816 to the conclusion of World War I in 1918, the highest frequencies of militarized disputes were, respectively, European, "extra-regional" (involving states from different regions), and in the Americas. Since most of the extra-regional disputes involved major powers "engaging states outside the major powers' regions, almost all militarized interstate disputes prior to 1919 were products of American and European politics." Regarding post-1945 dispute patterns, Gochman and Maoz (1984:604–606) note:

> [P]articularly after World War II . . . Asia and the Middle East have become the most conflict-prone regions . . .; Europe has been the least conflict prone . . . Turning to the question of the severity of disputes in the different regions . . ., we find that the use of force has been least prominent in European disputes (62.1% involved some use of force) and most prominent in Middle Eastern disputes (91.7%). However, the reverse has been true with regard to the resort to war: Europe has been the most war prone (15.7% of all disputes) and the Middle East (5.0%), the Americas (4.9%), and Africa the least war prone.

Gochman and Maoz interpret these post-World War II distributions to reflect differences in capabilities: minor powers, with capability constraints, more frequently use force short-of-war, whereas major powers have the capabilities to engage in war with greater ease.

Summary

The Gochman and Maoz (1984) findings are unique in terms of temporal span – producing inter-regional comparisons over a period of almost two centuries. Their findings with regard to frequencies of militarized interstate disputes from 1816 to 1945 conform to expectations: most conflicts involved the European major powers and the United States. In the post-1945 period – on a per-state basis – the Middle East, Asia, and Africa become the most conflict-prone. Hence, the weight of conflict events has shifted from the older regional subsystems of Europe and America in the nineteenth and early twentieth centuries, to the newer regional subsystems of Africa, the

Middle East, and Asia in the post-1945 period.[1] The Gochman and Maoz post-World War II distributions are consistent with other studies involving shorter temporal periods. It may be concluded that regional subsystems display considerable variation in patterns of conflict and war, with the newer subsystems experiencing comparatively more intra-regional violence than the older subsystems.[2]

---

[1] Weede (1996b:132ff) contends that the conflict-proneness of these Third World regions in the post-1945 period was due to the absence of "Pax Atomica," "Pax Democratica," and "Pax Sovietica," and Singer and Wildavsky (1993) suggest that the bifurcation of conflict patterns will persist well into the twenty-first century. They argue that the world is currently divided into "zones of peace, wealth, and democracy" and "zones of turmoil, war, and development." The former zones include Western Europe, the United States, Canada, Japan, and the Antipodes; the latter zones encompass the territory of the former Soviet Union, Eastern and Southeastern Europe, Africa, Asia, and Latin America. The basic thesis presented by Singer and Wildavsky is that the zones of peace will be nonviolent due to the low probability of wars between the democratic states that inhabit them. They argue that political relationships among these democratic countries will not be influenced by relative military capabilities and that hostile alliance systems between states in the zones of peace will not coalesce. In sum, states in these areas of the world will be internally peaceful, will engage in nonviolent relations with other developed democracies, and will remain liberal and progressive. The projection of life within the zones of turmoil is quite different. In these zones, political relationships will be determined by relative power, the suffering of mass populations will be the norm, and large-scale systematic violence will be a constant threat. In short, the zones of turmoil will be characterized by "wars and revolutions, . . . mass murders, famines, and epidemics caused by governments or by wars" (Singer and Wildavsky 1993:38).

Holsti (1995) also discusses zones of war and peace. However, unlike Singer and Wildavsky, Holsti postulates that it is peaceful relations among groups *within* states, rather than democratic government, *per se*, that produces peaceful relations *between* states. He argues that "strong states" – characterized by peaceful inter-group and state–group relations, governmental legitimacy, and consensus on the objectives of governance – are necessary for creating zones of peace. As Holsti (1995:334) notes:

> It follows that regions populated by large numbers of weak and/or failing states will be zones of war, areas of high incidence of both internal and interstate armed conflicts, while regions containing large numbers of states of medium strength will be no-war zones. There may be frequent militarized crises, arms competition, and ad hoc alliance-making, but the incidence of internal wars will be relatively low, and the incidence of interstate wars negligible. South America since the early twentieth century fits this profile. Finally, regions containing a predominance of strong states will be "pluralistic security communities," where both internal and interstate wars will be almost unthinkable. Western Europe since 1945, North America since the 1920s, and the South Pacific region concentrated on Australia and New Zealand, fit this pattern.

Holsti argues that the democratic peace thesis is insufficient as an explanation for the absence of wars, and offers South America as an example of a no-war zone where there has been a notable lack of democracy for extended periods over the last century. See Russett and Ray (1995:320–321) for a discussion on this last point.

[2] Mearsheimer (1990) and Kennedy (1993) are less optimistic regarding the prospects

Attributes

Aggregate system-level behaviors have been explained on the reductionist basis of the attributes of the units comprising the system and on the basis of the attributes of the system itself. While the principal focus of many recent data-based studies is on the effects of attributes of the international system (e.g., polarity, alliances, norms, etc.) on system-level patterns of war and peace, some analyses have examined the effects of these factors on a regional (or subsystemic) level. The following section discusses a number of regional studies dealing with the conflict effects of spatial dependence/heterogeneity, population density, subsystem polarity, and norms opposing the use of force.

Spatial dependence/heterogeneity

O'Loughlin and Anselin (1991) examine the patterns of conflictual and cooperative behaviors (COPDAB) for 42 African nations in terms of national attributes, spatial dependence, and spatial heterogeneity for the years 1966 through 1978. The national attribute set includes geographic size, regime-type, level of social mobilization, trade volume, military expenditures, location in a "shatterbelt,"[3] and the

for European peace in the post-Cold War world. For example, Mearsheimer (1990:142–143) suggests that the next few decades in Europe will probably not be as violent as the first 45 years of the twentieth century, but will be "substantially more prone to violence than the past 45 years." His thesis rests on the transformation of Europe from a bipolar system (under superpower domination) to a multipolar system with five major states (Russia, Germany, France, Britain, and Italy) plus a number of minor powers. As Mearsheimer notes: "The resulting system would suffer the problems common to multipolar systems, and would therefore be more prone to . . . wars and major crises. Power inequalities could also appear; if so, stability would be undermined further." Kennedy's (1993:251–253) projections for the European region focus less on capability differentials and more on ethnic and economic schisms. In Eastern Europe and in the territory of the former Soviet Union, ethnic divisions have already led to violence. Kennedy suggests that in the Czech Republic, Slovakia, Romania, Hungary, Turkey, Greece, and Macedonia, internal and external war is a strong possibility. Moreover, the deteriorating economic condition in the countries of the former Soviet Union and in Romania has exacerbated the pressures leading to mass migration of populations already set in motion by the Yugoslav civil war.

[3] "Shatterbelts" (Cohen 1973, 1982) are geographic areas where indigenous cultural, religious, and political schisms are aggravated by the intervention of external major powers attracted by the economic or strategic significance of the region. For example, the Middle East and Southeast Asia were areas of superpower competition in the post-World War II period. In an empirical test (COW database) of the shatterbelt thesis, Kelly (1986) reports that in the twentieth century almost 80 percent of major power wars have been conducted in shatterbelt areas. However, he argues that the

date of independence. The spatial analysis focuses on the effects of dependence (diffusion) and heterogeneity (differentiation of national characteristics). O'Loughlin and Anselin's results indicate that African states interact primarily with their immediate neighbors, and that either conflictual or cooperative behavior "beyond that [contiguous] level is rare and insignificant for the African system as a whole" (1991:58). They conclude that both spatial dependence (through border contact) and spatial heterogeneity are present in the African subsystem and should be taken into account in studies of this region's behavior.

Population density

Bremer, Singer and Luterbacher (1973) examine the war-proneness of the European state subsystem for the period between 1816 and 1965 in terms of population density and urbanization measures (COW database). Population pressures that threaten to outstrip available resources have been offered as political explanations for expansionist foreign policies in Europe and Asia in the 1930s: the geopolitical work of Karl Haushofer exemplifies this view (Dorpalen 1942; Whittlesey 1966; Sloan 1988). However, Bremer, Singer and Luterbacher report that at the level of the European interstate subsystem, an indicator of population pressure (density) and two indicators of war (total deaths from war and total deaths from intra-European war) were negatively associated; although other measures of "crowding" revealed positive relationships to war-proneness, none of the correlations was statistically significant. The authors conclude that for the European state subsystem, population density and levels of urbanization do not account for patterns of regional war.

Polarity

Hopf (1991) attempts to test Waltz's (1979) thesis regarding the inherently greater stability of bipolar systems over multipolar power configurations using data for European nations from 1495 to 1559. According to Hopf's (1991:479) calculations, the European subsystem was multipolar (six major powers) from 1495 to 1521 and bipolar (two major powers) from 1521 to 1559. The results of the analysis indicate that for the European region during that period, the amount of

propensities toward violent conflict in such areas exist independently of external intervention.

warfare is roughly equivalent irrespective of polarity. Hopf offers an alternative explanation for patterns of war based on the shifting balance of advantage between offensive and defensive forces: advantages of defense over offense minimize the occurrence of warfare and enhance the stability of the system.

Norms

Kegley and Raymond (1986) explore the effects of normative constraints on the use of force in patterns of militarized disputes for the European subsystem between 1815 and 1980 (COW database and Transnational Rules Indicator Project [TRIP] data). Their results indicate that normative constraints on the use of force fluctuate over time, and they provide a focused comparison of two periods – the Metternichean Concert of 1816 to 1848 and the Bismarckian Concert of 1849 to 1870 – with the period between 1816 and 1848 manifesting high constraints and the period between 1849 and 1870 manifesting low constraints. Although both periods experienced roughly the same number of serious disputes, none of the disputes escalated into wars during the (high-constraint) Metternichean Concert, whereas the post-Metternichean period exhibits four wars between major powers. However, Kegley and Raymond note that such constraining normative orders are rare, short-lived, and exceptionally fragile.

Summary

Quantitative empirical studies of specific regional subsystems have yielded interesting results in the area of conflict and war. O'Loughlin and Anselin (1991) demonstrate that within the African subsystem states principally interact with immediate neighbors and that conflictual or cooperative behavior with more distant states is rare. They also report evidence of the spatial dependence (diffusion) of behavior through border contact within the African context.

The remaining studies in this section focused on the European state subsystem – the most economically and technologically advanced region of the world over the last five centuries. Hopf (1991) reports the lack of a substantive connection between European subsystem polarity and warfare for the period 1495–1559, and suggests that fluctuation in war-proneness is due instead to shifts in advantage between offensive and defensive forces.

Bremer, Singer and Luterbacher (1973) examine the possible connection between population pressure and warfare for the European state subsystem in the nineteenth and twentieth centuries. Despite the historical use of this issue as a justification for expansionist foreign policies, the evidence within the European context reveals no substantive statistical relationship between these variables. Lastly, Kegley and Raymond (1986) explore the conflict effects of normative constraints on the use of force in the European subsystem. The findings in their study suggest a limited ability of nonviolent norms to reduce the frequency of wars, although they note that such constraining international orders tend to be rare and ephemeral. In sum, these studies suggest that attributes of certain geographic regions affect patterns of conflict and war.[4] In some contexts, the integration of specific regional attributes with more general factors associated with conflict may be necessary in the construction of an accurate explanation of regional war.

Contagion

The possible "contagion" or "diffusion" of international conflict, whether in the form of war or less serious modes of dispute, constitutes an interesting theoretical and empirical question in the study of international politics. The issue of contagion/diffusion processes in various forms of domestic conflict constitutes a closely related area of research (e.g., Spilerman 1970; Lieberson and Silverman 1965; Midlarsky 1970, 1978; Midlarsky, Crenshaw and

---

[4] Huntington (1993) has proposed that attributes cutting across regions may provide a focal point for future conflict. Specifically, he suggests that the "fault lines between civilizations" are becoming the critical areas of violence and war as the political and ideological forces of the Cold War disappear. In essence, Huntington argues that the 1,300-year-old military interaction between Western Christianity and Islam is likely to dominate international politics for the foreseeable future. According to Huntington (1993:30–31) the most significant fault line

> runs along what are now the boundaries between Finland and Russia and between the Baltic states and Russia, cuts through Belarus and Ukraine . . ., swings westward separating Transylvania from the rest of Romania, and then goes through Yugoslavia almost exactly along the line now separating Croatia and Slovenia from the rest of Yugoslavia . . . The peoples to the north and west of this line are Protestant or Catholic . . .; they are generally economically better off than the peoples to the east . . . The peoples to the east and south of this line are Orthodox or Muslim . . .; they are generally less advanced economically; they seem much less likely to develop stable democratic political systems.

Although Huntington allows that conflict and violence may occur between or within states comprising the same civilization, he argues that these conflicts are likely to be less intense and less expansive than cross-civilization conflicts.

Yoshida 1980; Li and Thompson 1975). These studies – dealing with the spread of domestic violence within national boundaries as well as the spread of domestic violence across national boundaries – treat conflict as both "cause" and "effect." The question at issue is whether there is something about an act of violence that makes the subsequent occurrence of violence in other areas more or less probable. The metaphors used in these analyses tend to be drawn from medicine (contagion) or from physical processes (diffusion). At the national level, the issue involves the spread of internal violence; at the level of interstate relations it involves the spread of war. Yet another related area of research involves questions of "addiction" or "reinforcement;" specifically, these processes refer to the probability that a war engagement by a nation will lead to another war engagement by the same nation (e.g., Most and Starr 1980; Garnham 1983; Levy and Morgan 1986). An examination of system-level war-contagion processes will be presented in chapter 6. This section will focus on a set of quantitative empirical studies that involve contagion/diffusion processes at the regional level of analysis.

Contagion/diffusion

Bremer (1982) examines regional patterns of coercive interstate behavior (involving the threat or use of force [COW database]) for the period between 1900 and 1976 by means of Poisson distribution models. He finds little evidence of inter-regional coercive contagion, but strong evidence that coercive behavior is contagious intra-regionally. In a related study, Faber, Houweling and Siccama (1984) analyze the spatial and temporal distances between wars (COW database) within five regions of the world for the period extending from 1816 to 1980. In addition to interstate and extra-systemic wars, they also include civil wars in the data analysis. The "spatial distance" between wars is defined as the geographical distance between locations of successive wars; "temporal distance" is defined as the time-lapse between successive wars. The Faber, Houweling and Siccama findings indicate that the location and timing of previous conflicts have positive and significant effects on subsequent war location and timing only within each region. They conclude that war outbreaks are not contagious across space (between regions) but are clustered in space and time (within regions). These findings are consistent with Bremer's (1982) conclusions.

Houweling and Siccama (1985) subsequently produce a more

detailed analysis of space–time interaction within specific regions. Using the COW database (1816–1980) on interstate, extra-systemic, and civil wars for the five geographic regions of Europe, Western Hemisphere, Middle East, Asia, and Africa, Houweling and Siccama report no evidence of worldwide contagion of interstate war but significant space–time interaction (contagion) in the outbreak of regional war for both Europe and Asia.

Three other analyses relevant to regional contagion focus on Africa. Two of these studies are by Starr and Most (1983, 1985), the third is by Kirby and Ward (1987). Starr and Most include the factor of "borders" in their examination of contagion/diffusion processes in the African region. The studies cover the temporal periods of 1960–1972 and 1960–1977 (with five-year lags) and utilize data from Kende (1978) and from the COPDAB Project. Their results indicate that nations with wars on their borders have a higher probability of engaging in war in a subsequent time period than do nations without border wars. Starr and Most conclude that war in Africa tends to diffuse spatially across states through common borders.

Kirby and Ward (1987) also produce a spatial analysis of African conflict. The period covered by their study is from 1948 to 1978 with data drawn from the COPDAB Project. Their findings are consistent with those of Starr and Most: specifically, Kirby and Ward note that hostile interactions between African states are significantly affected by existing conflicts among bordering nations.

Summary

The results of the six studies summarized in this section suggest that a militarized conflict or war contagion/diffusion process operates at the regional level. The analyses by Bremer (1982), Faber, Houweling and Siccama (1984), and Houweling and Siccama (1985) explore the probabilities of both inter- and intra-regional contagion – and conclude that conflict spreads within but not across geographical regions. The Starr and Most (1983, 1985) and Kirby and Ward (1987) studies focus on the African region alone. Their conclusions suggest that border contact increases the probability of war contagion.

Hower and Zinnes (1989:3) express reservations to this apparent consensus. They note that for a "contagion" process to occur, the second conflict event must involve a different nation than the states which were involved in the initial event. Moreover, they argue that some contact must be shown to have existed between the nations through which the contagion process supposedly operated. The studies by Starr and Most and by Kirby and Ward meet the "contact" criterion more closely than the Faber *et al.* and Bremer research designs, although Hower and Zinnes (1989:3) allow that nations in the same region may be presumed "to have contact with one another." In sum, on the basis of the evidence reviewed here, it is concluded that conflict contagion does occur on a regional basis.[5]

Cycles

This section will examine a number of studies relevant to the issue of cycles of conflict and war in geographical regions. The thesis of periodicities in great power war is most commonly associated with the work of Modelski (e.g., 1983) and Thompson (e.g., 1988), although Gilpin (1981) and Wallerstein (1984), among others, also discuss cycles of war among the strongest states in the international system. Despite the fact that the states in the European subsystem are the most prominent international actors in the post-1648 period, these cyclical explanations of war are not limited to particular geographical regions. For example, Gilpin discusses a cycle of pre-modern empires, followed by a cycle of rising and declining hegemonic powers. Wallerstein also identifies cycles of hegemonic succession that are linked to changes in world economic production. Modelski is the most specific, positing 100-year cycles of world leadership beginning in the fifteenth century. These theories account for hegemonic struggles that have moved beyond the European context.[6] The focus of the following analysis is on a set of quantitative studies of cycles that are specifically addressed to regional conflict, although they implicitly or explicitly incorporate elements of systemic-level theories.

Cycles

Farrar (1977) explores the possibility of cycles of war in the European state subsystem for the period between 1494 and 1973. Drawing on data from Wright ([1942], 1964), Farrar identifies three types of war: "probing" war (i.e., minimal violence causing little change), "adjusting" war (i.e., moderate violence but does not threaten the status

[5] For literature reviews and opposing interpretations of the evidence on this subject, see Hower and Zinnes (1989) and Most, Starr and Siverson (1989).
[6] See Goldstein (1988), Thompson (1988), and Levy (1991) for discussion of cycles in global politics. See chapter 6 on this subject.

hierarchy), and "hegemonic" war (i.e., massive violence that threatens or alters the hierarchy). Farrar concludes that these wars occur in a sequential pattern – probing, adjusting, and hegemonic wars tend to follow in that order. In sum, Farrar describes the war dynamic of the European state subsystem as first testing, then adjusting, and then fundamentally altering the hierarchical order. The complete cycle of war-types runs for approximately 100 years and is repeated four times during the period between 1494 and 1973.

Thompson (1996) examines the power transition hypothesis (Organski 1958; Organski and Kugler 1980) for the European state subsystem in terms of a modified long cycle mechanism. Specifically, he posits that wars are more probable when a rising regional challenger catches up with and then passes a declining regional leader. Two contests are relevant in this portion of his analysis: France versus Spain (1490–1690), and Germany versus France (1820–1940). The sole index of regional leadership is the relative size of the army. Thompson reports moderate empirical support for his hypothesis, with approximately 57 percent of the 14 cases of transitions associated with the outbreak of war, in comparison to the 23 percent (47 cases/11 wars) linked to non-transition intervals. However, he notes that there is no evidence of regular, spaced, repetitive cycles in these regional conflicts and concludes that regional, global, and regional–global capability transitions interact to produce the long cycles of global warfare.

Equilibrium

Midlarsky (1984) develops an equilibrium explanation of conflict behavior which posits that a balance (equilibrium) in the number of militarized disputes begun and ended in a given time period will be associated with the absence of systemic war. His analysis covers the European state subsystem for the period between 1816 and 1914 (COW database) and his findings indicate significant differences between the nineteenth-century pattern of conflict behavior (which did not result in widespread warfare), and the pattern in the early twentieth century (which did lead to extensive warfare). Specifically, Midlarsky reports an overall equilibrium in the onset and conclusion of militarized disputes in the nineteenth century that was absent in the twentieth century. Midlarsky concludes his analysis by relating the instability of the European conflict equilibrium in the early twentieth century to Modelski's theory of long cycles of global war.

Summary

The analyses reviewed in this section produce mixed results on the issue of regional cycles of war. All three studies focused on the European state subsystem – albeit with substantially different populations and time periods. Farrar reports European war cycles of roughly 100 years beginning in 1494; Thompson concludes that regional power transitions are moderately related to war, but that no regular cycles are evident at the level of the European region; and Midlarsky notes an equilibrium in the frequency of onset and termination of nineteenth-century European disputes that breaks down in the first decade of the twentieth century – an instability which he associates with the outbreak of global war. If evidence in support of long cycles of global war is included here (e.g., Modelski 1983; Thompson 1988) as a principally European-based phenomenon, then the hypothesis of cyclical wars beginning in the late fifteenth century gains a modicum of support. However, long cycle theory is not Europe-specific, and its most convincing evidence is based on measures of leadership shares of the global pool of sea power – a pool which includes (at times) a number of non-European nations. Thompson's (1996) findings on power transitions and war on the European continent suggests a mechanism of conflict, but he notes that cycles of war are not apparent in this regional data.

Evaluation

Over the last two centuries, major powers rather than minor powers have been the most dispute-prone states (Gochman and Maoz 1984); major powers have also been the most probable war participants (Bremer 1980; Small and Singer 1982; Eberwein 1982); and major powers rather than minor powers are most likely to engage in "severe" wars as measured by battle-deaths (Geller 1988). As a result – at least since 1816 – members of the European state subsystem have been involved in a disproportionately large number of destructive interstate and extra-regional wars. In the decades since 1945, however, regional shifts in the frequencies of interstate conflict activity have become evident. In the post-World War II period (following the breakdown of the colonial empires) the newer regional subsystems of Asia, the Middle East, and Africa now account for roughly half of all militarized interstate disputes. Since capabilities appear to be strongly related to war behavior, it may be projected that as the capacity of these new states to conduct military operations increases, their frequencies of war will also increase.

In terms of intra-regional behavior patterns, O'Loughlin and Anselin (1991) demonstrate that most interaction within the African subsystem is among contiguous states, with little contact (either conflictual or cooperative) among distant states. They also report evidence of the spatial diffusion of behavior. These tendencies, when linked with increasing military capabilities, may be expected to lead toward increased conflict and war on the African continent. A similar dynamic may also operate in the Middle East and Asia.

The implications of the findings on the European state subsystem are less clear. Bremer, Singer and Luterbacher (1973) report no substantive evidence of a relationship between population pressure and warfare in the European context for the nineteenth and twentieth centuries. However, the disruptive effects of the mass migration of populations from the less developed to the more developed regions of the world is a component of a number of recent trend analyses (e.g., Kennedy 1993). Hopf (1991) provides limited evidence from the European region of a decrease in war frequency linked to an increase in the military advantage of defensive forces over offensive forces. It has been argued that this thesis, when applied to nuclear weapons, suggests that the spread of secure, second-strike capabilities may reduce the utility of war as an instrument of foreign policy (e.g., Quester 1977; Waltz 1981, 1990; Bueno de Mesquita and Riker 1982). Mearsheimer (1990) specifically suggests that the managed proliferation of nuclear weapons in Europe may provide the best deterrent to future war in the region.[7] The study by Kegley and Raymond (1986) on the effectiveness of normative constraints on the use of force is less sanguine. Their findings indicate the limited efficacy of norms constraining the use of violence and the occurrence of war in the European subsystem between 1816 and 1870. They specifically note the fragility and brevity of such international normative orders.

The thesis regarding the "contagiousness" of conflict and war on an *intra*-regional basis is supported by the evidence. Despite the apparent absence of such a relationship at the *inter*-regional level, a space–time

---

[7] This argument also is made in the context of Middle Eastern regional war by Rosen (1977). For a discussion of the issue of nuclear weapons and deterrence within the context of the Cold War – and the difficulty of extrapolating from those patterns into the future – see Kegley and Raymond (1994:38–45).

conflict diffusion/contagion process appears to operate within geographic regions.

In conclusion, there is cumulative evidence regarding the difference in patterns of conflict and war across geographic regions. Proportional shifts in the distribution of militarized disputes have occurred from the pre-1945 to the post-1945 period, with the newer regional subsystems exhibiting greater conflict tendencies than in the past. Intraregional processes of conflict diffusion have influenced these patterns, and increasing military capabilities in the newer regional subsystems may be expected to further exacerbate their conflict potential.

6   War-prone systems

Introduction

In 1961, Singer noted that the analysis of the international system provides the most comprehensive level for the study of interstate relations. He observed that formation and dissolution of alliances, shifting capability distributions among major powers, and the effectiveness of international organizations and norms all could be subsumed within system-level study. However, 30 years later, Wayman and Singer (1991) state that the production of substantive data-based findings on associations between system-level characteristics and war has been less successful than dyadic-level studies. While this observation is valid, it is nevertheless possible to extract a series of consistent and cumulative empirical findings on war from the quantitative literature on international systems (references listed in appendix 2, table A.4). Many of the difficulties associated with early systemic-level studies stemmed from conceptual ambiguity in the construction of measures or the misspecification of variables. However, these problems do not fundamentally detract from the set of important observations on the factors associated with war-prone international systems.

Polarity/alliance

The literature of international politics is rife with discussions on the effects of the "polarity" of the international system on war. Unfortunately, due to the ambiguity of the concept of polarity and the multiple ways in which it can be operationalized, confusion rather than clarity has characterized the debate. The essence of this confusion involves the question of whether the polarity of the international system is determined by the number of major states or by the number of distinct clusters of states emerging from the configuration of alliances. For example, should a system with five major states that have coalesced into two opposing alliances be categorized as multipolar or bipolar? For the purposes of classifying data-based studies in this area, the following terminology will be used: the *polarity* of the international system is determined by the number of major actors. Possible configurations include *unipolarity* (one dominant state), *bipolarity* (two major states of approximately equal capabilities), and *multipolarity* (three or more major states of approximately equal capabilities).[1] As Snyder and Diesing (1977:420) assert:

> "poles" . . . are *states*, not alliances or "blocs" of states. Alliances and blocs are types of *relations* between states in the system that are influenced by the prevailing structure but do not constitute that structure. Thus the rough equality between the two alliances prior to 1914 did not make the system bipolar, nor did the loosening of the U.S. and Soviet blocs during the 1960s and early 1970s make that system multipolar.

Alliance configuration has often been discussed in terms of the *polarization* of the international system. For example, Kegley and Raymond (1994:54–55) argue that:

> whereas polarity pertains to the distribution of power [the number of major states], *polarization* refers to the propensity of countries to cluster in alliance . . . Thus a system with multiple power centers can be said to be moving toward a greater degree of polarization if its members gradually form two separate blocs whose interactions with others are characterized by increasing levels of conflict while the interactions among themselves become more cooperative.

Alliance configuration, like the number of major states (polarity), is viewed as a factor that affects uncertainty, and therefore the outbreak of war (Hower and Zinnes 1989:8). In both instances, opposing theoretical schools have developed regarding the war effects of the number of major actors and the formation or configuration of alliances. For example, some analysts argue that unipolar systems should be the least war-prone of the various system structures (e.g., Organski 1958; Gilpin 1981; Modelski 1983; Wallerstein 1984; Thompson 1988), while others maintain that this characteristic should inhere in bipolar systems (e.g., Waltz 1979:174–177) or in multipolar

[1] See Waltz (1979:161–169) for a discussion of bipolar and multipolar system structures.

structures (e.g., Morgenthau [1948], 1967:332–335).[2] Similar arguments exist with regard to alliances. Specifically, some theorists suggest that alliances deter war by maintaining military equilibrium (e.g., Holsti, Hopmann and Sullivan 1973), whereas others argue that alliances may increase tension, generate counter-coalitions, and raise the probability of war (e.g., Jervis 1976). As in the case of dyadic capability distributions (e.g., parity or preponderance), the war effects of polarity and alliance hinge, in part, on their roles in either enhancing or reducing uncertainty: unipolarity and firm alliances may reduce the level of uncertainty for decisionmakers,[3] but whether this decreases the probability of war by reducing misperception or increases the probability of war by simplifying an aggressor's calculations remains indeterminate (Levy 1989b:235).

Polarity

Explanations regarding polarity and war range from the "stable order" imposed by the dominant state in a unipolar system (e.g., Organski 1958; Modelski 1972; Gilpin 1981), to "balanced power" in a bipolar configuration (e.g, Waltz 1979), to "flexibility in alignment" in multipolar systems (e.g., Deutsch and Singer 1964; Morgenthau [1948], 1967). Data-based evidence, however, is mixed.

Mansfield (1988) examines international wars over the period from 1495 to 1980 and reports that the mean number of wars initiated per

---

[2] Midlarsky (1988:44–78) examines both mathematically and historically the multiple issues inherent in these opposing positions. See James (1995) for a discussion of extant theory on the war effects of system-level variables.

[3] Both Blainey (1973) and Snyder and Diesing (1977) argue that ambiguity in alliance commitments can increase uncertainty. For example, Blainey (1973:65) describes this situation on the eve of World War I:

> In every capital city [decisionmakers] had to predict whether their own allies would support them, whether the allies of the enemy would join in the war, and whether uncommitted nations would fight, give economic aid, or remain aloof.

Similarly, Snyder and Diesing (1977:430–431) note:

> Alliance considerations introduce complications into assessments of relative power by the direct protagonists in a crisis . . . [B]oth parties must calculate carefully the likely degree of allied support on both sides, since such support will be critical to the outcome. Negotiating positions and threat postures will be heavily affected by expectations about the interests and intentions of allies and other third parties.

Although Snyder and Diesing argue that alliance commitments are more critical to war outcomes in multipolar systems than in bipolar systems, it is obvious that expectations of alliance behavior could easily influence war decisions in bipolar systems as well. See Paul (1994:31–33) for a discussion of alliance support and war calculations in asymmetric conflicts. Here, too, ambiguity in alliance commitments may affect patterns of war initiation for both stronger and weaker states.

year was higher during eras when a "hegemonic" state (unipolarity) dominated the system than during eras when hegemony was absent. However, both Thompson (1986) and Spiezio (1990) report opposite results for unipolarity. Thompson's analysis covers a period similar to Mansfield's (1494–1983 [COW database], Modelski and Thompson database), and specifies categories of bipolarity, multipolarity, and near-unipolarity, in addition to unipolarity. Thompson's evidence suggests that warfare was least likely to occur when the system was unipolar or near-unipolar; he also reports that bipolar and multipolar systems were equally war-prone. Spiezio's study covers the more limited temporal period of 1815–1939 (COW data) in terms of the rising and falling economic/military capability base of Great Britain. He reports that the size of Britain's capability base was negatively and significantly associated with the frequency of war in the international system and concludes that his findings support the unipolar thesis that conflict is inversely related to the capabilities of the hegemonic state.

Brecher, James and Wilkenfeld (1990) and Wayman (1984) examine the effects of polarity in terms of international crises and war magnitude (i.e., total nation-months of war). The Brecher *et al.* analysis covers the temporal span of 1929–1985 (ICB database) for international crises using system categories of bipolarity and multipolarity. They report that the mean number of international crises per year was higher for the bipolar period (1945–1962) than for the multipolar era (1929–1939). However, based on an analysis of major power crisis involvement, they conclude that bipolarity is a more "stable" structure than multipolarity. Wayman (1984) examines the dependent variable of major power war magnitude for bipolar and multipolar periods over the years 1815–1965 (COW database). He reports that periods characterized by "power multipolarity" were much more likely to evidence high levels of war magnitude than were periods of "power bipolarity." These differences were statistically significant.

Hopf (1991) and Levy (1984) examine the frequency, magnitude, and severity of wars using polarity (Hopf) and "system size" (Levy) as predictors. Hopf's database includes warfare in the European subsystem for the restricted temporal period of 1495–1559. The system is classified as multipolar for the years 1495–1520 and as bipolar for the years 1521–1559. Hopf reports that the amount of warfare during these two periods was essentially equivalent. He concludes that polarity has little relationship to patterns of war for the historical period under examination. Levy (1984) explores a possible linear association between the number of great powers (system size) and war for the extended temporal span of 1495–1975. His findings coincide with those of Hopf; he reports that the frequency, magnitude, and severity of war in the international system is unrelated to the number of major powers in the system.

The cumulative findings in the area of polarity and warfare are mixed. Aside from the evidence of Thompson (1986) and Spiezio (1990) on an inverse relationship between the presence of an hegemonic state (unipolarity) and warfare, other findings indicate high numbers of crises during bipolar periods (Brecher, James and Wilkenfeld 1990) but lower war magnitudes than with multipolar systems. The study with the longest time-line and the most extensive set of war variables (Levy 1984) indicates the lack of a substantive linear relationship between the number of great powers and warfare.

Alliances

Quantitative empirical research in the area of alliances and warfare has produced a set of more consistent results than with system-level polarity and war. Three early studies by Singer and Small (1966, 1968, 1974) defined the problem and established the analytic model. Despite some conceptual ambiguity between alliance formation (aggregation), alliance configuration (polarization), and polarity (number of major states), the results of these analyses have been widely accepted. The basic hypothesis, simply stated, is: "The greater the number of alliance commitments in the system, the more war the system will experience" (Singer and Small 1968:251). The two early studies cover all nations for the period between 1815 and 1945; the third analysis extends the period to the years between 1815 and 1965 (COW database). Categories of alliance commitments include defense pacts, neutrality pacts, and ententes. The results of all three studies indicate the lack of a substantive statistical correlation between system-level alliance formation (aggregation) and the frequency of war for the entire period under analysis. In a subsequent study, Bueno de Mesquita and Lalman (1988) examine the effects of alliances on the occurrence of major power war in Europe for the period between 1815 and 1965. They conclude that alliance configuration (polarization) among the strongest nations does not appear to affect the probability of warfare in the major power system. In sum, the frequency and occurrence of war is unrelated to system-level alliance formation or configuration.

Other analyses produce generally consistent evidence with regard to alliance effects on the seriousness (magnitude, severity, and duration) of wars. Wallace (1973) examines war duration (nation-months of war) and war severity (battle-deaths) in terms of alliance polarization for the years 1815–1964 (COW database). He reports a strong curvilinear relationship between alliance polarization and both war duration and severity: specifically, periods in which alliance clustering in the international system is either extremely high or extremely low are likely to be associated with wars of great duration and severity. Similarly, Bueno de Mesquita (1978) examines war duration as a function of alliance configuration for the years 1816 to 1965 (COW database) and reports a statistically significant positive correlation between alliance polarization and the duration of wars. Lastly, Wayman (1984) provides additional evidence of a connection between alliance configuration and the magnitude of major power war. Wayman's analysis covers the period between 1815 and 1965 for all wars in the major power system (COW database). He defines war magnitude as the total nation-months of major power war involvement and reports that the clustering of major powers into two opposing alliances is significantly correlated with a subsequent increase in the magnitude of war. In sum, alliance polarization appears to be positively associated with the magnitude, severity, and duration of war.

Brecher, James and Wilkenfeld (1990) provide some insight into the crisis effects of alliance polarization. Using the ICB database for the years 1929–1985 and examining the frequency of international crises in periods with and without opposing alliance systems, they report the highest mean number of crises for system-periods characterized by polarized alliances.

Levy's (1981) analysis of great power alliances and warfare for the period between 1495 and 1975 also produces some notable conclusions. He examines a possible connection between the number of great powers engaged in alliances and the "amount" (i.e., frequency, duration, extent, magnitude, severity, intensity, and concentration) of war, and he reports that periods of high great power alliance formation (number of alliances and number of powers forming alliances) are characterized by relatively low levels of warfare. With regard to the occurrence of war, Levy (1981: 610) concludes his analysis by noting that "for none of the last five centuries have wars generally been preceded by alliances," and he argues that there is no apparent causal connection between great power alliance formation and the onset of war.

Summary

The results of data-based studies on polarity and warfare are mixed with no definitive linear pattern evident regarding unipolar, bipolar, and multipolar configurations and the occurrence of war. The only polar structure that appears to influence conflict probability is unipolarity. At least part of the difficulty in identifying a stable pattern may be the result of an interaction effect between factors at multiple analytic levels, as the onset (occurrence/initiation) of major power warfare is determined less by the number of major powers than by the static and dynamic capability distributions and policy objectives among the strongest states themselves. More precisely, the onset of wars among major powers is heavily affected by their relative capabilities and by their orientation toward the status quo. Every international system possesses a hierarchy based on relative capabilities, and the extent of the capability differential between the leading state and potential challengers matters. If the hierarchy is clear, with the leading state in possession of a substantial capability advantage over its nearest potential rival, then the probability of action to rearrange the hierarchical order is likely to be low. However, if the capability advantage of the leading state is small or is eroding, other states may choose to attempt to alter the hierarchy. The challenges may be directed against the leading state or lesser states within an increasingly unstable international order. This logic is found in the works of Organski, Modelski, Gilpin, Wallerstein, and others. Studies by Doran (1989), Geller (1992b, 1996), and Houweling and Siccama (1993) have presented empirical analyses of these complex cross-level dynamics and indicate that changes in the hierarchical arrangement of major powers are associated statistically with the onset of great power warfare.

In sum, shifts in system-level power structure appear to have an interactive effect with dyadic capability distributions in the onset of both major power and global wars. As the international system moves from a high concentration of resources in the leading state toward multipolarity (power diffusion), lower-order conflict among the set of major states will become increasingly probable, due to the weakening of the principal defender of the hierarchy. Movement toward power parity within these secondary nation-dyads triggers violent interactions that – though not related to system leadership – are still of considerable consequence. This suggests that the erosion of the system-level power structure links lower-order wars among major powers to system-shaping global wars. In this way, power distributions at both the systemic and dyadic levels of analysis interact synergistically to produce war among the set of major powers. The stability of the hierarchy rather than the number of major powers appears to be the critical factor.[4]

The evidence regarding system-level alliances and warfare is clear. The onset (occurrence/initiation) of war is unrelated to either alliance formation (aggregation) or configuration (polarization). However, the magnitude, duration, and severity (or "seriousness") of war does show consistent and significant correlation with the configuration of alliances. This is not surprising since alliance is a principal mechanism by which small wars become big wars – war spreads through alliances. Hence, the greater the extent of alliance polarization in the system, the higher the probability that the wars that do occur will be of greater magnitude, duration, and severity.[5]

Attributes

The first section of this chapter examined the results of data-based studies on the effects of polarity (i.e., the number of major states) and

---

[4] The inconsistencies between many system-level classifications of polarity and estimates of the presence or absence of hegemony are a function of either operational measure selection or, in a more fundamental way, of analytic focus. For example, in some instances, identification of polarity/hegemony depends on the indicator of "power" that is used. As a case in point, note that Organski and Kugler (1980) use GNP – and by that measure alone in the post-1945 period the United States was far superior to the Soviet Union: nevertheless, the Cold War era is usually referred to as one of military bipolarity. However, the principal distinction between the theories of power transition, hegemonic decline, etc. and many system-level classifications of polarity is one of analytic focus: theories of power transition, long cycles of world leadership, and hegemonic decline emphasize the power *differentials* (by whatever measure is used) between the *strongest nation* and its potential *challengers*, whereas many system-level classifications of polarity (e.g., Waltz 1979; Nye 1990) focus on the *number* of states with *approximately equal* capabilities. Hence, for Organski and Kugler, Modelski, and Gilpin the nineteenth century was unipolar (with British hegemony), and the post-1945 period was unipolar (with United States hegemony), whereas for Waltz the nineteenth century was multipolar (with approximate equality of power among Britain, France, Russia, Austria-Hungary, and Germany) and the post-1945 period was bipolar (with approximate equality between the United States and the Soviet Union).

[5] See Kim and Morrow (1992) and Vasquez (1993) on alliances and the spread of war.

alliances (i.e., formation and configuration) on patterns of war. This section will examine the effects of system-level capability concentration (i.e., the distribution of capabilities across the set of major states), the impact of subsystem (i.e., state-level) characteristics, the effects of borders, and the influence of global economic cycles on patterns of war. The importance of system-level capability concentration as a factor promoting or inhibiting war again relates to the theoretical issue of decisionmaking "certainty/uncertainty." The effects of subsystem (state-level) characteristics on system-level behavior involves reductionist theory. However, the attributes of states influence and are influenced by (or interact with) system structure. Therefore, the system-wide distribution of state-level attributes is an appropriate factor in the analysis of war-prone systems. The issue of contiguity and war is raised again – this time at the system level – by an examination of the number of borders and the frequency of war in the interstate arena at different time points. Lastly, evidence relating to the war effects among major powers of expansion and contraction in the global economy – a proposition drawn from Neo-Marxist theory – is explored.

Capability concentration

The distribution of capabilities is an element that is intrinsic to war decisions. However, as Singer, Bremer and Stuckey (1972) argue, some explanations of war emphasize "uncertainty" (e.g., misjudgment, misperception, faulty expectations, etc.), whereas other explanations emphasize "certainty" (e.g., clarity, order, and predictability). They suggest that the concentration of capabilities among major powers heavily influences the level of decisionmaker certainty or uncertainty – capability concentration enhances certainty, whereas deconcentration reduces it – and that a capability concentration index[6] may

---

[6] The concentration of capabilities in the system and the polarity (the number of major states) of the system are different measures of the systemic distribution of power. A standard index of capability concentration devised by Ray and Singer (1973) is:

$$CON_t = \sqrt{\frac{\sum_{i=1}^{N_t} (S_{it})^2 - 1/N_t}{1 - 1/N_t}}$$

where

therefore be used to test war explanations based on the level of decisionmaking certainty or uncertainty. Using six variables reflecting three dimensions of national capabilities (military, demographic, and economic) for the set of major powers over the period between 1820 and 1965 (COW database), Singer, Bremer and Stuckey regress three measures of capability concentration against the variable of major power nation-months at war. The results indicate a negligible (non-significant) association between the concentration of capabilities and "magnitude" (nation-months) of war for the entire period 1820–1965.

Bueno de Mesquita (1981b) replicates the Singer, Bremer and Stuckey analysis with a simple alteration: he measures war occurrence (a dichotomous event – either present or absent) instead of war magnitude (total nation-months) over five-year periods (COW database). His results are consistent with theirs – the concentration of capabilities is statistically unrelated to the occurrence of major power war over the period between 1820 and 1965. Bueno de Mesquita and Lalman (1988) also examine a more extensive set of system-level attributes ("tightness" and "polarity") along with capability concentration ("balance") for major powers between 1815 and 1965 and report, once again, that system-level capability concentration is unrelated to the occurrence of major power war.

Subsystem (state-level) attributes

A number of quantitative empirical studies have examined a possible relationship between the frequencies of civil wars and the frequencies of international disputes and wars. Specifically, both Maoz (1989) and Hoole and Huang (1989) pose the question of whether the amount of system-level interstate conflict is affected by the amount of state-level civil war or revolution in the international system. Maoz uses militarized interstate dispute counts (COW database) between 1815 and 1976 as his dependent variable and searches for correlations with the number of revolutionary state formations/transformations. His basic hypothesis – that the number of interstate conflicts in the system will

S_{it} = the proportion of the aggregate capabilities possessed by the major
powers that major power i controls in year t
N_t = the number of major powers in the system in year t
This is a statistical measure that takes on values from zero to one and reflects the aggregate inequality of capabilities as distributed among all major powers in the system. It is not directly related to the number of major powers in the system. See Mansfield (1994:72–75) for a discussion of this statistic.

increase when a large number of states are experiencing revolutionary regime changes – is supported statistically. Hoole and Huang, using international and civil war data (COW Project) for the limited temporal period of 1947–1980, report that changes in the amount of system-level international war are significantly affected by changes in the amount of civil war occurring in the interstate system. The results of both the Maoz and Hoole and Huang studies indicate that international and domestic conflict are part of an interactive global process.

In a related study, Maoz and Abdolali (1989) examine the homogeneity/heterogeneity of the international system in terms of the distribution of democratic and autocratic regimes and its effects on the frequencies of system-level disputes and wars for the period between 1816 and 1976 (COW database). They report that the proportion of both democratic/democratic interaction opportunities and autocratic/autocratic interaction opportunities exhibits significant positive effects on the frequency of disputes and significant negative effects on the frequency of war. In other words, the greater the homogeneity of regime-types (either democratic *or* autocratic), the lower the frequency of war. Maoz and Abdolali conclude that the homogeneity/heterogeneity of regimes in the international system affects the amount of system-level international conflict.

Two studies – by Wallace (1971) and East (1972) – focus on a possible relationship between states' status discrepancies and international violence/war. Wallace measures differences between a state's "ascribed" and "achieved" status and examines correlations with indicators of the magnitude (total nation-months) and severity (total battle-deaths) of wars over the period between 1820 and 1964. With time-lags of 10 and 20 years, he produces statistically significant correlations and concludes that peace in the international system appears to require the elimination of large differences between the "achieved" and "ascribed" status of its members. East, in a similar study for 120 nations for the limited period of 1948–1964, also reports a moderate relationship between status discrepancy and international violence.

Borders

Two studies by Starr and Most (1976, 1978) examine a possible relationship between the total number of borders in the international system and the number of new war participations in the system.

Using data from Richardson (1960), the COW Project, and SIPRI for the years 1946 through 1965, they report that the total number of borders in the international system is positively and significantly correlated with war participations in both the COW and SIPRI data sets. These results provide system-level evidence for the borders/ contiguity theses that were discussed at the monadic and dyadic levels of analysis.

Global economic cycles

Goldstein (1988) presents an exhaustive analysis on "long waves" in economic factors and wars. He combines 55 economic time series and several war series (Levy 1983 [1495–1975], COW database [1815–1975]) covering the period 1495–1975 for great power wars in a single data set. The war indicators employed in the analysis include severity (battle-deaths), intensity (ratio of battle-fatalities to the European population), incidence (presence or absence of war in a given year), and frequency (number of wars occurring in a given period). Among his findings, Goldstein reports that only the severity of great power war correlates strongly with economic long waves.

Mansfield (1988) attempts to test for the presence of an association between the phase of the Kondratieff economic long cycle and the mean number of wars begun per year in the international system between 1495 and 1980. The application of Kondratieff "waves" – the expansion and contraction of the global capitalist economy – to the occurrence of major power war has been explored by Modelski (1981)[7] and Wallerstein (1984). Mansfield's data-based study reports that the

---

[7] Although there is an interface with the Kondratieff wave thesis, Modelski's (1981, 1983) basic long cycle theory posits 100-year cycles of increasing power diffusion and subsequent global warfare followed by a high level of military/economic capability concentration in a single state (i.e., strong unipolarity) resulting in global order. His thesis holds that as the international system moves from a unipolar concentration of resources toward multipolarity, the conflicts among major states will become increasingly intense, leading ultimately to global war. Modelski (1981:64–65) suggests that the global political order is a type of exchange system involving transactions among those who provide and consume political goods. Principal among these goods are international order, security, territorial rights, and stability in the world economy. According to Modelski, in each century since 1500 the global system of transactions has been regulated by a single world power which possesses preponderance in the military capability of global reach (i.e., sea power). Each long cycle opens with the rise of a new world power out of the preceding global war; however, due to competitive erosion of its power position relative to other major states, the cycle moves through successive phases of delegitimation and deconcentration, culminating in another bout

mean number of wars begun during the upward phase of the Kondratieff cycle is greater than the mean number during the downward phase. This relationship is statistically significant, but the tendency for wars to vary with Kondratieff periods only appears when all wars are examined. The association does not hold for major power wars alone, as is maintained in the principal arguments of Modelski and Wallerstein.

Summary

The quantitative empirical findings in the area of system attributes and system-level conflict and war are consistent and cumulative. The studies dealing with capability concentration and major power war indicate the absence of a substantive relationship. One reason for these results may be found in the construction of the concentration index – a measure of aggregate *system-level* concentration or dispersion. If major power wars are based on estimates of capabilities, then the *relative* capabilities of *specific* opponents may be of greater consequence than the aggregate concentration/dispersion of power throughout the system. The clarity or ambiguity of the system-level major power hierarchy takes on more meaning when relative capabilities of antagonists are measured (e.g., Geller 1992b, 1996; Houweling and Siccama 1993; Weede 1994).

The results of the set of studies relating subsystem (state-level) attributes to system-level patterns of conflict and war are also interesting, with the global counts of civil and revolutionary wars revealing positive associations with global dispute and war frequencies. Starr (1994:482) has moved impressively toward identifying the elements involved in such a connection. Specifically, he has argued that:

> we must first differentiate between the ways in which revolution could lead to war and the ways in which war could lead to revolution. Looking at revolution-to-war, two basic relationships emerge – in what ways revolution would lead a state to *attack* another, or in what ways revolution would make a state an attractive *target* for another state. War-to-revolution may be based upon war as an agent of change, as a factor in the growth of domestic discontent, as a factor in the weakening of governmental legitimacy and/or strength, or as a factor in the changing resource base of opposition

of global war over leadership succession. The focus of long cycle theory is on explaining five global wars (see pp. 115–17, 119–120, 120 n.4).

groups. Whether a war is won or lost also must be factored into the
war-to-revolution relationship.

Starr (1994:495–496) goes on to discuss how the "interaction opportunity" model of conflict diffusion (Most and Starr 1980) can be
applied in an explanation of the revolution/war nexus:

> This model proposes that positive spatial diffusion would be en-
> hanced by the presence of violent conflict (either civil war, large-scale
> collective violence, or interstate war) in neighboring states, based on
> the heightened salience of conflict in proximate areas. This salience
> derives from: (1) a newly heightened uncertainty in the neighboring
> states as to the changing policies of a new government, possible
> ideological change and its interaction with either a newly strength-
> ened or weakened government and state; (2) a newly heightened
> uncertainty in the neighboring states as to their own viability or that
> of their neighbors. The neighbor must discern whether it has a newly
> strengthened or weakened country on its borders.

Starr (1994:501) then cites a recent study by Wallensteen and Axell
(1993) that identifies 82 armed conflicts for the period 1989–1992 and
notes that a connection between revolution and war is identifiable in
40 of these conflicts.

A second pattern relating state-level attributes to system-level
frequencies of conflict is the finding of a negative linkage between
regime homogeneity and international war – global conflict levels
vary in relation to the distribution of regime-types. Specifically, Maoz
and Abdolali (1989) report that an increase in the interaction opportunities of autocratic dyads is associated with a decrease in the global
frequency of war – just as in the case of democratic pairs.[8]

The findings on the positive relationship between the total number
of borders in the interstate system and the frequency of war participations in the system mirror the results on borders/contiguity and war
at the monadic and dyadic levels of analysis. The number of borders
and contiguity correlate positively with conflict and war at the state,
dyad, and system levels.

Lastly, evidence of system-level frequencies of all wars alternating
with phases of the Kondratieff cycle is interesting and superficially

---

[8] See Gleditsch (1994) for a discussion of shifts from positive to negative correlations
between system-level democratization and war-proneness. Gleditsch also reviews
results on the democratic peace proposition drawn from the monadic and dyadic
levels of analysis.

consistent with the formulations of Modelski and Wallerstein. However, these periods of global economic expansion and contraction are linked theoretically only to the occurrence of great power war, rather than to frequencies of all wars (which include minor power wars as well). Hence, empirical support of the Kondratieff thesis as an explanation for major power wars is, at this point, lacking.

Time

Comparisons of the frequency and seriousness of wars over time provide evidence of the historical war-proneness of the international system. Studies in this area tend to fall in one of two categories: simple scatterplots or frequency counts of wars over time (or by historical period); and tests of war-randomization – i.e., the use of time as a variable in predicting patterns of subsequent war. Many of these latter studies involve additional hypotheses of war contagion (diffusion) and war-weariness (negative reinforcement). This section will focus only on those analyses that attempt to measure war-proneness over time or to use time as a possible predictor from past to subsequent patterns of war. The issue of system-wide war contagion will be examined in the next section of this chapter.

Frequencies

Eckhardt and Azar (1978a, 1978b) produce frequency counts of conflict events and cooperative events over the period between 1945 and 1975. These categories are defined by the coding scheme of the COPDAB Project and involve scale points and weights assigned to specific events. Eckhardt and Azar report that the distribution of both cooperative and conflict events for the 1945–1975 period was not stable, but curvilinear. Generally, the frequencies of both cooperative and conflict events increased from 1945 to 1969 and decreased from 1969 to 1975. In terms of overall numbers, the authors note that there were more cooperative events than there were conflict events over the three-decade period.

In a conceptually clearer analysis, Stoll (1982) examines major power disputes and wars (COW database) for the more extensive period between 1816 and 1976. He reports that the number of serious subwar disputes per year averaged 1.84 in the post-World War II era, whereas the number of subwar disputes for the 1816–1945 period averaged only 1.28 per year. However, Stoll notes that fewer serious disputes actually escalated to war in the post-World War II era than in the pre-World War II period.

The most complete examination of the frequencies of militarized subwar disputes and wars is found in Gochman and Maoz (1984). Reporting on the distributions in their Militarized Interstate Dispute (MID) database for the years 1816 through 1976, Gochman and Maoz (1984:590–593) note that in terms of raw frequencies, disputes have not occurred evenly across time. They divide the 161-year period into historical eras, beginning with the "Concert of Europe" (1816–1848), which they note is the least dispute-prone period – with an average of 1.7 disputes begun per year. The second period, "European National Unification" (1849–1870), produces an average of 4.2 disputes begun per year and is the third most peaceful era of the set. The next period, the "Bismarckian Era" (1871–1890), shows a decline in dispute frequency to 3.4 disputes begun per year which reflects "the relative orderliness of the time." The fourth period, the "Age of Imperialism" (1891–1918), shows a sharp rise in the average number of disputes begun per year to 6.1. The fifth period, the "Interwar and World War II Era" (1919–1945), reveals an even greater frequency than the previous period, averaging 6.7 disputes begun per year. Finally, the raw frequencies indicate that the "Nuclear Era" (1946–1976) is by far the most disputatious period, averaging 12.7 disputes begun per year. However, as Gochman and Maoz (1984:592–593) note:

> The absolute frequency of disputes over time . . . does not reflect changes in the size of the international system. If it is assumed that the greater the number of states, the greater the number of conflict opportunities, then controlling for the number of states . . . allows for a more meaningful comparison of the conflictfulness of the interstate system during the various periods of the temporal domain.

When they introduce this control, they discover that the moving average flattens out and there is no substantial increase in the adjusted frequency of disputes over time. Gochman and Maoz (1984:593) conclude that "the apparent increase in the disputatiousness of inter-state relations over the past century and a half is, at least in part, a function of the growth in the size of the interstate system." A final observation of the analysis indicates that in the post-World War II era, war was a less frequently reached dispute level than in any of the pre-World War II periods.

Examining a longer time-line but for a smaller population, Levy

(1982a) produces some interesting information on the frequency and seriousness of great power wars between 1495 and 1975. Here, wars only include conflicts involving military forces of two or more "great powers" and resulting in at least 1,000 battle-deaths. Levy also examines war "seriousness" – a concept including: duration (years); extent (number of great powers engaged); magnitude (total number of nation-years of war); severity (battle-deaths); intensity (ratio of battle-deaths to total European population); and concentration (ratio of battle-deaths to nation-years of war). His analysis indicates that great power war has been decreasing in frequency but increasing in seriousness over time.[9]

Randomization

Singer and Small (1972, 1974) are among the first to examine the question of war randomization. Specifically, they pose the question of whether new war initiations are more likely to take place in the years immediately following the occurrence of an interstate war. Using the COW database for the period between 1816 and 1965, they report that years in which wars began were statistically neither more nor less likely to be followed by another war initiation in the next year. In other words, at the level of the international system, war initiations are random.

Levy and Morgan (1986) provide corroborative evidence in their analysis of war in the great power system for the period from 1500 to 1975. Their study distinguishes between "great power wars" (involving one or more great powers) and "general wars" (which involve nearly all great powers and result in very high numbers of casualties). Of their findings, Levy and Morgan report that the "probability of war is independent of the period of time since the last war." They also note that there is no evidence supporting the hypothesis "that more serious wars generate a greater inhibition against subsequent war" (Levy and Morgan 1986:46). In short, the

---

[9] Reaching further back in history, Cioffi-Revilla (1995, 1996) has reported preliminary results from the Long-Range Analysis of War (LORANOW) Project covering the areas of Mesopotamia (3000 BC to 539 BC), China (2500 BC to AD 220), Mesoamerica (900 BC to AD 1600), Greece–Rome (500 BC to "0"), Japan–Korea (600 BC to AD 1600), and East Central Europe ("0" to AD 1000). His findings (1996:10) on war frequencies indicate a lower onset rate for these areas (0.2 wars/year) than for the modern international system of AD 1500 to the present (1.1 wars/year).

systemic distributions of great power wars and general wars appear to be random with respect to time.

In an interesting study, Goldstein (1988:243–244) reexamines Levy's (1983) database for long cycles of great power war severity (battle-fatalities) using the methodology (spectral analysis) employed by Singer and Small (1972, 1974). Goldstein reports "a clear bulge in the AFC (Auto-Correlation Function) peaking around fifty to sixty years. Depending on the exact formulation, . . . the peak is either just barely, or not quite significant at the .05 level." Goldstein concludes that the existence of long waves of great power war severity is corroborated.

Midlarsky (1986) examines the frequencies of major power disputes and wars from 1816 to 1964 (COW database), and suggests that "systemic war" results from the conjunction of an ambiguous hierarchy and a disequilibrium in the frequencies of conflicts (disputes and wars) begun and terminated within a given period of time. Midlarsky defines hierarchy in terms of clear capability differentials between states within the same alliance system.[10] The system is in a state of equilibrium if the number of disputes begun and ended in a specified time span are balanced. Using these definitions, Midlarsky identifies the period between 1816 and 1899 as stable, and the periods of 1893–1914, 1919–1939, and 1946–1964 as unstable. He concludes that systemic or global wars are more likely to occur during periods characterized by an absence of hierarchical equilibrium.

Summary

The analyses discussed in this section indicate that from 1816 to 1976 the adjusted frequencies of militarized disputes occurring in the international system are stable over time once the control factor of system size is introduced. In other words, as the number of states has increased, so has the frequency of militarized disputes. With regard to great power wars, the tendency from the end of the fifteenth century to the last quarter of the twentieth century has reflected a decrease in the frequency of great power warfare but an increase in the destructiveness of those wars. The evidence regarding all system-level war initiations at one-year intervals and the elapsed time between the

---

[10] In this case, "hierarchy" refers only to internal alliance structures rather than to the rank-order structure of states by capability in the international system.

occurrence of great power wars is consistent with that of random distributions.

Contagion

The question of war contagion at the regional level was raised in chapter 5. This section examines quantitative empirical evidence of war contagion at the level of the international system. Awareness of a possible "contagion" or "diffusion" process with regard to social phenomena can be traced to the late nineteenth century with the formulation of "Galton's problem" (Naroll 1968). In a meeting of the Royal Anthropological Institute in 1889, Sir Francis Galton argued that cultural traits often spread through a diffusion process. Hence, the appearance of similar phenomena in different spatial–temporal settings may not be independent of one another, but rather connected through a process of contagion or diffusion. The contagion/diffusion issue has been raised in the study of race riots, coups d'état, revolutions, and alliance formation. Richardson (1960) was the first to attempt to test for a contagion process in war. Five recent data-based studies of possible war contagion at the systemic level of analysis illustrate the problem.

Contagion/diffusion

Bremer (1982) examines the question of whether coercive behavior (threats of force/use of force) in the international system is contagious. His data include all militarized disputes for the years between 1900 and 1976 (COW database). "Contagion" is said to have occurred if the use of force by one actor increases the probability that another actor will use force in the future. Bremer's analysis indicates that the system-wide number of disputes per month is not significantly different from a modified Poisson distribution. Although his findings indicate that a contagion process operates at the regional level, he concludes that the use of force has not been contagious at the global level between 1900 and 1976.

Faber, Houweling and Siccama (1984) explore evidence of diffusion for civil, interstate, and extra-systemic wars over the period between 1816 and 1980 (COW database). Their analysis examines both the spatial and temporal distances between the locations and timing of successive war initiations, using lags of between one and five years. Their results indicate that war outbreaks are contagious within regions, but not across regions (i.e., globally). In a subsequent study, Houweling and Siccama (1985) use a different statistical technique (David and Barton's Q test) more appropriate to the analysis of space–time interaction. The results of this study also indicate that interstate war outbreaks worldwide for the period between 1816 and 1980 (COW database) evidence no "epidemicity": interstate war outbreaks do not show a global pattern of space–time interaction.

Most and Starr (1980) examine new war participations in the international system for the restricted temporal period between 1946 and 1965 (COW and SIPRI databases). "War diffusion" is said to occur if states bordering on a state already at war become more likely (positive spatial diffusion) or less likely (negative spatial diffusion) to engage in war in the years subsequent to a war experience of one of its neighbors. Using ratios to compare war initiations across time periods, they report evidence in support of a positive spatial diffusion process. This analysis also identifies a possible mechanism for the spread of war through contiguity (shared borders).

Levy's (1982b) study of war contagion is limited to great power wars (i.e., wars involving at least one great power). The temporal domain for his analysis extends from 1495 to 1975, and his variables include both the frequency and "seriousness" (duration, extent, magnitude, severity, and concentration) of wars. His results indicate the absence of a substantive connection between either the frequency or seriousness of great power war in one period, and the frequency or seriousness of war in a subsequent period (three- and five-year intervals). Levy concludes that a war contagion process among great powers does not exist.

Summary

Positive findings of war contagion/diffusion at the regional level of analysis are consistent and cumulative. However, the results of studies at the systemic level are ambiguous. One possible explanation for the discrepancy of findings between the regional and systemic levels may be found in the mechanisms by which war diffuses: border contact and alliances. Contiguity is a factor at the local and regional levels and, historically, alliances are more commonly drawn within regions rather than extra-regionally. The absence of consistent findings of war contagion at the systemic level may be due to weak global effects of the factors (contiguity/alliance) responsible for regional war diffusion. At this point, evidence regarding the systemic diffusion of war must be considered tentative and preliminary.[11]

Norms/intergovernmental organizations

A relatively small set of quantitative empirical studies has focused on the conflict effects of international norms and organizations. Standard definitions describe norms as expectations of action in given situations (e.g., Parsons 1951:11–12). International norms pertain to expectations of action regarding the behavior of states. As Kegley and Raymond (1994:122) note, normative rules of international order are set by the great powers to serve their interests. These "rules of the system" are designed to maintain the international hierarchy, to benefit the dominant state and its allies, and are enforceable only through the self-interested actions of the great powers. Vasquez (1993:283) describes variation in the structure of norms in this fashion:

> System-wide rules and norms usually reflect custom. Every peace within the system helps establish a set of norms, rules, and conventions about how states should relate to each other and when war can serve as a way of resolving issues . . . At certain critical moments in history, however, major states attempt to develop in a more formal manner a set of rules and decision games. This typically occurs after a major global war, when the victors sit down . . . to establish a new world order. Formal attempts at rule making usually derive from a mutual realization that prior interaction games, especially total war, should be avoided and replaced by less costly ways of conducting politics.

Kegley and Raymond (1994) dichotomize normative orders in international politics on the basis of the normative positions regarding the use of force, treaty violations, and spatial constraints on state authority. The fundamental distinction is between a "permissive" or a "restrictive" normative order. As described by Kegley and Raymond (1994:55):

> The expectations of proper action expressed by international norms define the "cultural climate" within which great-power interaction takes place. At any time this rudimentary political culture communicates prevailing opinions about acceptable patterns of state behavior. Whereas a permissive normative order advances rules that

---

[11] For opposing evaluations of the evidence on this subject, see Most, Starr and Siverson (1989); Hower and Zinnes (1989).

accept the use of force as an instrument of statecraft and allow nations to repudiate agreements whenever they wish to free themselves from treaty obligations, a restrictive order encompasses rules that limit force, uphold the sanctity of treaties, and promote the development of rules governing the spatial limits of state authority.

Restrictive norms may be undermined when actors violate them successfully in the pursuit of their foreign policy objectives. Prohibitions, such as against the use of force, disintegrate as additional actors resort to violence. As the prohibited form of behavior becomes more commonplace, a norm that legitimizes the use of force emerges (Vasquez 1993:244). Intergovernmental organizations (IGOs) generally reflect attempts to institutionalize restrictive normative orders.

Norms

Three studies by Kegley and Raymond (1981, 1982, 1986) provide quantitative empirical evidence regarding the impact of international norms on patterns of war. Using data from the Transnational Rules Indicator Project (TRIP) and the COW Project database, Kegley and Raymond (1981) examine the effect of norms favoring pacific modes of dispute resolution (e.g., arbitration, illegality of war) on the frequencies of serious disputes and wars among major powers for the period between 1815 and 1974. Based on a content analysis of 244 legal treatises composed over the 160-year span, they attempt to test a set of conflict propositions utilizing measures reflecting acceptance of forcible retaliation and arbitration norms. The results of their analysis indicate that with the exception of a significant relationship between "acceptance of retorsion" (the legal use of force in retaliation for hostile actions) and the frequency of war, there appears to be little substantive association between arbitration norms, beliefs about the legality of war, and the frequencies of serious disputes and wars among major powers.

In a subsequent study, Kegley and Raymond (1982) examine the occurrence, magnitude, severity, and intensity of war in terms of norms supporting commitment to treaty obligations for the "great power" and "central power" systems between 1820 and 1939. Once again, TRIP and COW databases were used in the analysis. They report findings indicating that treaty commitment correlates inversely with measures of war magnitude, severity, and intensity for both the central and great power systems, and they conclude that international systems characterized by norms supporting treaty commitments are more likely to be peaceful than systems lacking those normative rules.

Kegley and Raymond (1986) also examine the efficacy of international norms constraining the use of force on patterns of militarized disputes and wars within the European state system (TRIP and COW databases). In this study, 244 legal treaties concluded between 1815 and 1980 were content analyzed and classified according to their emphasis on peaceful dispute resolution measures. They report that there has been considerable fluctuation in support for norms constraining the use of force, and that these fluctuations evidence no apparent periodicities (i.e., "dispute norms become salient irregularly, and for different lengths of time"). A focused comparison of two time periods with strong (1816–1848) and weak (1849–1870) normative constraints indicated that although both periods experienced approximately the same number of serious disputes, none of these disputes escalated into wars during the period of strong normative constraints, whereas the period characterized by weak constraints exhibited four wars between major powers. However, as Kegley and Raymond (1986:223–224) note:

> if norms can make a contribution to a reduction of war's frequency *in highly favorable circumstances*, this conclusion must immediately be followed by the qualification that even in auspicious environments norms cannot bring the incidence of war under control unless consensus is achieved about the uses to which force short of war can be put . . . The historical tendency for these preconditions to materialize only irregularly, and then for only limited periods of time, does not augur well for the ability of norms to maintain peace in other systems, under other circumstances, and over prolonged periods.

Intergovernmental organizations

Two quantitative empirical studies – producing divergent conclusions – are relevant to the question of the effects of IGOs on patterns of war and peace. Singer and Wallace (1970) conducted a correlation analysis between the number of IGOs, membership in IGOs, and the frequency, magnitude, and severity of interstate war (COW database) for the international system from 1816 to 1964. Time lags of five and 10 years between the number of IGOs and war were also explored. Singer and Wallace report results indicating that IGOs tend to be created after periods characterized by high levels of warfare, but that the number of IGOs in the international system or the extent of membership in

IGOs does not appear to substantively affect the amount of system-level war.

In a related study, Schahczenski (1991) employs Wallensteen's (1984) definitions of historical periods characterized by "particularistic" policy orientations (i.e., state pursuit of special interests at the expense of existing IGOs) and periods characterized by "universalistic" policy orientations (i.e., efforts to organize relations among states) in an analysis of patterns of system-level disputes and wars between 1816 and 1976 (COW database). Schahczenski's findings uniformly indicate that universalistic periods were less conflictual than were particularistic periods: universalistic periods were characterized by fewer militarized disputes, fewer dispute participants, fewer interstate wars, and fewer major power wars than particularistic periods. He concludes that collective efforts among major powers to establish limited international orders have a positive effect on the promotion of international peace.

Summary

The data-based findings on the efficacy of peaceful international norms and the establishment of IGOs as means of reducing system-level violence are not encouraging. Norms constraining the use of force or proclaiming the illegality of war do show some ability to reduce war behavior. However, as Kegley and Raymond (1986:213) note: "the historical evidence indicates that these conditions are met only rarely, and that the formation of such an international security regime is ephemeral." In contrast, acceptance of retorsion norms is positively and significantly associated with both militarized dispute and war frequencies. The findings indicating an inverse relationship between treaty commitments and the magnitude, severity, and intensity of war may be interpreted as the effect of an "uncertainty reduction" measure in the decisionmaking calculus: alliances that appear firm are less likely to be tested than alliances that appear tentative. The results involving the effects of IGOs on system-level conflict are less consistent, but not particularly hopeful. There is an empirical tendency for IGOs to be established at the conclusion of massive wars. However, the historical success of diplomatic institutions and procedures for nonviolent conflict resolution is punctuated by catastrophe. As Vasquez (1993:283) notes:

> Some of these formal rule-making efforts, like the Peace of Westphalia and the Congress of Vienna, have been highly successful in

resolving the issues that led to war and mitigating the use of violence. Others, such as the Versailles system, have been disastrous, bringing about the very war they tried to prevent.

Holsti (1991) provides insight into factors that may produce at least limited respite from system-wide war, but his eight prerequisites of peace[12] describe an international system fundamentally different from anything that has ever existed.

Evaluation

The data-based evidence regarding factors associated with war-prone international systems is mixed. Characteristic of these findings is the evidence on system polarity and war. A principal tenet of realpolitik maintains that the distribution of capabilities is a primary factor in the war-proneness of the system. This assumption has led to debates about the relative peacefulness of unipolar, bipolar, and multipolar configurations. However, attempts to answer the question through quantitative empirical analysis have been marred by ambiguity over what characteristics of war (e.g., occurrence, frequency, magnitude, duration, or severity) should be associated with polarity, as well as by problems resulting from the misspecification of variables (e.g., incorporating alliances in measures of polarity).

The onset (occurrence/initiation) of war has been connected empirically with capability distributions among challengers and defenders of the status quo. The evidence suggests that the onset of major power warfare is principally determined by a state's orientation toward the status quo and its relative ability to challenge or defend it, rather than by the number of major states in the system. Moreover, an interaction effect between the rising/declining capabilities of the leading state in the hierarchy relative to those of potential challengers

---

[12] Holsti's (1991:336–339) prerequisites for a relatively peaceful international order include: (1) a system of governance (i.e., the presence of actors or agencies able to make and enforce rules of order); (2) legitimacy (i.e., an order based on justice and self-determination); (3) assimilation (i.e., acceptance within an international order of defeated opponents); (4) a deterrent system (i.e., the presence of a coalition strong enough to enforce the norms of the system); (5) procedures and institutions for conflict resolution (i.e., mechanisms for resolving disputes without violence); (6) consensus on war (i.e., agreement on norms opposing war); (7) procedures for peaceful change (i.e., methods providing for the gradual evolution of the status quo); and (8) anticipation of future issues (i.e., sensitivity to problems that may precipitate future conflict).

as well as dyadic-level capability balances among lesser major powers have been identified as factors influencing the onset of great power wars. In short, the stability of the hierarchy – rather than the number of major powers – appears to be the critical factor.[13]

The evidence on alliances and warfare is consistent and cumulative. The frequency and occurrence of war are unrelated to either system-level alliance formation (aggregation) or configuration (polarization). However, the magnitude, duration, and severity (or "seriousness") of war is substantively connected to alliance configuration – for the simple reason that war spreads through alliances. Therefore, the greater the system-level alliance polarization, the greater the probability that the wars that do occur will engage more states, employ larger amounts of destructive capabilities, last longer, and produce more fatalities. Alliances turn small wars into big wars.

The evidence on subsystem political attributes and system-level warfare is also intriguing. Specifically, global counts of civil and revolutionary wars reveal positive associations with global interstate dispute and war frequencies: an apparent nexus between revolution and war has been identified in system-level studies. Similarly, the inverse relationship between regime homogeneity and international war provides an interesting pattern linking subsystem attributes and system-level attributes. The more homogeneous the distribution of regime-types in the international system, the lower the global frequencies of war.

Finally, it could be argued that the positive relationship between the number of borders in the international system and the frequency of war in the system is simply the result of an increase in the number of states: as the number of actors increases, the frequency of war increases. However, this evidence also conforms with findings on borders and war at the state and dyadic levels, and therefore cannot be easily dismissed on the basis of the expansion of the number of units within the system. Borders (proximity/contiguity) and war are linked empirically at multiple analytic levels.

Cross-time comparisons of the international system have also produced some interesting results. For example, the distribution of militarized disputes over time (1816–1976) has been shown to be

---

[13] See Thompson (1983a, 1983b), Doran (1983), Houweling and Siccama (1993), and Weede (1994) for a discussion of cross-level dynamics. Vasquez (1993) presents a related multi-level explanation for the onset of both World War I and World War II.

stable with the addition of the control factor of system size. However, the frequency of great power wars has diminished from the end of the fifteenth century to the last quarter of the twentieth century, while the destructiveness of those wars has increased over the same period.

The evidence of system-level war contagion/diffusion is less consistent than the evidence of this process at the level of the region. Contagion tends to be localized with prominent border effects; and, historically, alliances have been constructed within regional boundaries. The weak global effects of both contiguity and alliance – the principal mechanisms for the diffusion of war – may explain the difference in the contagion findings between the regional and systemic levels of analysis.

Lastly, the few examples of quantitative empirical research on the conflict effects of nonviolent international norms and the presence of IGOs do not provide a source for optimism. Norms constraining the use of force in international affairs show no substantive relationship to the frequency of militarized disputes, but do indicate some ability to reduce the occurrence of war. However, these norms appear irregularly, for short periods of time, and only under highly unusual circumstances. Moreover, there is an empirical tendency for IGOs to be established at the conclusion of massive wars, but little evidence of any association between the number of these organizations or extent of membership in IGOs and the amount of system-level warfare.

In conclusion, the evidence on factors associated with war-prone international systems is diverse and, in some instances, cumulative, consistent, and compelling. An unstable hierarchy with a declining leader, alliance polarization, revolution, and increasing border contacts are all related to increases in the occurrence, frequency, or seriousness (magnitude, duration, severity) of war. That the number of militarized interstate disputes (standardized by system size) has been stable over time and that the frequency of great power wars has decreased over time, must be balanced against the trend toward the increasing destructiveness of war and the weakness of international norms and organizations in substantively reducing interstate conflict. The system-level prognosis is disquieting.

7   Case study: Iran/Iraq War (1980)

Introduction

The onset of the Iran/Iraq War (1980) is explained on the basis of empirical uniformities established by systematic quantitative analyses. As Hempel (1966:68) notes, scientific explanations of individual events may be provided through inductive subsumption under probabilistic laws, as well as through deductive subsumption under universal laws. The following inductive explanation demonstrates that the case of the Iran/Iraq War is a specific instance of a set of patterns which have appeared in a much larger number of cases.

The Iran/Iraq War of 1980 conforms to a set of probabilistic laws based on empirical regularities identified at the dyadic level of analysis. These two states: shared a common border (contiguity); had nondemocratic regimes (absence of joint democracies); were economically underdeveloped (absence of joint advanced economies); and exhibited an unstable military balance (a capability shift in 1979 and a transition in 1980). Add to this the classification of the dyad as an "enduring rivalry" (based on the frequency of previous militarized conflicts) and the existence of an unresolved territorial dispute (over the Shatt al'Arab waterway), and the occurrence of dyadic war with initiation by the militarily superior challenger of the status quo (Iraq) was a high-probability event consistent with a broad array of empirical war patterns. Although the nonoccurrence of the event is not precluded logically due to the inductive form of argument, nevertheless the war may be considered "explained" by its subsumption under probabilistic laws.[1] The following sections will discuss these empirical patterns within the context of the Iran/Iraq War of 1980.

---

[1] For a similar explanatory epistemology, see Vasquez (1996b).

Contiguity

Empirical pattern: The presence of a contiguous land or sea (separated by 150 miles of water or less) border increases the probability of war within a dyad.

Shatt al'Arab

As Grummon (1982:3–7) notes, border disputes between Iraq and Iran go back at least as far as the sixteenth century with the Ottoman–Safivid rivalries. Territorial and border conflicts continued into the twentieth century, principally regarding sovereignty over the Shatt al'Arab river. The 130-mile Shatt al'Arab is the product of the confluence of the Tigris and Euphrates rivers and constitutes the Iran/Iraq border for its last 55 miles leading into the Persian Gulf.

The Shatt and its surrounding area have economic importance for both states, but especially for Iraq. The sole Iraqi port with commercial significance is Basra, situated approximately 47 miles up the Shatt. Export pipelines for petroleum follow along the river bank and a crude oil depository is located at al'Faw, near the estuary of the river on the Persian Gulf.

The Iraqi coastline on the Persian Gulf (approximately 50 miles in length) is not suitable for port development. The physical contours of the northern point of the Persian Gulf determine that Basra will continue as the principal Iraqi port and that the Shatt al'Arab river will serve as Iraq's major economic link to the Gulf. In essence, Iraq's most important economic asset is vulnerable to disruption due to lack of control over its access to the Persian Gulf through the Shatt al'Arab river.

Iran's economic interests are also affected by access to the Persian Gulf through the Shatt al'Arab. The Iranian port of Khorramshahr is located at the confluence of the Shatt and Karun rivers (approximately 45 miles north of the estuary of the Shatt) and serves as a railhead for the Trans-Iranian railroad system, in addition to its role in facilitating shipping to the Gulf. Due to overland transportation costs and its location near major population centers, the port of Khorramshahr is an important element in the Iranian economy. However, despite the significance of the Shatt al'Arab to Iranian commerce, the river does not constitute the pressure point for Iran that it does for Iraq. Iran possesses other Persian Gulf ports and numerous oil export facilities outside the area of the Shatt al'Arab.

As already noted, disputes between the Ottoman and Persian governments regarding sovereignty over the territory around the Shatt al'Arab began in the sixteenth century. However, by the nineteenth century the basic outline of territorial control had been established: the area east of the Shatt belonged to Iran, while the area to the west belonged to the Ottomans (and to Iraq as the successor state). Nevertheless, despite this general division of the land, a precise border was not delineated in the nineteenth century.

The discovery of oil in Khuzistan in 1908 increased the stakes associated with boundary demarcations. The Constantinople Accords of 1913 established the border at the low water mark of the eastern (Iranian) river bank, but Iran was dissatisfied with the boundary created by the 1913 accords, and a new treaty was produced in 1937 that adjusted the border in the area around Abadan. In this treaty, the border was established according to the *thalweg* principle (i.e., the border of two states separated by a river should be drawn down the center of the major navigable channel of the river). However, the remaining border demarcation (below Abadan) was left at the low water mark of the eastern shore in accordance with the provision of the 1913 accords. In 1975 another treaty was negotiated that adopted the *thalweg* principle as the method for establishing the entire Shatt al'Arab boundary. It was this treaty that Saddam Hussein declared null and void just prior to Iraq's invasion of Iran in 1980.

Summary

Sovereignty over territory around the Shatt al'Arab river had been an issue in contention for over 400 years. In the latter part of the twentieth century, access through the southern portion of the Shatt leading to the Persian Gulf became a critical economic necessity for Iraq. The contiguous border between Iran and Iraq provided both the issue in dispute and the physical opportunity to settle the question of control through the use of military force.

Political systems

Empirical pattern: The absence of joint democratic governments increases the probability of war within a dyad.

Iran

Banks (1995:400–408) describes Iran as a former monarchy that, following the revolution of the late 1970s, became an Islamic Republic in 1979 on the basis of a referendum, with its current constitution also adopted by referendum in the same year. The constitution created in 1979 established Shi'ite Islam as the official religion of the state and gave "supreme power" to the Muslim clergy. The Ayatollah Ruhollah Khomeini was designated as the religious leader (*velayat faghi*) of the nation for life:

> The *faghi* is supreme commander of the armed forces and the Revolutionary Guard, appoints the majority of members of the National Defense Council, can declare war (on recommendation of the Council), and can dismiss the president following a legislative vote of no-confidence or a ruling of the Supreme Court. An elected Council of Experts, composed of 83 mullahs, appoints the country's spiritual leader and has broad powers of constitutional interpretation. The president, the country's chief executive officer, is popularly elected for a four-year term, as is the unicameral *Majlis*, to which legislative authority is assigned . . . A Council of Constitutional Guardians (successor to the Revolutionary Council), encompassing six specialists in Islamic law appointed by the *faghi* and six lawyers named by the High Council of the Judiciary and approved by the legislature, is empowered to veto presidential candidates and to nullify laws considered contrary to the constitution or the Islamic faith . . . Political parties are authorized to the extent that they "do not violate the independence, sovereignty, national unity, and principles of the Islamic Republic" . . . With the civil courts instituted under the monarchy replaced by Islamic Revolutionary Courts, judges are mandated to reach verdicts on the basis of precedent and/ or Islamic law. The legal code itself continues to undergo frequent changes. (Banks 1995:403)

Iraq

Banks (1995:408–415) describes Iraq as a republic following a military coup which toppled the monarchy in 1958. The constitution is an amended version of a document which dates back to 1968. As of 1979, Saddam Hussein has been the designated President of the Republic and Chairman of the Revolutionary Command Council:

> Constitutional processes were largely nonexistent during the two decades after the 1958 coup . . . It was not until . . . 1980 that elections were held for a unicameral National Assembly. The [Revo-

lutionary Command Council] was not, however, dissolved, effective power remaining concentrated in its chairman, who continued to serve concurrently as president of the Republic. The president has broad powers of appointment and is also commander in chief of the Armed Forces. The judicial system is headed by a Court of Cassation and includes five courts of appeal, courts of the first instance, religious courts, and revolutionary courts that deal with crimes involving state security. (Banks 1995:410)

Summary

On two measures of democratic government reported by Taylor and Jodice (1983:58–65) – "political rights" and "civil rights" – Iran and Iraq rank at or near the bottom of a list of over 140 states for 1979.

The first measure, a "political rights" index, is coded by Raymond Gastil and published by Freedom House. As Taylor and Jodice (1983:60) note:

> Political rights involve the right to play a part in determining who will govern one's country and what the laws will be. Countries are coded with scores ranging from 1 (highest degree of liberty) to 7 (lowest degree of liberty).

On this index (for 1980) Iran had a score of 5 and Iraq had a score of 7. The second measure, a "civil rights" index (also coded by Gastil and published by Freedom House), is defined in Taylor and Jodice (1983:64) as follows:

> Civil rights are those rights the individual has vis à vis the state. Particularly important are the freedom of the press and the other media and the independence of the judiciary. Countries are coded with scores ranging from 1 (greatest civil liberty) to 7 (least civil liberty).

On this index (for 1980) Iran had a score of 5 and Iraq had a score of 7.

On the basis of the scores reported for both the "political rights" and "civil rights" indices, neither Iran nor Iraq could be considered to possess democratically-based political systems[2] at the onset of war in 1980. Moreover, neither political system placed serious constraints on war decisions by the dominant leaders, nor did the systems incorporate norms of nonviolent conflict resolution.

---

[2] See Ray (1995a:chapter 3) for a discussion of definitions of democracy and a critique of Gastil's indices.

Economic development

Empirical pattern: The absence of joint advanced economic systems increases the probability of war within a dyad.

Iran

The Iranian economy in 1980 can be classified as underdeveloped with principal economic activity focused in the area of primary product resource extraction (i.e., petroleum). Hence, the export of a natural resource constituted the main source of government revenue and foreign exchange. Banks and Overstreet (1981:246) note that both the economy and the society of Iran were organized around agriculture until the early 1960s, when Muhammad Reza Shah Pahlavi instituted a program of rapid development: "During the next decade and a half, the proportion of gross domestic product (exclusive of oil revenue) contributed by agriculture dropped from nearly 50 percent to approximately 20 percent, and Iran became a net importer of food." This shift in economic activity was accompanied by a major relocation of the population from rural to urban areas, reducing the previous concentration of the vast mass of the population in rural areas to approximately 50 percent and the proportion of the work force engaged in agriculture to under 40 percent. A five-year plan (1973–1978) instituted by the Shah was designed to increase agricultural production annually by 7 percent, increase industrial production by 17 percent, and increase oil and gas production by 51 percent. However, these projected goals were not achieved due to planning deficiencies, inflation, and an enormous outflow of capital. By the middle of 1979, the effects of the Islamic Revolution had produced "a 12 percent contraction in goods and services, accompanied by a 40–70 percent falloff in the manufacturing sector" (Banks and Overstreet 1981:246). Other serious economic dislocations preceding the war with Iraq in 1980 included unemployment and inflation rates of nearly 50 percent, and a decline in petroleum exports between 1979 and 1980 of over 40 percent.

Iraq

The Iraqi economy in 1980 can be classified as underdeveloped with principal economic activity focused in the area of primary product resource extraction (i.e., petroleum). Hence, the export of a natural resource constituted the main source of government revenue and foreign exchange. Banks and Overstreet (1981:249) note that in 1980 agricultural activity employed over 50 percent of the population but produced only 25 percent of the national income. In 1979, Iraq surpassed Iran as the second-ranking producer of petroleum in the Middle East. Other natural resources important to Iraq's economy in 1980 were phosphates, sulphur, copper, chromite, and gypsum. The manufacturing sector of the economy – nationalized since 1964 – was "not highly developed, and expansion [was] slowed by shortages of skilled labor and recurrent political instability" (Banks and Overstreet 1981:249).

Summary

The analysis of economic and social dislocations resulting from development has been an area of intense interest in the social sciences. For example, dependency theorists (e.g., Frank 1967; Stallings 1972; Sunkel 1972) have argued that underdeveloped areas of the world have been used as raw materials suppliers for developed, capitalist states (such as Britain, France, Germany, Japan, and the United States). The formation of an export enclave in an underdeveloped, dependent state produces a distorted indigenous economy with a strong export sector that coexists with a traditional, rural/agricultural economic system. Whatever internal economic changes occur in these dependent states are tailored to the requirements of the metropolitan powers. In short, international trade forces these dependent states to produce primary goods for export. Foreign investment capital flows to this area of the economy, and hence these sectors become even stronger, while other economic sectors stagnate. Concomitants of the process are the disintegration of internal linkages among different areas of a dependent economy and the persistence of underdevelopment.

Although the relevance of the dependency thesis to petroleum-exporting states is a matter of debate, it is nevertheless clear that Iran and Iraq have economic systems based on trade of a primary product. Taylor and Jodice (1983:226–229) report that in 1975, trade accounted for 89.9 percent of Iraq's GNP (23rd in a ranking of 136 states) and for 55 percent of Iran's GNP (53rd in the same ranking). A second measure – a concentration index of export commodities – places these figures in the proper context. Taylor and Jodice (1983:230–232), using a measure of concentration of export commodities within a state's total exports[3] for 1975, report a score of 0.936 for Iran (3rd in a ranking of 121 states) and a score of 0.306 for Iraq (47th in the same ranking).

In sum, by the onset of the Iran/Iraq War in 1980, both economic systems were almost totally dependent upon the export of a single primary product for government revenue and foreign exchange. Hence, their joint classification as economically underdeveloped. That the border dispute underlying the outbreak of war involved control of the Shatt al'Arab waterway linking the Persian Gulf to major oil ports of both countries indicates the exposure of this critical sector in each economy and the overall vulnerability of both economic systems to external disruption.

Capability balance

Empirical pattern: The presence of an unstable capability balance (i.e., shift/transition) increases the probability of war within a dyad.

Iran

Subsequent to the overthrow of the regime of Muhammad Mossadeq in 1953, Muhammad Reza Shah Pahlavi embarked on a long-term modernization program for the armed forces of Iran (which had supported him rather than Mossadeq in the internal power struggle). For example, military spending in 1966 accounted for approximately 5.6 percent of Iran's GNP, whereas by 1978 over 15 percent of its GNP went to the military sector.[4]

In 1978, Iranian ground forces were grouped into three field armies. The combat forces included three armored divisions, three infantry divisions, and four independent brigades; the air force in 1978 had an estimated strength of 460 combat aircraft; and the navy in 1978 included three destroyers, eight frigates, three diesel submarines, and 24 missile patrol boats. In 1979, the armed forces numbered 415,000 men (Cottrell and Bray 1978:34–46; United States ACDA 1984:30).

However, following the revolution in 1979, the Iranian officer corps

---

[3] The concentration index of export commodities was developed by Hirschman (1945:157–162). "Concentration" is defined as the sum over all export divisions of the squares of the proportions of total exports accounted for by each division. Concentration scores are higher (1.000 is the maximum) with fewer export divisions and the greater the value of the largest divisions (Taylor and Jodice 1983:232).

[4] See Cottrell and Bray (1978) and United States ACDA (1976, 1984).

was purged and military expenditures were sharply reduced (to approximately 7.3 percent of GNP). Moreover, as a result of the occupation of the American Embassy in Teheran, arms and spare-parts shipments from the United States were halted. In sum, the impressive pre-1979 military machine constructed by the Shah had become of questionable efficacy after the revolution (Grummon 1982).

Iraq

Since the establishment of the *de facto* one-party regime in 1968, Iraqi leaders have moved to substantially increase the state's military capabilities. The growth in the state's armed forces between 1972 and 1980 is reflected in almost every indicator of military strength. In 1972, Iraq spent approximately 14 percent of its GNP in the military sector. In 1980, its military expenditures represented 21 percent of the nation's GNP (United States ACDA 1984:30).

In 1978, Iraq had 212,000 men in the armed services, divided as follows: an army composed of 180,000 personnel; a navy consisting of 4,000 personnel; and an air force comprising 28,000 personnel. In 1977, the army consisted of four armored divisions, two mechanized divisions, four infantry divisions, one independent armored brigade, one independent infantry brigade, one special forces brigade, and the Republican Guard mechanized brigade. For the same year, the combat wing of the Iraqi air force totaled 339 aircraft. In 1978, the most significant elements in the Iraqi navy were 10 patrol boats equipped with surface-to-surface missiles. During the period of the Iraqi military buildup, the Soviet Union was extensively involved in the training of Iraq's military forces. By 1978, there were an estimated 2,000 Soviet advisors in Iraq acting in this capacity (Cottrell and Bray 1978:27–34).

Summary

The issues of power and capability measurement have been discussed in chapters 3 and 4. Standard methods of capability measurement employed by the Correlates of War (COW) Project involve the computation of capability indices. An estimate of the relative capability balance between Iran and Iraq in the 10-year period before the onset of war in 1980 has been generated through the use of two of these indices.

The COW National Capability data set encompasses six measures covering three dimensions of national power in yearly entries for every state in the world. Two measures involve military capabilities (military expenditures and military personnel); two measures tap industrial capabilities (energy consumption and iron/steel production); and two measures involve demographic variables (total population and urban population).[5] To measure relative capabilities on a yearly basis for the Iran/Iraq dyad, a Composite Index of National Capability (CINC) was developed for each nation (cf. Bremer 1980:63–66). Yearly CINC scores were created by first obtaining the sum of the values on all six capability variables for the dyad. A summary score was then computed indicating the percentage share possessed by each nation of the total capability pool of the dyad for every year. In addition, a second measure of relative capability – one based on the military dimension (Mil. Cap.) alone – was calculated for the Iran/Iraq dyad. The military component of national capabilities was provided with a separate analysis under the assumption that nations which identify each other as security threats may react more readily to changes in the military balance than to shifts in more broadly-based measures of national capability. Here, the percentage share for each nation of the pooled military resources (expenditures and personnel) of the dyad was computed on a yearly basis (cf. Anderson and McKeown 1987; Gochman 1990a).

The final procedure involved the determination of both composite and military capability balances within the Iran/Iraq dyad. Multiple categories were established to distinguish among the various possible static and dynamic power balances at the time of war initiation and in the period before the 1980 war. Simple *inferiority* or *superiority* for initiator and target were determined by a comparison of CINC and Mil. Cap. scores at the point of war inception. The "stability" of the

---

[5] The National Capabilities data set includes all nation-states from 1816 through 1993. The capability indicators are as follows:

Military personnel – Number of active troops.

Military expenditures – Amount of financial resources allocated for military purposes; collected in native currency then expressed in one common currency for purposes of comparison (pound sterling 1816–1913 and US dollars 1914–1993).

Energy consumption – A composite indicator of coal, petroleum, hydroelectric and nuclear fuels consumed; units are standardized into metric tons and then transformed into equal energy values expressed as tons of coal.

Iron and steel production – Iron production for the period 1816–1899 and steel production for 1900–1993.

Urban population – Population for cities over 100,000.

Total population – Number of residents living in a nation.

For a discussion and critique of these and other capability measures see Moul (1989).

power balance over time was reflected by the use of two sets of measures. A "stable" or static balance of either *preponderance* or *parity* was determined by a consistent threshold differential of 20 percent or more in the 10-year period before the war in 1980. Specifically, the consistent minimum of a 60 percent share of the dyad's total capability pool held by one state was necessary to classify the balance as preponderant. This distribution provides a minimum capability ratio of ≥ 3:2 over time. A capability ratio lower than this threshold was classified as reflecting a static balance of parity. An "unstable" or dynamic balance involving either a power *shift* or *transition* was defined as a change in relative capabilities of 20 percent or more (e.g., a shift from a 60 percent/40 percent distribution of the capability pool to a 50 percent/50 percent distribution [a ratio shift of 3:2 to 1:1]), or a reversal of leading position (transition) within the dyad, in the 10-year period before the war in 1980.

By these measures, the capability balance between Iran and Iraq during the 10-year period preceding the 1980 war was unequal and stable (0.67/0.33) when measured by relative CINC score (with Iran preponderant), whereas the distribution was equal and unstable (0.49/0.51) when measured by relative Mil. Cap. score (with Iraq possessing simple superiority). Moreover, a shift (in 1979) and a transition (in 1980) in relative military capabilities – both in Iraq's favor – occurred immediately before the onset of war.

In sum, the balance in military capabilities between Iran and Iraq during the 10-year period before the outbreak of war in 1980 was changing to Iraq's advantage. The shift passed the 20 percent threshold in 1979 and a transition occurred in 1980. With Iran in turmoil following the revolution in 1979, the purge of the Iranian military command, and weapons shipments to Iran under suspension by the United States, the changing balance of capabilities provided the prospect for the successful use of force by a militarily superior Iraq.

Enduring rivals

Empirical pattern: The presence of an enduring rivalry increases the probability of war within a dyad.

Iran/Iraq

The subject of enduring rivalries has been discussed in chapter 1. Briefly stated, current empirical work suggests the importance of a subset population of dyads (within the set of all nation-dyads) defined by long-term conflicts. These conflict-prone dyads, or "enduring rivals," account for a disproportionately large amount of the violence which occurs in the interstate system. Two analyses by Goertz and Diehl (1992, 1993) estimate that long-term rivals are responsible for almost half of the wars, violent territorial changes, and militarized disputes that have occurred in the last two centuries. Accordingly, recent studies have focused on these dispute-prone dyads in an effort to gain a better understanding of the factors associated with a large proportion of interstate conflict. For instance, Gochman (1990a:147) has argued that shifts in relative capability might be expected to have a particularly strong effect on the interaction of rival states with a history of violent conflict.

Multiple definitions of enduring rivals with widely varying criteria have been used in the construction of population sets. For example: Wayman (1982, 1996) includes any major power dyad which engages in two or more militarized disputes within a 10-year span; Diehl (1985) defines a major power rivalry as any dyad exhibiting three or more militarized disputes within a 15-year span; the Gochman and Maoz (1984) set includes all dyads which have engaged in a minimum of seven militarized disputes during the period from 1816 to 1980. The databases compiled from these criteria sets vary in terms of total rivalries, number of dyads by power status, average number of disputes, average duration of rivalry, and number of wars.[6]

In an interesting approach, Wayman and Jones (1991) developed a highly restrictive definition of enduring rivals which excludes all short- and medium-term conflict dyads from consideration. This definition delineates a small set of long-term rivalries which are responsible for almost 40 percent of all militarized disputes[7] occurring between 1816 and 1986, despite the fact that the rivalries constitute only about 8 percent of all dyad-years for that period. These are the most conflict-prone dyads in the interstate system.

---

[6] See Goertz and Diehl (1993) and Goertz (1994) for the definitions and criteria used in constructing these, and other, rivalry data sets, and for discussion of the various populations produced by the criteria.

[7] The Militarized Interstate Dispute (MID) data is a component of the Correlates of War (COW) Project database. By definition, "[A militarized] interstate dispute is a set of interactions involving the explicit, overt, and government-directed threat, display, or use of force in short temporal intervals" (Maoz 1982:7). The MID data set also includes

For the analysis presented here, enduring rivalries were defined according to the time/density dispute criteria established by Wayman and Jones (1991:5–6):

1. *Severity* – There must exist at least five reciprocated militarized disputes involving the same two states, such that each of these disputes lasts a minimum of thirty days . . .
2. *Durability* – There must be at least twenty-five years between the outbreak of the first dispute and the termination of the last dispute . . .
3. *Continuity* – When the gap between any two militarized disputes exceeds ten years . . . [the] rivalry. . .[continues] only if the territorial domain and issues remain unresolved and there is at least one . . . dispute within a period of twenty-five years.

These time/density criteria produced a set of 29 enduring rivals for the period between 1816 and 1986. Table 7.1 identifies the enduring rivalries by power status of each dyad and periods of rivalry. Twenty of these rivalries engaged in at least one war. Table 7.2 identifies the warring rival dyads. The Iran/Iraq dyad appears in this list.

Summary

The Iran/Iraq dyad constitutes an enduring rivalry from 1934 to 1986[8] on the basis of these criteria. Over this period of 53 years, Iran and Iraq engaged in 17 militarized disputes. Fourteen of these disputes occurred between 1960 and 1980. Thirteen of these disputes involved the limited use of force by at least one state. Nine of these disputes involved the limited use of force by both states. The last dispute involved the onset of war in 1980.

---

a five-level hostility scale with a coded action for both the initiator and target in the dispute. The levels of hostility (LH) are:

LH1 – No military confrontation action (target)
LH2 – Threat to use force
LH3 – Display of force
LH4 – Use of force
LH5 – War (Small and Singer 1982 criteria).

See Gochman and Maoz (1984) for a description of this data set.
[8] At the time of this analysis, 1986 was the last coded year in the MID database.

Table 7.1. *Enduring rivalries, 1816–1986*

Major power dyads	Dates
England (UK)/France	1816–1840
Austria-Hungary/Italy[a]	1861–1918
France/Prussia (Germany)	1850–1945
Russia (USSR)/Japan	1895–1945
USSR/China[b]	1950–1986
USA/USSR	1946–1986
USA/China	1950–1974

Major/minor power dyads	Dates
England (UK)/USA	1816–1861
Russia (USSR)/Turkey	1816–1918
Austria-Hungary/Italy	1843–1860
Russia (USSR)/China	1898–1949
USA/Mexico[c]	1899–1921
Japan/China	1874–1945
Italy/Turkey	1880–1926
China/India	1950–1986

Minor power dyads	Dates
Greece/Turkey	1829–1922, 1958–1986
USA/Mexico	1836–1898
Chile/Argentina	1843–1902, 1952–1984
USA/Spain	1850–1898
Bolivia/Chile	1857–1920
Ecuador/Peru	1858–1986
Peru/Chile	1872–1921
Bolivia/Paraguay	1887–1938
Iran/Iraq	1934–1986
India/Pakistan	1947–1986
Egypt/Israel	1948–1979
Syria/Israel	1948–1986
Afghanistan/Pakistan	1949–1986
North Korea/South Korea	1949–1986
Thailand/Cambodia	1954–1986
Somalia/Ethiopia	1960–1986
Israel/Jordan	1948–1986

Notes:
[a] Italy reclassified from minor power to major power after 1860. Austria-Hungary/Italy rivalry begins as major/minor in 1843 and continues to 1860 with that power status.
[b] China reclassified from minor power to major power after 1949. Russia (USSR)/China rivalry begins as major/minor in 1898 and continues to 1949 with that power status.
[c] USA reclassified from minor power to major power after 1898. USA/Mexico rivalry begins as minor/minor in 1836 and continues to 1898 with that power status.

Table 7.2. *Warring rivals, 1816–1986*

Major power dyads
Austria-Hungary/Italy[a] France/Prussia (Germany) Russia (USSR)/Japan USA/China
Major/minor power dyads
Russia (USSR)/Turkey Japan/China Italy/Turkey China/India Austria-Hungary/Italy[a]
Minor power dyads
Greece/Turkey USA/Spain Bolivia/Chile Peru/Chile Bolivia/Paraguay Iran/Iraq India/Pakistan Egypt/Israel Syria/Israel North Korea/South Korea Somalia/Ethiopia USA/Mexico

Note:
[a] Italy reclassified from minor power to major power after 1860. Austria-Hungary/Italy rivalry begins as major/minor in 1843 and continues to 1860 with that power status.

Conclusion

The historical event of the Iran/Iraq War (1980) has been described in the format of a case study. However, the critical factors leading to this war have been identified as empirical uniformities common to a broad set of wars. The dyadic-level factors of contiguity, absence of joint democratic regimes, absence of joint advanced economies, presence of an unstable capability balance, and presence of an enduring rivalry all increased the probability of war.

The detailed case analysis reveals how these factors combined to produce the war in question: the territorial dispute and the opportunity to exercise military force were created and facilitated by the contiguous border; the autocratic structure of both regimes placed few constraints on war decisions of the leadership, and there was an absence in both political systems of norms associated with nonviolent conflict resolution; the vulnerability to disruption and collapse of both primary product resource extraction economies increased the security threat; the shifting military balance with a transition in Iraq's favor in 1980 created the prospect for the successful use of force; and the classification of the dyad as an enduring rivalry with a history of chronic military interaction all made the onset of war highly likely.

Scientific explanation of individual events may be provided by their inductive subsumption under probabilistic laws. The preceding analysis demonstrates that the Iran/Iraq War was a high-probability event consistent with a broad array of empirical patterns and that it was a specific instance of a set of intersecting uniformities which have appeared in a much larger number of war cases.

8   Case study: World War I (1914)

Introduction

The onset and seriousness of World War I (1914) is explained on the basis of empirical uniformities established by systematic quantitative analyses. Scientific explanations of individual events may be provided through inductive subsumption under probabilistic laws, as well as through deductive subsumption under universal laws. This inductive explanation demonstrates that the case of World War I is a specific instance of a set of patterns which have appeared in a much larger number of cases.[1]

World War I conforms to a set of probabilistic laws based on empirical regularities identified at the state, dyadic, and systemic

---

[1] Whereas the explanation of war presented in this book treats all wars as the product of a set of factors drawn from multiple analytic levels, Vasquez (1993) provides an explanation based on a typology of wars. His first distinction is between "wars of rivalry" (between states possessing approximately equal capabilities) and "predatory wars" (where states are unequal in capabilities). A second distinction involves the differences between "limited" and "total" wars. The third distinction separates "dyadic" wars from "complex" wars which involve three or more states. Vasquez argues that rivalry wars – between equals – begin over territorial disputes. Realist foreign policy practices designed to demonstrate resolve and increase power only serve to escalate the dispute, enhancing the position of hardline policy proponents in both governments. As tension increases, further provocative steps are taken until one side initiates violence. These wars have, in specific cases, expanded beyond their original participants to become world wars. These events occur through a diffusion process produced by the conjunction of three system-level attributes: a multipolar distribution of capabilities; a polarized (tight, two-bloc) alliance structure; and approximate parity in capabilities between the two blocs. Thus, according to Vasquez, world wars are only a special class of rivalry wars – subject to the same causal processes but expanding as a result of the confluence of the three system-level conditions.

levels of analysis. The states involved in the onset of the war were contiguous or proximate major powers (Austria-Hungary, Russia, Germany, France, and Great Britain); three of these major powers (Germany, Great Britain, and Russia) were moving through critical points in their power cycles; two of these major powers had an unstable capability balance (Germany and Great Britain had recently experienced a power transition); three of these major powers lacked democratic political systems (Austria-Hungary, Germany, and Russia); and the international hierarchy was unstable with a declining leader (Great Britain). Add to this the classification of the Germany/France dyad as an "enduring rivalry" and the highly polarized alliance systems (Germany/Austria-Hungary and Great Britain/France/Russia), and the occurrence of a war of enormous magnitude, duration, and severity was a high-probability event consistent with a broad array of empirical war patterns. Although the nonoccurrence of the event is not precluded logically due to the inductive form of argument, nevertheless the war may be considered "explained" by its subsumption under probabilistic laws. The following sections will discuss these patterns within the context of World War I.

Proximity/contiguity

Empirical pattern: Proximity increases the probability of war between states; the presence of a contiguous land or sea (separated by 150 miles of water or less) border increases the probability of war between states.

Geography

As Keylor (1992:3–34) notes, one of the most striking characteristics of international politics at the inception of the twentieth century was the extent to which European states dominated peripheral areas of the globe. Beginning in the sixteenth century, European power and influence spread through the Americas, Africa, and Asia; by the first decade of the twentieth century, the power of European states had thoroughly penetrated the Southern hemisphere.

Two of the nations that were active in nineteenth-century expansionism were Great Britain and France. British colonial expansion was principally driven by economic factors: the "imperial system contribute[d] to the efficient operation of the worldwide network of trade and investment upon which . . . Great Britain depended for her economic prosperity" (Keylor 1992:6). French motivation for external influence and control stemmed from a different source. Specifically, toward the end of the nineteenth century the vulnerability of France to German military power led the French government to promote financial investment in the Russian, Austro-Hungarian, and Turkish empires, as well as in the nascent Balkan states. The purpose of this investment was to surround Germany (the principal continental rival of France) with a cordon of states dependent on French financial support and therefore subject to French influence. In addition, France also engaged actively in colonial expansion and held the second-ranking empire (behind Britain's) by the early twentieth century.

Two other European states, Germany and Russia, also attempted to expand into the periphery toward the end of the nineteenth century. In 1897, Kaiser William II announced his intention to pursue a *Weltpolitik* (world policy) in the less-developed regions of the world for the purpose of enhancing German military, economic, and political power. The prospect of Germany – the principal European land power – competing against British and French imperial interests in Africa and Asia produced insecurity in London and Paris. As a result, Britain and France submerged their disputes over control of colonial territories and established an entente to oppose Germany's move toward a global role.

The other major European power to engage in a policy of imperial expansion during the last half of the nineteenth century was Russia. Russian access to the major oceans of the world was constrained by the absence of ports that were not ice-bound during winter months. The principal Russian ice-free ports were located on the Black Sea, but the straits (the Bosporus and Dardanelles) connecting these ports to the Mediterranean could be closed easily by the state holding the two shorelines, and for hundreds of years the empire of Ottoman Turkey had exercised that control. Hence, Turkish sovereignty over the narrow waterway and over the contiguous Balkan peninsula denied Russia a secure route to the Mediterranean for its trade and naval power. During the last half of the nineteenth century, Russian tsars attempted to increase their influence in the Balkans and thereby break the geographical constraints on the projection of Russian power.

The results of this expansionist drive by Russia toward the Mediterranean at the expense of Turkey were the Crimean War (1854–1856) and the Congress of Berlin (1878) in which other major powers combined to thwart Russian aims. In the next two decades, the

Ottoman Empire ceded authority over the Slavic population of the Balkans creating the independent states of Serbia, Romania, Bulgaria, and Montenegro, while the remainder of the territory was wracked by revolutionary violence against continued Turkish domination.

The empire of Austria-Hungary – backed by Germany – attempted to fill the political vacuum in the Balkans. The creation of the Dual Alliance in 1879 committed Germany to the reinforcement of Habsburg power in Southern Europe. Confronted with the combined opposition of both Germany and Austria-Hungary, the Russian government was compelled to postpone its expansion toward the Mediterranean through the Balkans, and in 1897, an agreement to preserve the status quo in the Balkans was struck by the leaders in Vienna and St. Petersburg.

Technology

Two technological innovations in the area of transport fundamentally changed the means of power projection at the close of the nineteenth century. Both involved the application of the steam engine in transportation. The first application was the use of coal-fueled steam engines in ships. By the 1850s, sail-driven ships were largely eliminated from the merchant and military navies of the sea powers. This technological achievement permitted the industrially advanced states of Europe to extend their commercial and military operations around the globe. The initial benefits of this technology were exploited by Great Britain, the dominant sea power of the era.

The second application of the steam engine in transport involved the development of the railroad locomotive, which permitted the continental empire of Russia to exercise substantially greater political and economic control over its territories. The steam-powered railroad engine also enabled Britain and France to move beyond the coastal regions of Africa into the interior of the continent. The military consequences of these two innovations were enormous. Railroad and steamship transport increased the size and mobility of military operations. Massive armies equipped by the industrial economies of the European states could now be transported rapidly to any point in the world.

Geopolitics

Geopolitics represents the combination of political and economic geography in the study of capability distributions, frontiers, and war.

According to one school of geopolitical thought (e.g., Friedrich Ratzel 1899),[2] the earth constitutes the environment for a struggle among great powers to gain control of resources, territory, and population. Given the unequal distribution of capabilities, the major states are condemned to compete for control of geographic areas that will supplement their strength.

The most comprehensive doctrine of geopolitics at the turn of the twentieth century appeared in Imperial Germany. As Keylor (1992:29–30) notes:

> To the underlying principle of German geopolitics – the definition of Eurasia as a geographical space to be filled by the political authority and military power of the strongest nation – was added the Malthusian doctrine of population pressure against food supply and the Social Darwinist concept of the competition of racial groups for survival in the uncongenial natural environment.

This multidimensional thesis provided the rationale for the eastward expansion of German power toward Russia.

The principal barrier to the geopolitical design of Germany was Great Britain with its dominant navy and string of colonies along the southern rim of Eurasia. British geopolitical thinking during this period was epitomized by the work of Halford Mackinder (1904) who divided the earth into two regions: the "world island" (comprising the continents of Europe, Asia, and Africa); and the peripheral areas (including North and South America, Australia, Japan, and the British Isles). The world island was the largest, most resource-rich, and most populous land mass on the planet. At the center of the world island was the pivot area, or "heartland," which coincided roughly with the tsarist Russian Empire. Pre-twentieth century technologies of transportation inhibited any single state's domination of Eurasia, but Mackinder believed that with the advent of the steam-powered locomotive and the installation of an extensive railway system, Eurasia was now vulnerable to domination by a single state. Given the resources of the combined land masses of Eurasia, control of this area would present the potential for the creation of unmatchable military power. For Mackinder, then, the geopolitical threat to Great Britain was the possible German seizure of Eastern Europe, followed by the conquest of Eurasia, and culminating in the domination of the world.

---

[2] For a discussion of the various schools of thought classified as geopolitics, see Whittlesey (1966).

This geopolitical conception of a global competition for power was held by the decisionmaking elites of the major states at the turn of the twentieth century. A tacit agreement among these states to avoid war was maintained until the summer of 1914. The trigger for the war involved the collision between Austria-Hungary and Russia over control of the Balkan peninsula, preceding the decision by their allies – Germany, France, and Britain – to move toward military engagement.

Summary

On June 28, 1914, Archduke Franz Ferdinand – the heir to the throne of the Austro-Hungarian Empire – was assassinated in the Bosnian capital of Sarajevo. The assassination was followed in less than six weeks by the onset of World War I. However, the roots of the war reach back to a security problem among the proximate and contiguous states of Europe. The Congress of Vienna in 1815 had established a concert among the five major powers of Europe – Great Britain, France, Prussia, Austria-Hungary, and Russia – designed to prevent domination of the area by a single state. This system was disrupted by the unification of Germany in 1871 and the creation of a new power in the center of Europe possessing resources, technology, military force, and an expansionist doctrine that threatened the security of neighboring states. As Kennedy (1987:197) argues:

> the broad outlines of [the] Great Power struggles were already being suggested in the 1890s . . . [Much] depended, as always, upon the immutable facts of geography. Was a country near the center of international crises, or at the periphery? Was it safe from invasion? Did it have to face two or three ways simultaneously?

In sum, despite the competition for territory among established and incipient empires in the peripheral areas of the globe, the proximate and contiguous borders of the major European powers at the beginning of the twentieth century provided the issues in conflict, the security threats, and the physical opportunity to deal with the problems through the use of military force.

Power status

Empirical pattern: The higher the status rank of a state, the greater the probability of its war involvement; the higher the status rank of a state, the greater the probability of its involvement in severe wars.

Major powers

There are strong *a priori* reasons to expect that extant patterns of war involvement (participation) and war seriousness (magnitude, duration, and severity) may be quite dissimilar for major powers and minor powers. For example, major powers may be more likely to engage in war because the hierarchy of which they are a part is structured and restructured primarily through the use of violence. Major powers tend to define their interests more broadly than do minor powers, and the pursuit of those interests may bring them more frequently into violent conflict with other states. Moreover, given the fact that major powers possess greater military capabilities than do minor powers, it is reasonable to assume that their wars will tend to be more destructive than those of minor powers.

The Correlates of War (COW) Project has compiled a list of major powers based on "scholarly consensus." Small and Singer (1982:45) identify the set of major powers from 1816 to 1980 as including: Austria-Hungary (1816–1918); Prussia (1816–1870); Germany (1871–1918, 1925–1945); Russia (1816–1917); USSR (1922–1980); France (1816–1940, 1945–1980); England (1816–1980); Italy (1816–1943); Japan (1895–1945); United States (1898–1980); and China (1949–1980). The COW Project has also compiled lists of international (i.e., interstate, imperial, and colonial) wars. Distinctions between these wars are based on the participants': membership in the interstate system; involvement in hostilities; and number of fatalities. For the period of 1816 through 1980, the COW Project reports 67 interstate wars and 51 extra-systemic (imperial and colonial) wars, for a total of 118 international wars (Small and Singer 1982:55–61).

The analysis of the war-proneness of states (1816–1980) is summarized as follows: France 22 wars, England 19 wars, Russia/USSR 19 wars, Turkey 18 wars, Sardinia/Italy 12 wars, China 11 wars, Spain 10 wars, Japan 9 wars, United States 8 wars, Austria-Hungary 8 wars, Greece 7 wars, and Prussia/Germany 6 wars. Five nations were involved in an average of more than one war per decade: France, England, Turkey, Russia, and Israel. The analysis of the severity of war experiences of states (1816–1980) produced the following list. Battle-deaths exceeding 750,000: Russia/USSR, Prussia/Germany, China, France, Japan, England, Austria-Hungary, Italy, and Turkey.

Small and Singer (1982:180) conclude their analysis as follows:

most of the war in the system has been accounted for by a small fraction of the nations, most of which would be found near the top of any hierarchy based on diplomatic status, military–industrial capability, or related indicators. It is not surprising that every one of the nations cited so far was a member of what we defined as the central system. Further, of the highly war-prone nations, only Turkey, Spain, and Greece at one time or another were not major powers.

Summary

The previous analysis demonstrates that most international (interstate, imperial, and colonial) war between 1816 and 1980 has been conducted by states classified as major powers. In fact, very few war-prone countries fall outside the major power category. Hence, Small and Singer (1982:180) conclude that "top-ranked nations [are] compelled to fight often and at length either to maintain their position or to achieve it." Bremer (1980:79), in a careful exploration of the possible linkage between the possession of power and its probability of use, discovered that the aggregate capability of nations is positively associated with both war frequency and war initiation. Bremer (1980:81) also reported that powerful nations tend to have more severe wars (measured by battle-deaths) than do weaker states, but that differences in capabilities do not appear to impact on levels of war duration or intensity. Another study (Geller 1988) corroborated this pattern on severity using Markov chain analysis to compare war behavior of major and minor powers and concluded that a nation's power status is a determinant of the scale of its wars.

World War I was fought by states that are the most probable war participants when classified by power status. These states are also the most probable participants in severe wars. The onset of World War I involved the military engagement of Austria-Hungary, Germany, France, Russia, and Great Britain, with subsequent involvement by Japan, Italy, and the United States. All of these states were classified as major powers for the period before the onset of the war. World War I produced approximately 8,555,800 battle-deaths (i.e., troop-fatalities) and remains one of the bloodiest wars in recorded history.

Power cycle

Empirical pattern: Passage through a critical point in the power cycle increases the probability of war involvement for a major power.

Power cycle theory

This formulation (i.e., Doran 1983, 1989; Doran and Parsons 1980) holds that certain critical points in a major power's cycle of increasing and decreasing capabilities (relative to the major power system's capability pool)[3] are associated probabilistically with both its initiation and involvement in war. The thesis maintains that major powers move through a general, cyclical pattern (i.e., power cycle) of capability growth, maturation, and decline. The pattern itself is a function of differential rates of development among the set of major powers. These differences result from variations in resource distribution, political development, and industrialization.

The power cycle thesis asserts that a state's foreign policy is shaped by its position on this capability cycle. According to Doran and Parsons (1980:947,949): "As a nation gains in power relative to others, its capacity to exercise leadership grows; as it falls behind, the capacity to influence international politics wanes . . . As the cycle evolves and the role changes, significant adjustments are required of the government and the society." Collectively, the evolution of the power cycles of the principal states defines the hierarchy of the international system (Doran 1983:427).

Doran identifies four critical points on the cycle: the lower turning point, the first (or rising) inflection point, the upper turning point, and the second (or declining) inflection point. These four points on the evolutionary curve of a state's relative capabilities – termed "critical points" – are important because they represent a disjuncture between a state's interests or aspirations and its actual capabilities. Due to the shift in direction or rate of capability growth, the state's leaders must reevaluate their relative position, capability base, and foreign policy objectives. Doran (1985:294) maintains that the foreign policy stakes at these critical points are enormous – involving status, security, and power – and are therefore more likely to lead to war involvement. It should be noted that power cycle theory measures time in decades and critical points are not considered to be instantaneous transforma-

---

[3] Although power cycle theory is established at the level of the monad, it is linked with the system of all major powers by means of capability measurement. As Houweling and Siccama (1991:643) note: "A critical point on a nation's capability trajectory is an absolute property of the nation concerned. However, the capability trajectory consists of the nation's shares [of the total resource pool available to the major power system as a whole at a given point] in time."

tions. Similarly, the perceptions of leaders as their states approach critical points may change in a gradual fashion. However, abrupt over-reaction to the points is considered more probable (Doran and Parsons 1980:951).

James and Hebron (1993:4–5) provide this description of the probable perceptions and policy shifts associated with the evolutionary cycle:

> The lower turning point . . . marks the formal entry of the state into the great power system. As a "junior" member of the great power club, its policy orientation is toward growth and positional enhancement. As such, [the lower turning point] may be characterized by a tendency towards nationalism and expansion. The rising inflection point . . . denotes the state's initial experience with a decline in the rate of increase of relative capability. Growth and development continue, but not at the same frantic pace. At the upper turning point, . . . the power of [the state] is (for the first time) in decline relative to others. Danger is created by the prospect of having to adjust its interests to a situation where relative capability cannot sustain the state's current role. This transition could stimulate aggressive foreign policy initiatives . . . Finally, at the declining inflection point, . . . power continues to diminish relative to competitors but at a reduced rate . . . [Proximity to the second inflection point] may encourage attempts to arrest further deterioration through a reactivated foreign policy. These efforts may be triggered by the profound hope that a reversal of fortunes holds out the promise of a restored position in the system.

Doran and Parsons (1980:952) suggest that the critical points most likely to produce the imprudent use of force or the encumbrance of unyielding foreign policy positions are the two inflection points (where the tangents reverse direction).

In short, power cycle theory holds that major power war results from a government's inability to adjust to shifts in its capacity to exercise power and influence. The critical points on the power cycle are especially likely to produce over-reaction, misperception, and the aggressive use of force in foreign policy.

Summary

The set of major powers identified by Doran and Parsons (1980:953) at the onset of World War I included Great Britain, France, Germany, Russia, Austria-Hungary, Italy, the United States, and Japan. The capability data employed to determine power cycles incorporated measures of: (1) iron and steel production; (2) population; (3) size of armed forces; (4) coal production; and (5) urbanization. For the period between 1896 and 1914, Doran (1989:384) reports the following critical points for the four highest-ranking states: Russia (lower turning point); Germany (upper turning point); Great Britain (declining [second] inflection point); and the United States (rising [first] inflection point).

In describing World War I in terms of imbalances in capability and role, Doran (1989:393) states that:

> World War I . . . was a war over how to reconstitute the nineteenth century balance of power system in a way that would (1) permit the balanced ascendancy of Russia and the United States on the outskirts of the old central system; (2) resolve the problems surrounding Austria-Hungary's inability to politically hold sway in its perch astride Central Europe in the region of the Balkans; and (3) in the process restore equilibrium in terms of power and interests among the declining Britain and France and the ascendant Germany. The war was a war to redress the excessive disequilibrium of power and role within the central system, a redress *requiring* either major adjustments of role by all the leading states or a redistribution of relative power.

That three of the most powerful states in Europe were passing through critical points in their power cycles at the turn of the twentieth century, with the consequent extremes of uncertainty and threat, made the onset of systemic war highly probable.[4]

Hierarchy

Empirical pattern: The presence of an unstable hierarchy among the major powers of the international system increases the probability of systemic war.

Unstable hierarchy

Shifts in system-level power structure have an interactive effect with dyadic capability distributions in the onset of war. The structural theories of Organski (1958), Gilpin (1981), Modelski (1983), Wallerstein (1984), and Thompson (1988) all suggest that systemic stability and world order are associated with the dominance of a single state. As

---

[4] See Doran (1995) for a detailed description of the elements of the power cycle as they relate to World War I.

the systemic distribution of power changes from a unipolar concentration of capabilities to a more diffuse multipolar balance, the disintegration of the hierarchy will lead to a challenge against the dominant state and result in global war. However, it also has been shown (Houweling and Siccama 1993; Geller 1992b, 1996)[5] that as the international system moves from a high concentration of resources in the leading state toward multipolarity (power diffusion), lower-order conflict among the set of major states will become increasingly probable, due to the weakening of the principal defender of the hierarchy. Movement toward power parity within these secondary nation-dyads triggers violent interactions that – though not related to system leadership – are still of considerable consequence. This suggests that the erosion of the system-level power structure links lower-order wars among major powers to system-shaping global wars. Hence, the decline of unipolar power concentration and the reordering of the hierarchy among the strongest states leads to secondary great power wars that precede system-shaping global wars. In this way, power distributions at both the systemic and dyadic levels of analysis interact synergistically to produce war among the set of major powers. The international hierarchy at the turn of the twentieth century was subject to these shifts in capabilities.

Germany

As Kennedy (1987:209) notes, two factors determined the enormous impact of the rise of imperial Germany on the international hierarchy. The first involved its geographical location: the unification of Germany in 1871 directly affected the geopolitical situations of both Austria-Hungary and France, and changed the relative positions of all major powers in Europe. The second factor involved the rates of German economic and military growth. By 1913, Germany had surpassed France, Russia, and Britain in material capabilities.

German industrial expansion between 1890 and 1913 was phenomenal. By the eve of World War I, its share of world manufacturing production (14.8 percent) was larger than Britain's (13.6 percent) and over twice that of France (6.1 percent). This industrial base provided Germany with the military tools required to alter the status quo, or with the resources necessary for producing those tools. For example, the transformation of the German navy from the sixth-ranking fleet in

---

[5] See chapter 6 (pp. 119–120).

the world to the second-ranking fleet (behind Britain's) took a mere 15 years. By 1914, the German High Seas Fleet consisted of 13 modern ("dreadnought") battleships, 16 older battleships, and 5 battle cruisers. In terms of construction, weapons, targeting and gunnery control, and night training, the German force was far superior to those of France and Russia, and a challenge to the British navy.

Although the German army was smaller than Russia's and approximately the same size as that of France, it retained an advantage over those states through its superior ability to mobilize and equip millions of reservists. German land forces also possessed quicker mobilization schedules, better staff training, and more advanced weaponry.

In other areas, however, Germany confronted serious obstacles. Because of its location in the center of Europe, it presented a security threat to other proximate or contiguous major powers. The power of its military forces created a potential danger to both France and Russia and served to push those states toward tighter relations. The rapid expansion of the German navy similarly led to British concern over the increase in German capabilities.

As Kennedy (1987:214–215) argues, Germany was the sole rising European state with the strength to challenge the existing order. However, the eastern or western expansion of its borders could only be accomplished at the expense of great power neighbors, and its explosive economic and military growth had already destabilized the international hierarchy.

Austria-Hungary

By the twentieth century, the Austro-Hungarian Empire was the weakest of the major powers and, by some indices, had already fallen from this rank. Its economic base was frail with a *per capita* level of industrialization substantially below that of the other major states and a share of world manufacturing production fluctuating around 4.5 percent in the decades before the onset of World War I. Moreover, it was the most ethnically diverse state in Europe, a situation that created an additional set of problems. Dissident groups within the Empire sought political independence, and looked toward Serbia and Russia for support. The cooperation of Czech and Hungarian army regiments was unreliable in certain circumstances, and the loyalty of other groups was also suspect. The army's weapons were bordering on the obsolete and, due to a lack of funds, military personnel were kept to a minimum and received little training.

By the first decade of the twentieth century, the Austro-Hungarian Empire was in a precarious position. Its ethnic divisions promoted internal unrest and its economic growth rate would not permit it closure on such powers as Britain or Germany. Its *per capita* defense expenditures were lower than those of most other major powers, and its conscription ratio of soldiers to available population was the lowest of any other continental nation. By 1913 Austria-Hungary was attempting to play the role of a great power with the resources of a second-rank nation.

France

In 1914 France had only one enemy, Germany, against which it concentrated its economic and military power. However, the effect of the large sums of money allocated toward strengthening the French navy at the turn of the twentieth century was dissipated by frequent changes in naval strategy. Vacillation between ship construction for a commerce-raiding strategy and an opposing force structure of battle-ships left the navy with a heterogeneous fleet of ships incapable of matching the naval forces of Britain or Germany (Kennedy 1987:219). The efficiency and loyalty of the army was also undermined by frequent disputes with political authorities, and poor relations characterized civil–military interaction until the eve of World War I.

Weakness in its economic base also constrained the power of France. In terms of mobile capital, France was enormously wealthy, and these financial resources were used to support the state's diplomacy. A principal example was the use of loans to modernize the Russian strategic railway system so that in the event of war, Russia could mobilize more quickly against their common opponent, Germany. However, in comparative perspective, the French economy was lagging behind that of Germany. By the early 1880s, Germany's proportion of European manufactured exports had surpassed that of France and by 1911 was almost twice as high. By 1914, the total industrial potential of France was only about 40 percent of Germany's. The growth rates of France's economic base were falling below those of Britain and Russia as well.[6]

In sheer size, the French army was competitive – a situation that was maintained through the conscription of over 80 percent of its eligible population. For example, France could mobilize 80 divisions

---

[6] See the comparative economic indices in Kennedy (1987:199–202).

from a population of 40 million, whereas Austria-Hungary extracted only 48 divisions from a population of 52 million. On the other hand, Germany could field over 100 divisions, and possessed an available manpower pool (almost 10 million men) double that of France. Due to its larger economy, Germany could afford to allocate a smaller proportion of its national income to the military sector than France, but still spend more in absolute terms. At the onset of World War I, German superiority over France in the quantities of machine guns and cannon was in the range of 2:1 and Germany held a near monopoly in heavy artillery.

Nevertheless, the French believed their prospects in war against Germany to be favorable. The army had adopted an offensive strategy over a defensive one, and the expectation was for a war of brief duration. What would be critical in such a contest was not the size of the economic base which could be mobilized during the war, but rather the immediate impact of existing forces. A second factor in France's favor was its 1904 entente with Britain. The German threat to British naval power and its potential dominance in Europe assured France of British support in the event of war. France was a major power in relative decline, but with support from Britain and Russia in a conflict with Germany, it could envision the prospect of victory.

Great Britain

The capabilities of Great Britain were imposing. By 1900, it possessed the largest empire in history. The British navy was the equal of the next two top-ranking fleets combined, it held a network of naval bases which circled the globe, and it operated the world's largest merchant fleet. Britain was also the principal beneficiary in the evolving global economy.

In comparative perspective, however, British power was in decline. The pinnacle of Britain's relative power was achieved a few decades after its military victory in 1815. Nevertheless, by 1870, British supremacy was eroding due to a shift in industrial capacity and the military forces that flowed from it. The erosion of Britain's economic base, in relative terms, was producing a fundamental alteration in the international hierarchy.

As Kennedy (1987:228) notes:

> Industrial production, which had grown at an annual rule of about 4 percent in the period 1820 to 1840 and about 3 percent between 1840 and 1870, became more sluggish; between 1875 and 1894 it grew at

just over 1.5 percent annually, far less than that of the country's chief rivals . . . Whereas in 1880 the United Kingdom still contained 22.9 percent of total world manufacturing output, that figure had shrunk to 13.6 percent by 1913; and while its share of world trade was 23.2 percent in 1880, it was only 14.1 percent in 1911–1913. In terms of industrial muscle, . . . imperial Germany had moved ahead.

On the positive side, the British ship-building industry was still the world's leader. In the first decade of the twentieth century, Britain produced 60 percent of the world's merchant tonnage and 33 percent of its warships. It was also enormously wealthy, and although it was among the leaders in military spending prior to 1914, it required a smaller percentage of its national income to maintain this position than any other major power in Europe. Geographically, the physical separation of the British Isles from continental Europe provided a strategic advantage: defense against invasion by opposing armies could be secured by sea power rather than land power.

Kennedy (1987:231) concludes that on balance – in the decades before the onset of World War I – Britain had been surpassed industrially by Germany and was experiencing intense competition in its commercial, colonial, and maritime operations. Nevertheless, he maintains that on the strength of its financial resources, industrial base, imperial holdings, and naval preeminence, it "was still probably the 'number-one' world power, even if its lead was much less marked than in 1850."

Russia

On the basis of sheer size alone, Russia was a legitimate member in the set of major European powers. For hundreds of years, Russian expansion toward the west, south, and east had increased the area under its control. It contained a population three times greater than Germany's and four times the size of Britain's. Its army was the largest of any European power's during the nineteenth century, and it maintained this advantage up to the outbreak of World War I. Russian military expenditures were also at or near the top of all European powers in the decade before 1914. Railroad construction, with French support, was proceeding at a rapid pace and a new naval fleet was under construction following the war with Japan in 1904–1905.

However, Kennedy (1987:233–238) argues that evaluations of Russian power in "absolute" and "relative" terms produce two opposing conclusions on Russia's capabilities:

To begin with, it was now much stronger industrially than it had been at the time of the Crimean War. Between 1860 and 1913 – a very lengthy period – Russian industrial output grew at the impressive annual average rate of 5 percent, and in the 1890s the rate was closer to 8 percent . . . Foreign trade . . . nearly tripled between 1890 and 1914, when Russia became the world's sixth-largest trading nation . . . By 1914, as many histories have pointed out, Russia had become the fourth industrial power in the world . . . Yet the assessment of Russian strength is worse when it comes to *comparative* output. Although Russia was the fourth-largest industrial power before 1914, it was a long way behind . . . Britain and Germany. In the indices of its steel production, energy consumption, share of world manufacturing production, and total industrial potential, it was eclipsed by Britain and Germany . . . Despite all its own absolute increases in industrial output in this period . . . Russia's productive strength was actually *decreasing* relative to Germany's.

In a conflict against Austria-Hungary and Germany, Russian military capabilities had to be considered problematical. The Russian army was composed of conscripted peasants, unsuited for modern industrialized war. In the areas of technical training, communications, troop movement, deployment and use of heavy artillery, machine guns, and aircraft, Russian weakness and inefficiency were evident. The Russian navy was modern, but the level of technical training for naval personnel was limited. Similarly, the number of miles of Russian railroad track in 1914 was high, but when compared to the enormous expanse of territory which had to be traversed for mobilization and troop movement, its inadequacy becomes clear.

Kennedy (1987:241) concludes his analysis of Russian capabilities by noting that the state was growing – in absolute terms – at a rapid rate. Its industrial base and military power were increasing; but it was not yet prepared in 1914 for war with Germany.

Summary

The empirical pattern of an unstable hierarchy is associated with the onset of systemic war. A data-based analysis of the major power hierarchy prior to 1914 will be used to illustrate the dyadic and systemic shifts in relative capabilities leading to the outbreak of World War I.

Information on capabilities for major power dyads over the 11-year period before the onset of World War I was drawn from the Correlates of War (COW) database. The COW National Capability data set encompasses six measures covering three dimensions of national power. Two measures involve military capabilities (military expenditures and military personnel); two measures tap industrial capabilities (energy consumption and iron/steel production); and two measures involve demographic variables (total population and urban population).[7] To measure relative capabilities on a yearly basis for each dyad, a Composite Index of National Capability (CINC) was developed for every state. Yearly CINC scores were created by first obtaining the sum of the values on all six capability variables for the dyad. A summary score was then computed indicating the percentage share possessed by each nation of the total capability pool of the dyad for every year. In addition, a second measure of relative capability – one based on the military dimension (Mil. Cap.) alone – was calculated for each dyad. The military component of national capabilities was provided with a separate analysis under the assumption that nations which identify each other as security threats may react more readily to changes in the military balance than to shifts in more broadly-based measures of national capability. Here, the percentage share for each nation of the pooled military resources (expenditures and personnel) of the dyad was computed on a yearly basis.

The final procedure involved the determination of capability balances within each dyad. Multiple categories were established to distinguish among the various possible static and dynamic power balances at the time of the onset of war. The "stability" of the power balance over time was reflected by the use of two sets of measures. A "stable" or static balance of either *preponderance* or *parity* was determined by a consistent threshold differential of 20 percent or more in the decade between 1903 and 1913. Specifically, the consistent minimum of a 60 percent share of the dyad's total capability pool by one state was necessary to classify the balance as preponderant. This distribution provides a minimum capability ratio of $\geq 3{:}2$ over time. A capability ratio lower than this threshold was classified as reflecting a static balance of parity. An "unstable" or dynamic balance involving either a power *shift* or *transition* was defined as a change in relative capabilities of 20 percent or more (e.g., a shift from a 60 percent/40 percent distribution of the capability pool to a 50 percent/50 percent distribution [a ratio shift of 3:2 to 1:1]), or a reversal of leading position within the dyad, in the 11-year period before the onset of World War I.

---

[7] See chapter 7, n.5.

Table 8.1. *Relative capability*

Measures of capability balance over time	
Variable	*Definition*
Static (stable) balance	
Preponderance/parity:	Relative capabilities (CINC/Mil. Cap. scores) differ by 20 percent or more (preponderance) or by less than 20 percent (parity) in the 11-year period between 1903 and 1913.
Dynamic (unstable) balance	
Shift/transition:	A change in relative capabilities (CINC/Mil. Cap. scores) of 20 percent or more (shift) or the passing of one state's capability score by the other state's capability score (transition), one or more times in the 11-year period between 1903 and 1913.

The operational definitions for these capability balances are given in Table 8.1.

A capability analysis based on these criteria for the three principal major power dyads of the United Kingdom (Britain)/Germany, France/Germany, and Germany/Russia produced the following results. The UK/Germany dyad reflected unstable distributions for both CINC and Mil. Cap. measures during the 11-year period before the onset of World War I. The relative capabilities of Britain and Germany – when measured by CINC scores – underwent three transitions between 1903 and 1913, with the last transition (to Germany's advantage) occurring in 1912. When capabilities were measured by Mil. Cap. scores, a similar pattern emerged. A shift in relative military strength (to Germany's advantage) occurs in 1907, followed by three transitions (in 1908, 1910, and 1913). The last transition in military capabilities, in 1913, was also to the advantage of Germany.[8]

In contradistinction, the France/Germany dyad reflected a stable capability balance for both CINC and Mil. Cap. measures for the 11-year period before World War I. The relative capabilities of France and Germany – when measured by CINC scores – was stable, with German preponderance, for the entire period. The ratio was approximately 2:1 in Germany's favor. When capabilities were measured by

---

[8] Dyads indicating close equality in capabilities – and where each state is increasing its power base – frequently will evidence multiple transitions in short periods of time.

Mil. Cap. scores, a pattern of stable parity emerges, with Germany possessing a small advantage.

The Germany/Russia dyad presents a mixture of patterns, with the differences determined by the capability measure used in the analysis. When relative capabilities were measured by CINC scores, a pattern of stable parity emerges, with a small advantage to Germany. However, when relative capabilities were measured by Mil. Cap. scores the pattern of a dynamic balance appears, with transitions in military strength occurring in 1907, 1909, and 1913. The last transition, in the year before the onset of World War I, was to the advantage of Germany.

The analysis of capability balances for the three great power dyads involved in the onset of World War I has revealed patterns of instability in military capability in two cases (UK/Germany and Germany/Russia), and one case of stable parity (France/Germany). When relative capabilities were measured by the more broadly-based CINC scores, the dyads exhibited two cases of stable parity (France/Germany and Germany/Russia) and one case of an unstable balance (UK/Germany). In all cases, the advantage went to Germany. Table 8.2 summarizes these relationships.

However, these dyadic capability balances present an incomplete picture of the international hierarchy in the decades leading up to World War I. The dynamic nature of the hierarchy over time can be depicted by a calculation of the capability trajectories of all major powers based on the total pool of available resources. Because the general stability of the hierarchy – and particularly the degree of advantage possessed by the strongest state over its nearest competitors – is associated with the probability of systemic war, this type of calculation can best illustrate the structure of the pre-1914 hierarchy.

The data in the following analysis is drawn from the COW National Capability data set and utilizes the same six measures covering three dimensions of national power.[9] Since this study focuses on the war behavior of a restricted class of major powers, a Composite Index of National Capability (CINC) was developed to reflect the *relative* capability scores of this *subset* of nations. Major powers were identified on the basis of COW coding procedures (Small and Singer 1982: 44–45). CINC scores were created by first obtaining the sum of major

---

[9] See chapter 7, n.5.

Table 8.2. *Dyadic capability balances, 1903–1913*

Dyad	Capability balance	CINC	CINC advantage	Mil. Cap.	Mil. Cap. advantage
UK/Germany	CINC: Unstable	1908 (Transition)	UK < GMY		
		1909 (Transition)	UK > GMY		
		1912 (Transition)	UK < GMY		
	Mil. Cap.: Unstable			1907 (Shift)	UK > GMY
				1908 (Transition)	UK < GMY
				1910 (Transition)	UK > GMY
				1913 (Transition)	UK < GMY
France/Germany	CINC: Stable	Preponderance	FRN < GMY		
	Mil. Cap.: Stable			Parity	FRN < GMY
Germany/Russia	CINC: Stable	Parity	GMY > RUS		
	Mil. Cap.: Unstable			1907 (Transition)	GMY > RUS
				1909 (Transition)	GMY < RUS
				1913 (Transition)	GMY > RUS

power values on each of the six capability variables; the percentage of the total value for all majors that was controlled by each nation on each of the six measures was calculated. A summary score was then computed indicating the percentage share of the *total* capability pool of all majors possessed by *each* major power. For example, in 1816 England controlled a 0.3301 share of the total capabilities possessed by all major powers, whereas France had a 0.1960 share of the pool. These summary capability scores (CINCs) combining the six variables were computed for all major powers on a yearly basis from 1816 through 1976. A further distinction was then drawn between those major powers (i.e., "great powers") that controlled at minimum a 0.1000 share of the capability base and those major powers whose CINCs were below 10 percent. This narrowed the set of major powers to between three and five states in a given year. The nations which met these criteria are as follows:

Great powers

1816–1859	England/UK, France, Russia, Austria-Hungary
1860–1864	England/UK, France, Russia
1865–1899	England/UK, France, Russia, Prussia/Germany
1900–1934	United States, England/UK, France, Russia/Soviet Union, Germany
1935–1945	United States, England/UK, Soviet Union, Germany
1946–1949	United States, Soviet Union, England/UK
1950–1976	United States, Soviet Union, People's Republic of China

A final procedure involved the computation of average CINC scores for each great power for five-year periods beginning in 1816.

The measure of hierarchical stability was constructed to reflect changes along a unipolar concentration/diffusion continuum. Composition of the measure involved the calculation of the average change in the lead nation's share of the capability pool of all great powers over ten-year periods beginning in 1820. An increase or decrease in the lead nation's average CINC score was noted between each successive period. The lead nation's CINC share for the years 1816 through 1819 constituted the initial baseline. A summary statement of unipolar concentration phases (combining contiguous ten-year periods) is as follows:

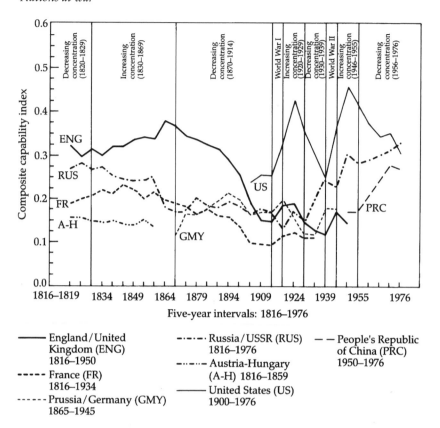

Figure 8.1 Hierarchy: great powers, 1816–1976

Phases of

Decreasing concentration	Increasing concentration
1820–1829	1830–1869
1870–1914	1920–1929
1930–1939	1946–1955
1956–1976	

The individual capability trajectories of the great powers and the shifts in power concentration are indicated in Figure 8.1.

Figure 8.1 depicts a dynamic international hierarchy of increasing instability in the decades between 1870 and 1914. The capability advantage of Britain begins a long decline while the trajectories of

Germany, France, and Russia exhibit convergence and transitions in the years immediately preceding the onset of World War I. The foregoing analysis has demonstrated that in the period from 1870 to 1914 the international system moved from a high concentration of resources in the leading state toward multipolarity (power diffusion). The principal defender of the status quo – Britain – lost its relative advantage over other great powers. Moreover, movement toward power parity within these great power dyads created security threats and hostile interactions that – though not related to system leadership – served as a trigger to global war. World War I may begin as a struggle over the Balkans between Russia and Austria-Hungary, but the rising national power of Germany, the security threat to France, and the decline of Britain all reflected an international hierarchy on the verge of violent collapse.

Political systems

Empirical pattern: The absence of democratic governments increases the probability of war between states.

Germany

Keylor (1992:44–45) characterizes the pre-1914 German political system as follows:

> The political structure of the German Reich, as defined by the federal constitution of 1871, may best be described as a facade of a parliamentary monarchy superimposed upon the edifice of an authoritarian state dominated by the reactionary, militarist, landowning aristocracy of Prussia. The hereditary position of German emperor was vested in the King of Prussia, who enjoyed the exclusive power to appoint and dismiss the head of government (the chancellor), to conduct foreign relations, to command the armed forces in time of war, to convoke and adjourn the bicameral parliament, and, through the chancellor, to initiate all domestic legislation. Prussian control of the upper house of the parliament (the Bundesrat) was preserved through a complex system of indirect and weighted representation together with the constitutional stipulation of a Prussian veto on legislation concerning military affairs. Even the lower house of the imperial legislature (the Reichstag), though elected by direct representation on the basis of universal male suffrage, was prevented from exercising the type of legislative authority associated with genuine parliamentary systems such as those of Great Britain and France. The head of government (the chancellor) was responsible to

the emperor, while his cabinet ministers were responsible only to him. This meant that a government was free to remain in office without a legislative majority so long as it retained the confidence of the hereditary ruler.

In short, neither the Bundesrat nor the Reichstag had much substantive power. This was particularly true with regard to foreign policy. The constitution placed these responsibilities solely in the control of the emperor. It was his privilege to determine the course of war or peace.

France

Kagan (1995:86–87) describes the political system of pre-World War I France as follows:

> By 1875 a series of fundamental laws had established a republican regime in France . . . The Third Republic, as it was called, had probably the most democratic constitution of any European state. The legislature . . . consisted of two houses, the Chamber of Deputies, whose members were elected by universal male suffrage for a four-year term, and a Senate, whose . . . members were elected indirectly for terms of nine years. The two houses were ostensibly equal, but in fact the directly elected, more democratic, Chamber of Deputies was the more powerful. Ministries and governments needed a majority in the Chamber to win appointment, and a vote of no confidence there brought them down. The two houses met jointly . . . to elect the President of the Republic who served a seven-year term. In practice he was usually only . . . a ceremonial figurehead . . . The true executive power rested with the Cabinet of Ministers. The real decisions were made in negotiations among the leaders of the parties, and the ministers were responsible to the Chamber. The French political system consisted of a multitude of parties . . . All governments, therefore, were composed of coalitions and could be dissolved by disagreements on a wide range of questions. Between 1890 and 1914 France had forty-three governments and twenty-six prime ministers.

The Third Republic was a democratically-based political system with both domestic and foreign policy issues subject to intense influence from partisan politics, press coverage, and the moods of public opinion.

Great Britain

Kagan (1995:89–90) argues that despite the democratic structure of the political system, few constraints on foreign policy decisionmaking existed in pre-1914 Britain. He characterizes the system in the following way:

> Great Britain . . . was formally a constitutional monarchy but in fact an increasingly democratic parliamentary government. Queen Victoria, Edward VII, and George V were little more than figureheads who reigned but did not rule. The true executive element in the constitution was the Cabinet, theoretically chosen by the monarch but really by the party holding a majority in the House of Commons. Led by a prime minister of the party's choosing, the Cabinet appointed officials, supervised the administration, and introduced legislation in Parliament. In turn, it was responsible to the Parliament. It could be expelled from office by a vote of no confidence or by failing to pass an important piece of legislation. For the most part the Parliament was divided between the major parties, Conservatives and Liberals. When the ruling party failed on a key vote it could resign and allow the other party to try to form a Cabinet or it could dissolve the Parliament and force new elections to determine which party could form the new government . . . Britain's true sovereign was Parliament, divided into two houses, Lords and Commons. Throughout this period Commons was the dominant member, but until 1909 the House of Lords had the right to delay or even to block legislation passed by the Commons. In that year the Lords were deprived of that power, and the Commons ruled without hindrance. The House of Commons was elected by popular vote for a term of six years, which might be shortened if the Cabinet dissolved it to hold new elections. The reform bills of the nineteenth century had broadened the franchise considerably, but it left as many as one third of the men of Britain without the vote.

With regard to foreign policy, Kagan notes that British Foreign Ministers had a high degree of autonomy, and that the Cabinet was not an effective instrument of control. Parliament had even less influence over foreign policy – required only to approve treaties that entailed financial commitments or to consent to the peacetime cession of territory.

Russia

Hammer (1974:21–24) describes the Russian political system in the years preceding World War I in the following terms:

> At the beginning of the twentieth century, the Russian Empire was the only European state which officially proclaimed itself to be an "autocracy." In theory, all legal power was vested in the person of the tsar . . . The ministers of the government were his personal

appointees . . . The laws of the empire were the tsar's decrees. Since there was no elected legislature, there was . . . no need for political parties in any form; and, until 1905, all political groupings which might voice opposition to the government were outlawed . . . In 1905, [following defeat in the Russo-Japanese War] there was a revolution against the autocracy; and in the face of popular rebellion, the tsar gave some ground. The censorship was ended, as was the formal ban on political parties. An elected national assembly, the Duma, was created. But even with these reforms, the Russian political system was far from democratic. The deputies to the Duma were elected indirectly, and the electoral system was devised to favor social groups . . . thought to be loyal to the tsar. When the first two elections produced deputies who were hostile to the regime, the Duma was dissolved and the electoral system revised.

In short, the introduction of a constitution and the creation of a legislature did not alter the fundamentally autocratic nature of the Russian political system.

Austria-Hungary

Kagan (1995:95–97) describes the political system of Austria-Hungary prior to World War I in the following way:

> In the Middle Ages the German family the Habsburgs began forging a great empire in central Europe from the borders of Russia and Rumania on the east to the Alps and the Adriatic in the west. Early in the twentieth century it was the third largest state in Europe, behind Russia and Germany. It was unique among the great powers in being a polyglot empire in which the ruling nationality was a small minority of the population. Of the Habsburg emperor's more than fifty million subjects in 1910 only about twelve million were Germans; ten million were Magyars, the ruling people of Hungary. The rest were Czechs, Slovaks, Poles, Ukranians, Rumanians, Serbs, Croats, Slovenes, Italians, Slavic Muslims, and a scattering of others. In 1867 the Habsburg realm was divided into two separate states called the Empire of Austria and the Kingdom of Hungary, united under a single flag and under the sovereignty of a single monarch [the emperor] . . . Each state had its own language, its own constitution, officials, and Parliament. In practice the Parliaments were powerless and ineffective.

In sum, in the years before the onset of World War I, Austria-Hungary established the external trappings of constitutional parliamentary government while in fact maintaining a system of bureaucratic absolutism. Emperor Franz Joseph (1848–1916) of Austria-Hungary, like the emperors of Germany and Russia, possessed ultimate decisionmaking power in questions of war or peace.

Summary

The preceding descriptions of the political systems of Germany, France, Great Britain, Russia, and Austria-Hungary on the eve of World War I suggest which systems were democratically-based and which systems were not. A more systematic, comparative approach to the issue of the presence or absence of democratic government can be undertaken by utilizing the ordinal data on political characteristics collected by Banks (1971). Banks' Cross-Polity Time-Series (CPTS) database contains four ordinal-scale variables on political characteristics relevant to the question of democratic government. This segment of the database includes all states for the period between 1815 and 1966.

Field J of the CPTS database involves "effective executive selection."[10] The ordinal variable includes entries for: (1) direct election; (2) indirect election; and (3) nonelective. Field K of the database comprises an ordinal variable for "parliamentary responsibility"[11] with the following entries: (0) irrelevant; (1) absent; (2) incomplete; and (3) complete. Field O of the database is an ordinal variable for "legislative effectiveness"[12] and has the following entries: (0) none; (1) ineffective; (2) partially effective; and (3) effective. Field P of the database is an ordinal variable involving "legislative selection"[13] and includes entries for: (0) none; (1) nonelective; and (2) elective.

To create a scale for "democracy" based on these four variables, Field J was recoded from (1) to (3) for increasingly democratic selection of the executive. Fields K, O, and P had original ordinal codings for increasing democratic attributes. Combining the four

---

[10] This variable includes methods of executive selection by: popular vote, committed delegates, uncommitted electoral college or elected assembly, and nonelective methods of selection. See Banks (1971) Field J for a precise description of the variable.

[11] This variable refers "to the degree to which a premier must depend on the support of a majority in the lower house of the legislature in order to remain in office." See Banks (1971) Field K.

[12] This variable includes entries for: no legislature, "rubber stamp" legislature, weak legislature, and autonomous legislature. See Banks (1971) Field O for a precise description of the variable.

[13] This variable includes entries for: no legislature, appointment by executive selection or hereditary right, ascription, and indirect or direct popular election. See Banks (1971) Field P for a precise description of the variable.

variables produces a democracy scale with a maximum score of 11 (highly democratic) and a minimum score of 1 (absence of democracy). For the year 1913, the following scores were calculated for the initial major power participants in World War I:

Democracy index: 1913

Great Britain	10
France	10
Germany	6
Austria-Hungary	5
Russia	5

Given that Germany, Austria-Hungary, and Russia possessed elective legislatures but of minimal effectiveness and responsibility, and also possessed nonelective executives, their rankings accurately reflect systems of democratic facade. The scores of both Britain and France are double those of Austria-Hungary and Russia, and are substantially higher than Germany's. On the basis of this comparative analysis, it may be concluded that only Britain and France possessed democratically-based political systems on the eve of World War I. Structural and normative constraints on war decisions of political leaders in Germany, Russia, and Austria-Hungary were insignificant. In fact, the case analysis suggests that structural constraints on British war decisions were also minimal. That World War I begins with the conflict over the Balkans between the non-democratic states of Austria-Hungary and Russia, and that the Dual Alliance of Austria-Hungary and Germany confronts the democratic states of Britain and France is consistent with the empirical pattern of war probabilities for opposing nations lacking matched democratic political systems.

Enduring rivals

Empirical pattern: The presence of an enduring rivalry increases the probability of war within a dyad.

France/Germany

The subject of enduring rivalries has been discussed in chapters 1 and 7. To briefly summarize, it has been noted that a small number of conflict-prone dyads – or "enduring rivals" – account for a disproportionately large amount of the violence that occurs in the interstate system. Multiple definitions of "enduring rivals" with different criteria for inclusion in the population set have been used in the compilation of databases. For example, Wayman (1982, 1996) includes any major power dyad that engages in two or more militarized disputes within a 10-year span; Diehl (1985) defines a major power rivalry as any dyad engaging in three or more militarized disputes within a 15-year span; Gochman and Maoz (1984) construct a set that includes all dyads which have engaged in a minimum of seven militarized disputes during the period from 1816 to 1980.

Huth, Bennett and Gelpi (1992) define rivalries in a different manner. Specifically, Huth *et al.* eliminate the frequency of militarized disputes as a criterion of rivalry and focus instead on dissatisfaction with the status quo, perception of security threat, and viability of the usage of military force. Concentrating on great powers alone, Huth *et al.* produce a set of 18 major power rivals for the period between 1816 and 1975.

The rivalries set used in the analysis of the Iran/Iraq War in chapter 7 was based on criteria established by Wayman and Jones (1991). This highly restrictive definition of enduring rivals excludes all short- and medium-term conflict dyads from consideration. The criteria delineate a small set of long-term rivalries which are responsible for almost 40 percent of all militarized disputes occurring between 1816 and 1986, despite the fact that the rivalries constitute only about 8 percent of the total dyad-years for that period. In short, these are the most conflict-prone pairs in the interstate system.

For the analysis presented here, enduring rivalries were again defined according to the time/density dispute criteria established by Wayman and Jones. These criteria involve the "severity," "durability," and "continuity" of the rivalry,[14] and produce a set of 29 enduring rivals[15] for the period between 1816 and 1986. Of these rivalries, seven involve major power dyads. Four of these major power dyads engaged in at least one war. Table 8.3 identifies the warring major power dyads and their wars. The France/Germany dyad appears in this list.

Summary

The France/Germany dyad constitutes an enduring rivalry from 1850 to 1945 on the basis of time/density dispute criteria. Over this period

---

[14] See chapter 7 (p. 152) for a description of these criteria.
[15] See chapter 7 (table 7.1) for a complete list of the enduring rivalries generated by these criteria.

Table 8.3. *Warring major power rivals, 1816–1986*

Rivalry	Wars	Year (initiation/entry)
Austria-Hungary/Italy	Seven Weeks' War	1866
	World War I	1915
France/Prussia(Germany)	Franco-Prussian War	1870
	World War I	1914
	World War II	1939
Russia(USSR)/Japan	Russo-Japanese War	1904
	Changkuofeng War	1938
	Nomohan War	1939
	World War II	1945
USA/China	Korean War	1950

of 96 years, France and Germany engaged in 17 militarized disputes (14 subwar disputes and 3 wars). Six of these militarized disputes occurred after the Franco-Prussian War (1870) and before the Treaty of Versailles (1919). The last of these six disputes involved the onset of World War I.

Alliances

Empirical pattern: The presence of polarized alliances increases the probability of the seriousness (magnitude/duration/severity) of war.

Alliances (1890–1914)

As many historians have noted, an important element in understanding certain characteristics of World War I involves the system of major power alliances and their subsequent polarization in the years preceding the outbreak of the war. With few exceptions, most of the interstate wars of the 1890s were dyadic conflicts (e.g., the Sino-Japanese War, the Greco-Turkish War, the Spanish–American War, etc.). However, by the end of the first decade of the twentieth century, the polarized alliance systems of the major powers led to the expectation that the next great war would be between coalitions.

Alliance diplomacy affected the behavior of all the major European states, including Britain, as a result of long-standing rivalries and perceived security threats. As Kennedy (1987:249) observes:

> The creation of fixed military alliances in peacetime – rarely if ever seen before – was begun by Bismarck in 1879, when he sought to "control" Vienna's foreign policy, and to warn off St. Petersburg, by

establishing the Austro-German alliance . . .; but the longer-lasting legacy of Bismarck's action was that Germany bound itself to come to Austria-Hungary's aid in the event of a Russian attack.

Bismarck's alliance objectives are described generally as short-term and defensive – to isolate France diplomatically and to organize opposition against a possible Russian invasion of the Balkans – but the alliance with Austria-Hungary in 1879 led to suspicion in both France and Russia that Berlin was constructing a coalition to be used against them in wartime.

The ability of France to recover Alsace–Lorraine and Russia's drive to expand in eastern Europe were blocked by German power. In the absence of other major continental alliance partners for either state, France and Russia sought coalition with each other. France could offer money (loans) and modern weaponry to St. Petersburg; Russia could provide military support for Paris. By 1894 the German/Austro-Hungarian alliance was matched by the Franco/Russian alliance.

These two coalitions appeared to stabilize the European situation. Kennedy (1987:250) argues that at this point:

> A rough equilibrium existed between the two alliance blocs, making the results of a Great Power conflict more incalculable, and thus less likely, than before. Having escaped from their isolation, France and Russia turned away to African and Asian concerns . . . Germany was also turning toward *Weltpolitik*.

One result of this colonial expansionism on the part of France, Russia, and Germany was to create a perceived security threat to the British Empire. Britain generally had maintained its separation from European political machinations, but the imperial maneuverings of the continental powers caused problems for British security and threatened the resources available to support it.

With the advent of the twentieth century, the extra-systemic "imperial rivalries" among the major powers began to have repercussions within the European theater. Specifically, Britain moved to end its isolation and consolidate its strategic situation. For example: concessions to the United States permitted the removal of British military resources from the western hemisphere; the implementation of the Anglo-Japanese alliance in 1902 alleviated the British strategic burden in China; and there was movement toward settling outstanding colonial issues with France.

Although these maneuvers appeared to affect only extra-systemic affairs, they nevertheless had an impact on European relations. Kennedy (1987:251) observes that:

> The resolution of Britain's strategical dilemmas in the western hemisphere . . . eased some of the pressures upon the Royal Navy . . . and enhanced its prospects of consolidating in wartime; and settling Anglo-French rivalries would mean an even greater boost to Britain's naval security . . . Finally, even the distant Anglo-Japanese alliance was to have repercussions upon the European states system, since it made it unlikely that any third power would intervene when Japan decided in 1904 to challenge Russia . . .; when that war broke out . . . the Anglo-Japanese treaty *and* the Franco-Russian alliance strongly induced . . . Britain and France respectively, to work with each other to avoid being drawn openly into the conflict.

Thus, the alliance between Austria-Hungary and Germany in combination with the Russo-Japanese War led to the entente of 1904 between France and Britain and ended their years of conflict.

Underlying the British–French entente was a mutual fear induced by the rising power of Germany. German political ambitions on the continent appeared to threaten French security, and the German High Seas Fleet had a range and configuration that suggested that British naval forces were its target. Yet another factor driving the British–French entente was the internal unrest in Russia which peaked during 1905. The uprising against the autocratic rule of the Tsar appeared to both France and Britain to reduce the role of Russia as a military counterweight to Germany. With the relative capabilities of Germany rising, the prospects for France – in the event of war – looked dire.

The British–French entente of 1904 was followed by the 1907 Anglo-Russian entente over Persia, Tibet, and Afghanistan. Although the agreement focused on the elimination of a set of nineteenth-century regional conflicts between London and St. Petersburg, it produced unease in Germany and a fear of encirclement by hostile states. The Anglo-German naval race of 1908–1909 added to the spiral of suspicion and threat growing between Britain and Germany.[16] When Austria-Hungary formally annexed Bosnia–Herzegovina during the Balkan crises of 1908–1909, Russian opposition to the move was met by a German ultimatum that Russia "accept the *fait accompli* or suffer

---

[16] For an analysis of the extended Anglo-German naval rivalry see Stoll (1992). For a study of the final years of the naval race before the onset of World War I see Maurer (1992).

the consequences" (Kennedy 1987:253). The reaction by the Tsar was to increase military expenditures and to move diplomatically closer to Britain and France.

Thus, by 1909 the polarization of the major power alliances was complete. Britain subsequently intervened on the side of France and against Germany in the Agadir (Morocco) crisis of 1911. By 1912, the states of the Balkan League had essentially eliminated the rule of the Ottoman Empire; developments in the Balkans threatened interests of both Austria-Hungary and Russia; and the 1914 assassination of Archduke Franz Ferdinand was followed by Austria-Hungary's action against Serbia and by Russia's military response.

Hence, the assassination in June of 1914 ignites a general crisis which culminates in World War I. Austria-Hungary rejects Serbian conciliation and attacks Belgrade. Russia mobilizes its military forces to assist its Serbian ally. Germany implements the Schlieffen Plan with its preemptive strike through Belgium against France. Britain joins the conflict on the side of France and Russia.

Summary

The polarized alliance systems did not precipitate the onset of World War I – they merely reflected the competing and complementary interests of the major powers and their perceived security threats. However, the alliances did produce a war of enormous magnitude, duration, and severity. As Kennedy (1987:256) notes:

> [H]ad the Russians been allowed to attack Austria-Hungary alone, or had the Germans been permitted a rerun of their 1870 war against France while the other powers remained neutral, the prospects of victory... seem incontestable. But these coalitions meant that even if one belligerent was heavily beaten in a campaign or saw that its resources were inadequate to sustain further conflict, it was encouraged to remain in the war by the hope – and promises – of aid from its allies... Thus, the alliance system itself virtually guaranteed that the war would *not* be swiftly decided, and meant in turn that victory in this lengthy duel would go – as in the great coalition wars of the eighteenth century – to the side whose combination of both military/ naval *and* financial/industrial/technological resources was the greatest.

In short, the polarized alliance systems of the major powers ensured that if a war did occur, it would be a war of truly devastating consequences.

Conclusion

The historical event of World War I (1914) has been described in the format of a case study. However, the critical factors leading to both the onset and seriousness of this war have been identified as empirical uniformities common to a broad set of wars. The state-level, dyadic-level, and systemic-level factors of proximity/contiguity, status-rank, power cycle, unstable hierarchy, absence of democratic governments in opposing coalitions, presence of an enduring rivalry, and presence of polarized alliances all increased the probability of the onset of a war of enormous magnitude, duration, and severity.

The detailed case analysis reveals how these factors combined to produce the war in question: the territorial issues in conflict, the security threats, and the physical opportunity to deal with the problems by military force were provided by the proximate and contiguous borders of the major European states; the high status-rank of Britain, Germany, France, Russia, and Austria-Hungary increased the probability of the use of force; the conjunctive passage of Britain, Germany, and Russia through critical points on their power cycles produced the extremes of decisionmaking uncertainty and risk; the rising national power of Germany, its security threat to France, and the decline of Britain as the leading state reflected an international hierarchy on the verge of violent collapse; the autocratic structures of the governments in Russia, Germany, and Austria-Hungary placed few constraints on war decisions by their leaders, and there was an absence of shared norms associated with nonviolent conflict resolution between the Dual Alliance and the democratic states of France and Britain; the presence of the enduring rivalry between France and Germany with its history of chronic, militarized interaction increased the probability of violent conflict; and the polarized alliance systems of Austria-Hungary/Germany and Britain/France/Russia all made the onset of a war of enormous magnitude, duration, and severity highly likely.

Scientific explanation of individual events may be provided by their inductive subsumption under probabilistic laws. The preceding analysis demonstrates that World War I was a high-probability event consistent with a broad array of empirical patterns and that it was a specific instance of a set of intersecting uniformities which have appeared in a much larger number of war cases.

9 Conclusion

In 1970, Singer outlined his scientific approach toward uncovering the causes of international war and speculated as to the outcome. Specifically, he postulated that state attributes, relational characteristics within dyads, and system-level attributes might combine in creating a potent source of war:

> It will almost certainly turn out that certain attributes do indeed make some nations more war-prone than others . . . I would, on the other hand, expect that these attributes – in order to exercise any consistent and powerful effect – have to interact with certain *relational* variables and with the attributes of the international system at the moment. A nation must, in a sense, be in the "right" setting if it is to get into war. Finally, there is little doubt that all of these ecological factors will have to be taken into account . . . if we are ever to understand the dynamic processes of behavior and interaction which are so large a part of conflict. (Singer 1970:537)

The analysis presented here has attempted to identify those factors and to demonstrate how they conjoin in influencing the onset of war among nations.

The preceding eight chapters of this book were designed to provide a scientific explanation of war in international politics grounded on data-based empirical research. The study began with an examination of two basic decisionmaking models – the rational and the nonrational – in relation to the explanatory framework of the volume. The central body of the book was organized around quantitative empirical research findings on the onset and seriousness of war drawn from the analytic levels of the state, dyad, region, and international system. Case analyses of the onset of two wars – Iran/Iraq (1980) and World War I (1914) – were provided as demonstrations of scientifically-based explanations of historical conflicts.

Principal among the objectives of this study was the effort to identify a series of probabilistic laws drawn from consistent empirical regularities at multiple analytic levels. The form of covering law model employed here involves explanation of an event as a result of the conjunction of a set of strong empirical patterns. The empirical patterns were not interrelated deductively, but rather were treated as inductive generalizations which, additively, increased the probability of the occurrence of the specified outcome. In other words, wars in the two case studies – Iran/Iraq and World War I – were explained by inductive logic given the empirical regularities (probabilistic laws) drawn from data-based research.

Because wars follow from decisions, any explanation of war must incorporate, explicitly or implicitly, a model of decisionmaking. Chapter 2 examined decisionmaking models on the basis of their assumptions about rationality. Nonrational models, whether focusing on cognitive psychology or organizational interests and routines, maintain that decisions are frequently distorted by systematic perceptual, cognitive, or bureaucratic biases. Although the definition of rationality is a subject of both philosophical and conceptual debate, minimal criteria for an instrumentally rational decision include the logical requirements of consistency and coherence in goal-directed behavior.

Due to the high information requirements, nonrational models of war based on psychological principles or bureaucratic interests and routines have primary applicability in detailed explanations of specific events. In contrast, rational models offer the simplifying assumption that psychological biases or organizational routines have minimal impact and that decisionmakers all calculate in basically the same manner. Accepting the simplifying assumption of rational decisionmaking facilitates the examination of other, nondecisional elements among the causes of war located at the analytic levels of the state, dyad, region, and system and permits these factors to be incorporated in a general explanation of interstate conflict without reference to specific leaders or bureaucratic/organizational elements within governments.

If states do not act similarly in similar situations, then perhaps variation in foreign policies is due to variation in the internal attributes of states. According to this logic, states with the same critical internal attributes will evidence similar patterns of war behavior, distinct from the patterns produced by states with different attributes. Chapter 3 focused on quantitative empirical research that related to the war-proneness of states. A set of consistent and cumulative empirical uniformities on the onset and seriousness of war were identified at the state level of analysis and were noted in that chapter. Factors increasing the probability of the onset (occurrence/ initiation) of war at the level of the state are:

- Power status (major power)
- Power cycle (critical point if major power)
- Alliance (alliance member)
- Borders (number of borders)

The factor identified as increasing the probable seriousness (magnitude/duration/severity) of war at the level of the state is:

- Power status (major power)

In contrast to state-level studies, dyadic analyses permit the examination of relational attributes for pairs of states that engage in conflict. Some of these elements have a substantial history in realist explanations on the causes of war (e.g., capability differentials, alliances, and arms races), while others have constituted cornerstones of liberal philosophy as elements associated with peaceful interstate relations (e.g., economic development, free trade, and democracy). Chapter 4 focused on quantitative empirical research that related to the war-proneness of dyads. A set of consistent and cumulative empirical uniformities on the onset of war were identified at the dyadic level of analysis and were noted in that chapter. Factors increasing the probability of the onset (occurrence/initiation) of war at the level of the dyad are:

- Contiguity/proximity (common border/distance)
- Political systems (absence of joint democracies)
- Economic development (absence of joint advanced economies)
- Static capability balance (parity)
- Dynamic capability balance (unstable: shift/transition)
- Alliance (unbalanced external alliance-tie)
- Enduring rivalry

Chapter 5 examined data-based research on war-prone regions. The initial section of the chapter focused on simple comparisons *between* geographic regions in terms of the number of crises, subwar disputes, and wars as well as inter-regional comparisons of processes of militarized dispute contagion. The second section of that chapter explored evidence relating to *intra*-regional patterns of conflict and war that may have been dependent upon spatial heterogeneity, population pressure, polarity, and normative constraints. The third section of the chapter examined evidence of war contagion as it pertained to patterns of intra-regional behavior. The final section in chapter 5 examined evidence of intra-regional cycles of war. One consistent and cumulative empirical pattern on the onset of war was identified at the regional level of analysis. The factor increasing the probability of the onset (occurrence) of war at the level of the region is:

- Contagion/diffusion (presence of an ongoing regional war)

Chapter 6 reviewed data-based research on war-prone systems. Here, certain system-level attributes such as polarity, alliances, capability concentration, Kondratieff economic cycles, normative constraints, and the presence of intergovernmental organizations were examined for war effects. A set of consistent and cumulative empirical uniformities on the onset and seriousness of war were identified at the systemic level of analysis. Factors increasing the probability of the onset (occurrence) of war at the level of the international system are:

- Polarity (weak unipolarity/declining leader)
- Unstable hierarchy
- Number of borders
- Frequency of civil/revolutionary wars

The factor identified as increasing the probable seriousness (magnitude/duration/severity) of war at the level of the international system is:

- Alliance (high polarization)

Case analyses of two wars – presented in chapters 7 and 8 – were provided as demonstrations of scientifically-based explanations of historical events. More specifically, the cases of the Iran/Iraq War (1980) and World War I (1914) were explained on the basis of empirical uniformities established through systematic quantitative analyses. The explanations in chapters 7 and 8 demonstrated that the Iran/Iraq War and World War I were specific instances of a set of patterns which have appeared in a much larger number of cases. In short, both wars were high-probability events consistent with a broad array of empirical patterns.

Wars are contests of power. They may develop over any of a large number of issues such as territory, security, wealth, or ethnicity. However, it is maintained that the presence or absence of certain factors increases the probability of the onset and seriousness of such contests. The analysis presented here has attempted to identify those factors and to provide an account of conflict using findings derived from over five decades of systematic, quantitative empirical research.

In sum, this book has offered an explanation of war in international politics based on covering laws. The approach has utilized the inductive–probabilistic logical form, and has identified a series of strong empirical patterns at multiple levels of analysis that are associated with both the onset (occurrence/initiation) and seriousness (magnitude/duration/severity) of war. It has demonstrated that the onset and seriousness of individual cases of dyadic and multistate war can be explained as resulting from the conjunction of factors identified as strong empirical patterns. Moreover, these patterns may be used to generate probabilistic predictions about war in specific cases.[1] Such policy-oriented work lies beyond the scope of this volume, but remains within the realm of its epistemological framework. Alternatively, as Nicholson (1996:43) argues, the implications of chaos theory in terms of the predictability of certain physical phenomena suggest that uncertainty may be a basic characteristic in the behavior of even simple deterministic systems. The study of international conflict may also reveal an inherently limited predictability – for specific cases – despite the existence of highly stable patterns. Limitations in prediction, however, do not weaken our ability to explain how and why wars occur. Of course, the onset of war ultimately turns on decisions. Structural forces influence and shape those decisions, but do not determine them entirely. In this sense, the conditions conducive to war may be present, but due to the element of human choice, the last step remains indeterminate.

---

[1] A published version of an attempt to forecast the severity (total battle-deaths) of the impending war between Iraq and United Nations forces in 1991 – based on historical patterns of conflict – may be found in Cioffi-Revilla (1991). Specifically, Cioffi-Revilla estimated the number of states involved in the war and the duration of the war and then used these estimates to predict the number of total battle-deaths, based on equations designed to account for the severity of historical wars.

Appendix 1
List of databases

COPDAB:	Conflict and Peace Data Bank (University of North Carolina)
COW:	Correlates of War Project (University of Michigan)
CPTS:	Cross-Polity Time-Series (State University of New York at Binghamton)
CREON:	Comparative Research on the Events of Nations Project (Ohio State University)
DON:	Dimensionality of Nations Project (University of Hawaii)
ICB:	International Crisis Behavior Project (University of Maryland)
LORANOW:	Long-Range Analysis of War Project (University of Colorado)
MIC:	Managing Interstate Conflict (University of Pittsburgh)
MID:	Militarized Interstate Dispute; Correlates of War (COW) Project (University of Michigan)
SIPRI:	Stockholm International Peace Research Institute
TRIP:	Transnational Rules Indicator Project (University of South Carolina)
WEIS:	World Event Interaction Survey (University of Southern California)

Appendix 2
Tables of references by category

Table A.1. *War-prone states: references by category*

National attributes	Regimes	Capabilities	Borders	Alliances	Status quo orientation
Bremer, Singer & Luterbacher (1973)	Brady & Kegley (1977)	Bremer (1980)	Boulding (1962)	Kemp (1977)	Geller (1994)
Cattell (1949)	Chan (1984)	Diehl & Kingston (1987)	Midlarsky (1975)	Levy (1981)	Gilpin (1981)
Cattell et al. (1952)	Dixon (1989)	Doran (1983)	Richardson (1960)	Singer & Small (1966)	Modelski (1983)
Cattell & Gorsuch (1965)	Domke (1988)	Doran (1985)	Rummel (1972)	Siverson & Starr (1990)	Organski (1958)
Choucri & North (1972)	East & Gregg (1967)	Doran (1989)	Siverson & Starr (1990)	Siverson & Sullivan Wish (1980)	Organski & Kugler (1980)
Choucri & North (1975)	East & Hermann (1974)	Doran & Parsons (1980)	Starr & Most (1976)	Vasquez (1993)	
Choucri, North & Yamakage (1992)	Enterline (1996)	Eberwein (1982)	Starr & Most (1978)	Weede (1970)	
Duval & Thompson (1980)	Gaubatz (1991)	Feierabend & Feierabend (1969)	Starr & Most (1983)		
East (1973)	Geller (1985)	Geller (1988)	Weede (1970)		
East & Gregg (1967)	Gleditsch (1992)	Houweling & Siccama (1991)	Wright (1964)		
Eberwein et al. (1979)	Gleditsch (1994)	James & Hebron (1993)			
Feierabend & Feierabend (1969)	Gregg & Banks (1965)	Kemp (1977)			
Geller (1985)	Haas (1965)	Köhler (1975)			
Richardson (1960)	Levy (1988)	Rummel (1968)			
Rummel (1963)	Mansfield & Snyder (1995)	Small & Singer (1970)			
Rummel (1967)	Maoz (1989)	Small & Singer (1982)			
Rummel (1968)	Maoz & Abdolali (1989)	Weede (1970)			
Rummel (1969)	Nincic (1990)	Wright (1964)			
Salmore & Hermann (1969)	Ray (1995b)				
Singer (1972)	Rummel (1968)				
Singer & Cusack (1981)	Rummel (1983)				
Thompson (1982)	Rummel (1985)				
Vincent (1981)	Russett (1990a)				
Vincent et al.(1973)	Russett & Monsen (1975)				
Wilkenfeld (1969)	Salmore & Hermann (1969)				
Wilkenfeld (1971)	Small & Singer (1976)				
	Stoll (1984)				
	Weede (1970)				
	Weede (1984)				
	Weede (1996a)				
	Wright (1964)				
	Zinnes & Wilkenfeld (1971)				

Table A.2. *War-prone dyads: references by category*

Capability balance	Contiguity	Arms race	Alliances	Regimes	Status quo orientation	Economic factors
Anderson & McKeown (1987)	Boulding (1962)	Altfeld (1983)	Bueno de Mesquita (1981a)	Babst (1972)	Anderson & McKeown (1987)	Barbieri (1996)
Bremer (1992)	Bremer (1992)	Diehl (1983)	Bremer (1992)	Bremer (1992)	Galtung (1964)	Blainey (1973)
Bueno de Mesquita (1978)	Bueno de Mesquita (1981a)	Diehl (1985)	Kim (1991)	Bremer (1993a)	Geller (1994)	Bremer (1992)
Bueno de Mesquita (1980)	Garnham (1976b)	Diehl & Kingston (1987)	Kim (1992)	Bueno de Mesquita & Lalman (1992)	Gilpin (1981)	Buzan (1984)
Bueno de Mesquita (1981a)	Gleditsch (1995)	Huntington (1969)	Kim & Morrow (1992)	Chan (1984)	Huth (1996)	Gasiorowski & Polachek (1982)
Bueno de Mesquita & Riker (1982)	Gleditsch & Singer (1975)	Intriligator (1969)	Mihalka (1976)	Dixon (1989)	Huth, Bennett & Gelpi (1992)	Hoffmann (1978)
Garnham (1976a)	Gochman (1990b)	Intriligator & Brito (1984)	Ray (1990)	Dixon (1993)	Huth, Gelpi & Bennett (1993)	Nye (1990)
Geller (1990)	Lemke (1995)	Majeski (1986)	Siverson & Tennefoss (1984)	Dixon (1994)	Levy (1987)	Oneal, Oneal, Maoz & Russett (1996)
Geller (1992a)	Mihalka (1976)	Morrow (1989)	Weede (1975)	Domke (1988)	Maoz (1982)	Sullivan (1974)
Geller (1993)	Moul (1985)	Richardson (1939)	Weede (1989)	Doyle (1986)	Midlarsky (1975)	Weede (1995)
Geller (1998)	Moul (1988)	Vasquez (1993)		Farber & Gowa (1995)	Morrow (1996)	
Gochman (1990a)	Rummel (1979)	Wallace (1979)		Gates, Knutsen & Moses (1996)	Organski (1958)	
Houweling & Siccama (1988)	Starr & Most (1976)	Wallace (1980)		Geller (1985)	Paul (1994)	
Huth, Bennett & Gelpi (1992)	Starr & Most (1978)	Wallace (1981)		Gleditsch (1995)	Ray (1995a)	
Huth & Russett (1993)	Vasquez (1993)	Wallace (1982)		James & Mitchell (1995)	Rummel (1979)	
Maoz & Abdolali	Vasquez (1995)	Wallace (1983)		Layne (1994)	Vasquez (1996a)	
Kim (1991)	Weede (1975)	Wallace (1990)		Levy (1988)	Wallace (1971)	
Kim (1992)		Weede (1980)		(1989)		
Kim (1996)				Maoz & Russett (1993)		
Kim & Morrow (1992)				Morgan & Campbell (1991)		
Lemke & Kugler (1996)				Morgan & Schwebach (1992)		
Mandel (1980)						

(continued)

Table A.2. (continued)

Capability balance	Contiguity	Arms race	Alliances	Regimes	Status quo orientation	Economic factors
Mihalka (1976)				Ray (1993)		
Modelski (1983)				Ray (1995a)		
Morrow (1996)				Rummel (1968)		
Moul (1988)				Rummel (1979)		
Organski & Kugler (1980)				Rummel (1983)		
Singer (1972)				Russett (1990b)		
Siverson & Tennefoss (1984)				Russett (1993)		
Small & Singer (1982)				Small & Singer (1976)		
Wang & Ray (1994)				Spiro (1994)		
Wayman (1996)				Waltz (1959)		
Weede (1976)				Weede (1970)		
				Weede (1984)		
				Wright (1964)		

Table A.3. *War-prone regions: references by category*

Comparisons	Attributes	Contagion	Cycles
Brecher (1984)	Bremer, Singer &	Bremer (1982)	Farrar (1977)
Brecher &	Luterbacher (1973)	Faber, Houweling	Gilpin (1981)
Wilkenfeld (1982)	Cohen (1973)	& Siccama (1984)	Goldstein (1988)
Bremer (1982)	Cohen (1982)	Garnham (1983)	Levy (1991)
Eckhardt & Azar	Holsti (1991)	Houweling &	Midlarsky (1984)
(1978a)	Hopf (1991)	Siccama (1985)	Modelski (1983)
Eckhardt & Azar	Huntington (1993)	Kirby & Ward	Thompson (1988)
(1978b)	Kegley & Raymond	(1987)	Thompson (1996)
Gochman & Maoz	(1986)	Levy & Morgan	Wallerstein (1984)
(1984)	Kelly (1986)	(1986)	Wright (1964)
Holsti (1995)	O'Loughlin &	Li & Thompson	
Houweling &	Anselin (1991)	(1975)	
Kuné (1984)		Lieberson &	
Houweling &		Silverman (1965)	
Siccama (1985)		Midlarsky (1970)	
Kende (1978)		Midlarsky (1978)	
Kennedy (1993)		Midlarsky, Crenshaw	
Mearsheimer (1990)		& Yoshida (1980)	
Singer &		Most & Starr (1980)	
Wildavsky (1993)		Spilerman (1970)	
Weede (1996b)		Starr & Most (1983)	
		Starr & Most (1985)	

Table A.4. *War-prone systems: references by category*

Polarity	Alliances	Attributes	Time	Contagion	Norms/IGOs
Doran (1989)	Brecher, James & Wilkenfeld (1990)	Bueno de Mesquita (1981b)	Cioffi-Revilla (1995)	Bremer (1982)	Holsti (1991)
Geller (1992b)	Bueno de Mesquita (1978)	Bueno de Mesquita & Lalman (1988)	Cioffi-Revilla (1996)	Faber, Houweling & Siccama (1984)	Kegley & Raymond (1981)
Geller (1996)	Bueno de Mesquita & Lalman (1988)	East (1972)	Eckhardt & Azar (1978a)	Houweling & Siccama (1985)	Kegley & Raymond (1982)
Gilpin (1981)	Holsti, Hopmann & Sullivan (1973)	Gleditsch (1994)	Eckhardt & Azar (1978b)	Levy (1982b)	Kegley & Raymond (1986)
Hopf (1991)	Jervis (1976)	Goldstein (1988)	Gochman & Maoz (1984)	Most & Starr (1980)	Kegley & Raymond (1994)
Levy (1984)	Kegley & Raymond (1994)	Hoole & Huang (1989)	Goldstein (1988)	Most, Starr & Siverson (1989)	Parsons (1951)
Mansfield (1988)	Kim & Morrow (1992)	Mansfield (1988)	Levy (1982a)	Naroll (1968)	Schahczenski (1991)
Modelski (1972)	Levy (1981)	Maoz (1989)	Levy & Morgan (1986)	Richardson (1960)	Singer & Wallace (1970)
Modelski (1983)	Singer & Small (1966)	Maoz & Abdolali (1989)	Midlarsky (1986)		Vasquez (1993)
Morgenthau (1967)	Singer & Small (1968)	Modelski (1981)	Singer & Small (1972)		Wallensteen (1984)
Organski (1958)	Singer & Small (1974)	Richardson (1960)	Singer & Small (1974)		
Spiezio (1990)	Snyder & Diesing (1977)	Singer, Bremer & Stuckey (1972)	Stoll (1982)		
Thompson (1986)	Vasquez (1993)	Starr (1994)			
Thompson (1988)	Wallace (1973)	Starr & Most (1976)			
Wallerstein (1984)	Wayman (1984)	Starr & Most (1978)			
Waltz (1979)		Wallace (1971)			
Weede (1994)		Wallace (1973)			
		Wallensteen & Axell (1993)			
		Wallerstein (1984)			
		Waltz (1979)			

References

Allison, Graham T. (1969) Conceptual Models and the Cuban Missile Crisis. *American Political Science Review* 63:689–718.

Altfeld, Michael F. (1983) Arms Races? – And Escalation? A Comment on Wallace. *International Studies Quarterly* 27:225–231.

Anderson, Paul A. and Timothy J. McKeown (1987) Changing Aspirations, Limited Attention, and War. *World Politics* 40:1–29.

Andriole, Stephen J., Jonathan Wilkenfeld and Gerald W. Hopple (1975) A Framework for the Comparative Analysis of Foreign Policy Behavior. *International Studies Quarterly* 19:160–198.

Babst, Dean V. (1972) A Force for Peace. *Industrial Research* (April):55–58.

Banks, Arthur S. (1971) *Cross-Polity Time-Series Data.* Cambridge: MIT Press.

Banks, Arthur S. (ed.) (1995) *Political Handbook of the World: 1994–1995.* Binghamton, NY: CSA Publications.

Banks, Arthur S. and William Overstreet (eds.) (1981) *Political Handbook of the World: 1981.* New York: McGraw-Hill.

Barbieri, Katherine (1996) Economic Interdependence: A Path to Peace or a Source of Interstate Conflict? *Journal of Peace Research* 33:29–49.

Bhaskar, Roy (1978) *A Realist Theory of Science* (2nd edition). London: Routledge and Kegan Paul.

(1986) *Scientific Realism and Human Emancipation.* London: Verso.

Blainey, Geoffrey (1973) *The Causes of War.* New York: The Free Press.

Blechman, Barry M. and Stephen S. Kaplan (1978) *Force Without War: U.S. Armed Forces as a Political Instrument.* Washington, DC: The Brookings Institution.

Bloch, Ivan [Jean de] (1898) *The Future of War.* New York: Doubleday and McClure.

Boulding, Kenneth (1962) *Conflict and Defense.* New York: Harper and Row.

Brady, Linda and Charles W. Kegley, Jr. (1977) Bureaucratic Determinants of Foreign Policy: Some Empirical Evidence. *International Interactions* 3:33–50.

References

Braithwaite, Richard Bevan (1953) *Scientific Explanation: A Study of the Function of Theory, Probability and Law in Science*. Cambridge: Cambridge University Press.

Braybrooke, David and Charles E. Lindblom (1963) *A Strategy of Decision: Policy Evaluation as a Social Process*. New York: The Free Press.

Brecher, Michael (1984) International Crises and Protracted Conflicts. *International Interactions* 11:237–297.

Brecher, Michael and Jonathan Wilkenfeld (1982) Crises in World Politics. *World Politics* 34:380–417.

Brecher, Michael, Patrick James and Jonathan Wilkenfeld (1990) Polarity and Stability: New Concepts, Indicators and Evidence. *International Interactions* 16:49–80.

Bremer, Stuart A. (1980) National Capabilities and War Proneness. In J. David Singer (ed.), *The Correlates of War: II. Testing Some Realpolitik Models*. New York: The Free Press, pp. 57–82.

(1982) The Contagiousness of Coercion: The Spread of Serious International Disputes, 1900–1976. *International Interactions* 9:29–55.

(1992) Dangerous Dyads: Conditions Affecting the Likelihood of Interstate War, 1816–1965. *Journal of Conflict Resolution* 36:309–341.

(1993a) Democracy and Militarized Interstate Conflict, 1816–1965. *International Interactions* 18:231–249.

(1993b) Advancing the Scientific Study of War. *International Interactions* 19:1–26.

Bremer, Stuart A. and Thomas R. Cusack (eds.) (1995) *The Process of War: Advancing the Scientific Study of War*. Amsterdam: Gordon and Breach Science Publishers SA.

Bremer, Stuart A., J. David Singer and Urs Luterbacher (1973) The Population Density and War Proneness of European Nations, 1816–1965. *Comparative Political Studies* 6:329–348.

Brzezinski, Zbigniew and Samuel P. Huntington (1963) *Political Power: USA/ USSR*. New York: Viking.

Buckle, Henry Thomas (1885) *History of Civilization in England* (3 vols.). London: Longmans, Green.

Bueno de Mesquita, Bruce (1978) Systemic Polarization and the Occurrence and Duration of War. *Journal of Conflict Resolution* 22:241–267.

(1980) An Expected Utility Theory of International Conflict. *American Political Science Review* 74:917–932.

(1981a) *The War Trap*. New Haven: Yale University Press.

(1981b) Risk, Power Distributions, and the Likelihood of War. *International Studies Quarterly* 25:541–568.

(1989) The Contribution of Expected-Utility Theory to the Study of International Conflict. In Manus I. Midlarsky (ed.), *Handbook of War Studies*. Boston: Unwin Hyman, pp. 143–169.

Bueno de Mesquita, Bruce and David Lalman (1988) Empirical Support for Systemic and Dyadic Explanations of Conflict. *World Politics* 26:1–20.

(1992) *War and Reason: Domestic and International Imperatives*. New Haven: Yale University Press.

Bueno de Mesquita, Bruce and William Riker (1982) An Assessment of the Merits of Selective Nuclear Proliferation. *Jounal of Conflict Resolution* 26:283–306.

Bueno de Mesquita, Bruce, David Newman and Alvin Rabushka (1985) *Forecasting Political Events: The Future of Hong Kong*. New Haven: Yale University Press.

(1996) *Red Flag Over Hong Kong*. Chatham, NJ: Chatham House Publishers, Inc.

Burgess, Philip and Raymond W. Lawton (1972) *Indicators of International Behavior: An Assessment of Events Data Research*. Sage Professional Papers in International Studies, vol. 1, no. 02–010. Beverly Hills: Sage.

Burrowes, Robert (1974) Mirror, Mirror, On the Wall. . .: A Comparison of Event Data Sources. In James N. Rosenau (ed.), *Comparing Foreign Policies: Theories, Findings, and Methods*. New York: John Wiley & Sons, pp. 383–406.

Buzan, Barry (1984) Economic Structure and International Security: The Limits of the Liberal Case. *International Organization* 38:597–624.

Buzan, Barry, Charles Jones and Richard Little (1993) *The Logic of Anarchy: Neorealism to Structural Realism*. New York: Columbia University Press.

Campbell, Donald T. and Julian C. Stanley (1963) Experimental and Quasi-Experimental Designs for Research. In N. L. Gage (ed.), *Handbook of Research on Teaching*. Chicago: Rand McNally, pp. 171–246.

Carr, Edward Hallett (1939) *The Twenty-Years' Crisis, 1919–1939: An Introduction to the Study of International Relations*. London: Macmillan Company.

Cattell, Raymond B. (1949) The Dimensions of Culture Patterns by Factorization of National Characters. *Journal of Abnormal and Social Psychology* 44: 443–469.

Cattell, Raymond B. and Richard L. Gorsuch (1965) The Definition and Measurement of National Morale and Morality. *The Journal of Social Psychology* 67:77–96.

Cattell, Raymond B., H. Breul and H. Parker Hartman (1952) An Attempt at More Refined Definition of the Cultural Dimensions of Syntality in Modern Nations. *American Sociological Review* 17:408–421.

Chan, Steve (1984) Mirror, Mirror on the Wall . . . Are Freer Countries More Pacific? *Journal of Conflict Resolution* 28:617–648.

Choucri, Nazli and Robert C. North (1972) Dynamics of International Conflict: Some Policy Implications of Population, Resources and Technology. *World Politics* 24:80–122.

(1975) *Nations in Conflict: National Growth and International Violence*. San Francisco: W.H. Freeman.

(1989) Lateral Pressure in International Relations: Concept and Theory. In Manus I. Midlarsky (ed.), *Handbook of War Studies*. Boston: Unwin Hyman, pp. 289–326.

Choucri, Nazli, Robert C. North and Susumu Yamakage (1992) *The Challenge of*

Japan Before World War II and After: A Study of National Growth and Expansion. New York: Routledge.

Cioffi-Revilla, Claudio (1991) On the Likely Magnitude, Extent, and Duration of an Iraq–UN War. *Journal of Conflict Resolution* 35:387–411.

(1995) War and Politics in Ancient China, 2700 B.C. to 722 B.C. *Journal of Conflict Resolution* 39:467–494.

(1996) Origins and Evolution of War and Politics. *International Studies Quarterly* 40:1–22.

Claude, Inis L., Jr. (1962) *Power and International Relations.* New York: Random House.

Cohen, Saul (1973) *Geography and Politics in a World Divided* (2nd edition). New York: Oxford University Press.

(1982) A New Map of Global Geopolitical Equilibrium: A Developmental Approach. *Political Geography Quarterly* 1:223–241.

Condorcet, Marie Jean Antoine Nicholas Caritat ([1794], 1955) *Sketch for a Historical Picture of the Progress of the Human Mind.* Trans. by June Barraclough. New York: Noonday Press.

Cottrell, Alvin J. and Frank Bray (1978) *Military Forces in the Persian Gulf.* Washington Papers, no. 60. Beverly Hills: Sage.

de Rivera, Joseph H. (1968) *The Psychological Dimension of Foreign Policy.* Columbus, OH: Charles E. Merrill.

Denton, Frank (1965) Some Regularities in International Conflict, 1820–1949. *Background* 9: 283–296. Santa Monica, CA: Rand Corporation.

Dessler, David (1991) Beyond Correlations: Toward a Causal Theory of War. *International Studies Quarterly* 35:337–355.

Deutsch, Karl W. and J. David Singer (1964) Multipolar Power Systems and International Stability. *World Politics* 16:390–406.

Diehl, Paul F. (1983) Arms Races and Escalation: A Closer Look. *Journal of Peace Research* 20:205–212.

(1985) Arms Races to War: Testing Some Empirical Linkages. *Sociological Quarterly* 26:331–349.

(1991) Geography and War: A Review and Assessment of the Empirical Literature. *International Interactions* 17:11–27.

Diehl, Paul F. and Jean Kingston (1987) Messenger or Message?: Military Buildups and the Initiation of Conflict. *Journal of Politics* 49:801–813.

Dixon, William J. (1989) "Political Democracy and War: A New Look at an Old Problem." Paper presented at the 30th Annual Convention of the International Studies Association, March 28–April 1, London, United Kingdom.

(1993) Democracy and the Management of International Conflict. *Journal of Conflict Resolution* 37:42–68.

(1994) Democracy and the Peaceful Settlement of International Conflict. *American Political Science Review* 88:14–32.

Domke, William K. (1988) *War and the Changing Global System.* New Haven: Yale University Press.

Doran, Charles F. (1983) Power Cycle Theory and the Contemporary State

System. In William R. Thompson (ed.), *Contending Approaches to World Systems Analysis*. Beverly Hills: Sage, pp. 165–182.

(1985) Power Cycle Theory and Systems Stability. In Paul M. Johnson and William R. Thompson (eds.), *Rhythms in Politics and Economics*. New York: Praeger, pp. 292–312.

(1989) Systemic Disequilibrium, Foreign Policy Role, and the Power Cycle: Challenges for Research Design. *Journal of Conflict Resolution* 33:371–401.

(1995) "The 'Discontinuity Dilemma' of Changing Systems Structure: Confronting the Principles of the Power Cycle." Paper presented at the 36th Annual Convention of the International Studies Association, February 21–25, Chicago, Illinois.

Doran, Charles F. and Wes Parsons (1980) War and the Cycle of Relative Power. *American Political Science Review* 74:947–965.

Dorpalen, Andreas (1942) *The World of General Haushofer*. New York: Farmer and Rinehart.

Doyle, Michael W. (1986) Liberalism and World Politics. *American Political Science Review* 80:1151–1169.

Duffy, Gavan (1994) Events and Versions: Reconstructing Event Data Analysis. *International Interactions* 20:147–167.

Duval, Robert and William R. Thompson (1980) Reconsidering the Aggregate Relationship Between Size, Economic Development, and Some Types of Foreign Policy Behavior. *American Journal of Political Science* 24:511–525.

East, Maurice A. (1972) Status Discrepancy and Violence in the International System: An Empirical Analysis. In James N. Rosenau, Vincent Davis and Maurice A. East (eds.), *The Analysis of International Politics: Essays in Honor of Harold and Margaret Sprout*. New York: The Free Press, pp. 299–319.

(1973) Size and Foreign Policy Behavior: A Test of Two Models. *World Politics* 25:556–576.

East, Maurice A. and Phillip M. Gregg (1967) Factors Influencing Cooperation and Conflict in the International System. *International Studies Quarterly* 11:244–269.

East, Maurice A. and Charles F. Hermann (1974) Do Nation-Types Account for Foreign Policy Behavior? In James N. Rosenau (ed.), *Comparing Foreign Policies: Theories, Findings, and Methods*. New York: John Wiley, pp. 269–303.

Eberwein, Wolf-Dieter (1982) The Seduction of Power: Serious International Disputes and the Power Status of Nations, 1900–1976. *International Interactions* 9:57–74.

Eberwein, Wolf-Dieter, Gisela Hubner-Dick, Wolfgang Jagodzinski, Hans Rattinger and Erich Weede (1979) External and Internal Conflict Behavior Among Nations, 1966–1967. *Journal of Conflict Resolution* 23:715–742.

Eckhardt, William and Edward Azar (1978a) Major World Conflicts and Interventions, 1945–1975. *International Interactions* 5:75–110.

(1978b) Major World Cooperation Events, 1945 to 1975. *International Interactions* 5:203–239.

References

Enterline, Andrew J. (1996) Correspondence: Driving While Democratizing (DWD). *International Security* 20:183–196.

Faber, Jan, Henk Houweling and Jan Siccama (1984) Diffusion of Wars: Some Theoretical Considerations and Empirical Evidence. *Journal of Peace Research* 21:277–288.

Farber, Henry S. and Joanne Gowa (1995) Polities and Peace. *International Security* 20:123–146.

Farkas, Andrew (1996) Evolutionary Models in Foreign Policy Analysis. *International Studies Quarterly* 40:343–361.

Farrar, L.L., Jr. (1977) Cycles of War: Historical Speculations on Future International Violence. *International Interactions* 3:161–179.

Feierabend, Ivo K. and Rosalind L. Feierabend (1969) Level of Development and International Behavior. In R. Butwell (ed.), *Foreign Policy and the Developing Nation*. Lexington: University of Kentucky Press, pp. 135–188.

Festinger, Leon (1957) *A Theory of Cognitive Dissonance*. Stanford: Stanford University Press.

Frank, André Gunder (1967) *Capitalism and Underdevelopment in Latin America – Historical Studies of Chile and Brazil*. New York: Monthly Review Press.

Galtung, Johan (1964) A Structural Theory of Aggression. *Journal of Peace Research* 1:95–119.

Garnham, David (1976a) Power Parity and Lethal International Violence, 1969–1973. *Journal of Conflict Resolution* 20:379–394.

(1976b) Dyadic International War, 1816–1965: The Role of Power Parity and Geographical Proximity. *Western Political Quarterly* 29:231–242.

(1983) "Explaining Major Power Bellicosity and Pacifism." Paper presented at the 24th Annual Convention of the International Studies Association, April 5–9, Mexico City, Mexico.

Gasiorowski, Mark and Solomon Polachek (1982) Conflict and Interdependence: East–West Trade and Linkages in the Era of Detente. *Journal of Conflict Resolution* 26:709–728.

Gates, Scott, Torbjørn L. Knutsen and Jonathon W. Moses (1996) Democracy and Peace: A More Skeptical View. *Journal of Peace Research* 33:1–10.

Gaubatz, Kurt Taylor (1991) Election Cycles and War. *Journal of Conflict Resolution* 35:212–224.

Geller, Daniel S. (1985) *Domestic Factors in Foreign Policy: A Cross-National Statistical Analysis*. Cambridge: Schenkman.

(1988) Power System Membership and Patterns of War. *International Political Science Review* 9:365–379.

(1990) Nuclear Weapons, Deterrence, and Crisis Escalation. *Journal of Conflict Resolution* 34:291–310.

(1992a) Power Transition and Conflict Initiation. *Conflict Management and Peace Science* 12:1–16.

(1992b) Capability Concentration, Power Transition, and War. *International Interactions* 17:269–284.

(1993) Power Differentials and War in Rival Dyads. *International Studies Quarterly* 37:173–193.

(1994) "Patterns of War Initiation Among Status Quo Challengers and Defenders." Paper presented at the XVIth World Congress of the International Political Science Association, August 21–25, Berlin, Germany.

(1996) Relative Power, Rationality, and International Conflict. In Jacek Kugler and Douglas Lemke (eds.), *Parity and War: Evaluations and Extensions of The War Ledger*. Ann Arbor: University of Michigan Press, pp. 127–143.

(1998) The Stability of the Military Balance and War among Great Power Rivals. In Paul F. Diehl (ed.), *The Dynamics of Enduring Rivalries*. Urbana: University of Illinois Press.

Gelpi, Christopher (1996) "Democratic Diversions: Governmental Structure and the Externalization of Domestic Conflict." Paper presented at the 92nd Annual Meeting of the American Political Science Association, August 29– September 1, San Francisco, California.

George, Alexander L. and Richard Smoke (1974) *Deterrence in American Foreign Policy*. New York: Columbia University Press.

Gibbs, Brian H. and J. David Singer (1993) *Empirical Knowledge on World Politics: A Summary of Quantitative Research, 1970–1991*. Westport, CT: Greenwood Press.

Gilpin, Robert (1981) *War and Change in World Politics*. Cambridge: Cambridge University Press.

Gleditsch, Nils Petter (1992) Democracy and Peace. *Journal of Peace Research* 29:369–376.

(1994) "Peace and Democracy: Three Levels of Analysis." Paper presented at the XVIth World Congress of the International Political Science Association, August 21–25, Berlin, Germany.

(1995) Geography, Democracy, and Peace. *International Interactions* 20:297–323.

Gleditsch, Nils Petter and J. David Singer (1975) Distance and International War, 1816–1965. In M.R. Khan (ed.), *Proceedings of the International Peace Research Association, Fifth General Conference*. Oslo: International Peace Research Association.

Gochman, Charles S. (1990a) Capability-Driven Disputes. In Charles S. Gochman and Alan N. Sabrosky (eds.), *Prisoners of War? Nation-States in the Modern Era*. Lexington, MA: Lexington Books, pp. 141–159.

(1990b) "The Geography of Conflict: Militarized Interstate Disputes Since 1816." Paper presented at the 31st Annual Convention of the International Studies Association, April 10–14, Washington, DC.

Gochman, Charles S. and Zeev Maoz (1984) Militarized Interstate Disputes, 1816–1976: Procedures, Patterns, and Insights. *Journal of Conflict Resolution* 28:585–616.

Goertz, Gary (1992) Contextual Theories and Indicators in World Politics. *International Interactions* 17:285–303.

References

(1994) *Contexts of International Politics.* Cambridge: Cambridge University Press.

Goertz, Gary and Paul F. Diehl (1992) The Empirical Importance of Enduring Rivalries. *International Interactions* 18:151–163.

(1993) Enduring Rivalries: Theoretical Constructs and Empirical Patterns. *International Studies Quarterly* 37:145–171.

Goldstein, Joshua S. (1988) *Long Cycles: Prosperity and War in the Modern Age.* New Haven: Yale University Press.

(1991) Reciprocity in Superpower Relations: An Empirical Analysis. *International Studies Quarterly* 35:195–209.

Gregg, Phillip M. and Arthur S. Banks (1965) Dimensions of Political Systems: Factor Analysis of *A Cross-Polity Survey. American Political Science Review* 59:602–614.

Grummon, Stephen R. (1982) *The Iran–Iraq War.* Washington Papers, no. 92. New York: Praeger.

Gurr, Ted Robert, Keith Jaggers and Will H. Moore (1989) "Polity II Codebook." Boulder, CO: Department of Political Science (mimeo).

Guttenplan, Samuel D. and Martin Tamny (1971) *Logic: A Comprehensive Introduction.* New York: Basic Books.

Haas, Ernst B. (1953) The Balance of Power: Prescription, Concept, or Propaganda? *World Politics* 5:442–477.

(1964) *Beyond the Nation-State.* Stanford: Stanford University Press.

Haas, Michael (1965) Societal Approaches to the Study of War. *Journal of Peace Research* 2:307–323.

Hagan, Joe D. (1987) Regimes, Political Oppositions, and the Comparative Analysis of Foreign Policy. In Charles F. Hermann, Charles W. Kegley, Jr. and James N. Rosenau (eds.), *New Directions in the Study of Foreign Policy.* Boston: Allen & Unwin, pp. 339–365.

Hammer, Darrell (1974*) U.S.S.R.: The Politics of Oligarchy.* Hinsdale, IL: Dryden Press.

Harre, Rom (1970) *The Principles of Scientific Thinking.* Chicago: University of Chicago Press.

Hazlewood, Leo A. (1973) Externalizing Systemic Stress: International Conflict as Adaptive Behavior. In Jonathan Wilkenfeld (ed.), *Conflict Behavior and Linkage Politics.* New York: David McKay Co., Inc., pp. 148–190.

Hempel, Carl G. (1966) *Philosophy of Natural Science.* Englewood Cliffs, NJ: Prentice-Hall.

Hensel, Paul and Henrik Sommer (1996) "Adding Event Data to the Study of Interstate Rivalry." Paper presented at the 37th Annual Convention of the International Studies Association, April 16–20, San Diego, California.

Herek, Gregory M., Irving L. Janis and Paul Huth (1987) Decision Making During International Crises: Is Quality of Process Related to Outcome? *Journal of Conflict Resolution* 31:203–226.

Hermann, Charles F., Maurice A. East, Margaret G. Hermann, Barbara G. Salmore and Stephen A. Salmore (1973) *CREON: A Foreign Events Data*

Set. Sage Professional Papers in International Studies, vol. 2, no. 02–024. Beverly Hills: Sage.

Herz, John (1959) *Political Realism and Political Idealism.* Chicago: University of Chicago Press.

Hilsman, Roger (1964) *To Move a Nation.* New York: Doubleday and Co., Inc.

Hirschman, Albert O. (1945) *National Power and the Structure of Foreign Trade.* Berkeley: University of California Press.

Hobson, John A. ([1902], 1954) *Imperialism.* London: Allen & Unwin.

Hoffmann, Stanley (1978) *Primacy or World Order: American Foreign Policy Since the Cold War.* New York: McGraw-Hill.

Hoggard, Gary (1974) Differential Source Coverage in Foreign Policy Analysis. In James N. Rosenau (ed.), *Comparing Foreign Policies: Theories, Findings, and Methods.* New York: John Wiley & Sons, pp. 353–381.

Hollis, Martin and Steve Smith (1990) *Explaining and Understanding International Relations.* Oxford: Oxford University Press.

Holsti, Kalevi J. (1985) *The Dividing Discipline: Hegemony and Diversity in International Theory.* Boston: Unwin Hyman.

—— (1991) *Peace and War: Armed Conflicts and International Order 1648–1989.* Cambridge: Cambridge University Press.

—— (1995) War, Peace, and the State of the State. *International Political Science Review* 16:319–339.

Holsti, Ole R. (1962) The Belief-System and National Images: A Case Study. *Journal of Conflict Resolution* 6:244–252.

Holsti, Ole R., P. Terrence Hopmann and John D. Sullivan (1973) *Unity and Disintegration in International Alliances: Comparative Studies.* New York: John Wiley & Sons.

Hoole, Francis W. and Chi Huang (1989) The Global Conflict Process. *Journal of Conflict Resolution* 33:142–163.

Hopf, Ted (1991) Polarity, the Offense–Defense Balance, and War. *American Political Science Review* 85:475–494.

Houweling, Henk and Jan Kuné (1984) Do Outbreaks of War Follow a Poisson-Process? *Journal of Conflict Resolution* 28:51–61.

Houweling, Henk and Jan G. Siccama (1985) The Epidemiology of War, 1816–1980. *Journal of Conflict Resolution* 29:641–663.

—— (1988) Power Transitions as a Cause of War. *Journal of Conflict Resolution* 32:87–102.

—— (1991) Power Transitions and Critical Points as Predictors of Great Power War: Toward a Synthesis. *Journal of Conflict Resolution* 35:642–658.

—— (1993) The Neo-Functionalist Explanation of World Wars: A Critique and An Alternative. *International Interactions* 18:387–408.

Howell, Llewellyn (1983) A Comparative Study of the WEIS and COPDAB Data Sets. *International Studies Quarterly* 27:149–159.

Hower, Gretchen and Dina A. Zinnes (1989) International Political Conflict: A Literature Review. *DDIR – Update* 3:1–14. Merriam Laboratory for

Analytic Political Research. University of Illinois at Urbana–Champaign (mimeo).

Hudson, Valerie M. (1995) Foreign Policy Analysis Yesterday, Today, and Tomorrow. *Mershon International Studies Review* 39:209–238.

Hume, David ([1748], 1894) *An Enquiry Concerning Human Understanding*. Oxford: Clarendon Press.

Huntington, Samuel P. ([1958], 1969) Arms Races: Prerequisites and Results. In Carl J. Friedrich and Seymour E. Harris (eds.), *Public Policy*. Cambridge: Harvard University Press, pp. 41–83; reprinted in Robert J. Art and Kenneth N. Waltz (eds.), *The Use of Force: Military Power and International Politics*. Lanham, MD: University Press of America, Inc., pp. 85–118.

(1993) The Clash of Civilizations? *Foreign Affairs* 72:22–49.

Huth, Paul K. (1996) *Standing Your Ground: Territorial Disputes and International Conflict*. Ann Arbor: University of Michigan Press.

Huth, Paul and Bruce Russett (1993) General Deterrence Between Enduring Rivals: Testing Three Competing Models. *American Political Science Review* 87: 61–73.

Huth, Paul, D. Scott Bennett and Christopher Gelpi (1992) System Uncertainty, Risk Propensity, and International Conflict Among the Great Powers. *Journal of Conflict Resolution* 36:478–517.

Huth, Paul, Christopher Gelpi and D. Scott Bennett (1993) The Escalation of Great Power Militarized Disputes: Testing Rational Deterrence Theory and Structural Realism. *American Political Science Review* 87:609–623.

Intriligator, Michael D. ([1964], 1969) Some Simple Models of Arms Races. Rand RM–3903–PR. Santa Monica, CA: Rand Corporation; reprinted in John E. Mueller (ed.), *Approaches to Measurement in International Relations: A Non-Evangelical Survey*. New York: Meredith Corporation, pp. 295–304.

Intriligator, Michael D. and Dagobert L. Brito (1984) Can Arms Races Lead to the Outbreak of War? *Journal of Conflict Resolution* 28:63–84.

James, Patrick (1988) *Crisis and War*. Montreal: McGill–Queen's University Press.

(1995) Structural Realism and the Causes of War. *Mershon International Studies Review* 39:181–208.

James, Patrick and Lui Hebron (1993) "Great Powers, Cycles of Relative Capability and Crises in World Politics." Paper presented at the 27th North American Meeting of the Peace Science Society (International), Syracuse University, November 12–14, Syracuse, New York.

James, Patrick and Glenn E. Mitchell II (1995) Targets of Covert Pressure: The Hidden Victims of the Democratic Peace. *International Interactions* 21:85–107.

Janis, Irving L. (1972) *Victims of Groupthink*. Boston: Houghton-Mifflin.

(1982) *Groupthink: Psychological Studies of Policy Decisions and Fiascos* (2nd edition). Boston: Houghton-Mifflin.

Janis, Irving L. and Leon Mann (1977) *Decisionmaking: A Psychological Analysis of Conflict, Choice, and Commitment*. New York: The Free Press.

Jervis, Robert (1968) Hypotheses on Misperception. *World Politics* 20:454–479.
    (1976) *Perception and Misperception in International Politics*. Princeton: Princeton University Press.
    (1984) *The Illogic of American Nuclear Strategy*. Ithaca: Cornell University Press.
Jones, Daniel M. (1989) "Enduring Rivalries, Dispute Escalation and Interstate War." Paper presented at the 23rd North American Meeting of the Peace Science Society (International), November 8, Columbus, Ohio.
Jones, Susan and J. David Singer (1972) *Beyond Conjecture in International Politics*. Itasca, IL: F. E. Peacock Press.
Joynt, C.B. (1964) Arms Races and the Problem of Equilibrium. In *Year Book of World Affairs 1964*. London: Stevens, pp. 23–40.
Kagan, Donald (1995) *On the Origins of War and the Preservation of Peace*. New York: Doubleday.
Kahn, Herman (1962) *Thinking About the Unthinkable*. New York: Avon Books.
    (1965) *On Escalation: Metaphors and Scenarios*. New York: Praeger.
Kahneman, Daniel and Amos Tversky (1979) Prospect Theory: An Analysis of Decision under Risk. *Econometrica* 47:263–291.
Kant, Immanuel ([1781], 1966) *Critique of Pure Reason*. Trans. by F. Max Müller. New York: Anchor Books.
    ([1795], 1939) *Perpetual Peace*. Original translation from the first English edition [1796]. New York: Columbia University Press.
Kaufmann, Chaim D. (1994) Out of the Lab and into the Archives: A Method for Testing Psychological Explanations of Political Decision Making. *International Studies Quarterly* 38:557–586.
Kegley, Charles W., Jr. (ed.) (1995) *Controversies in International Relations Theory: Realism and the Neoliberal Challenge*. New York: St. Martin's Press.
Kegley, Charles W., Jr. and Gregory Raymond (1981) International Legal Norms and the Preservation of Peace, 1820–1964: Some Evidence and Bivariate Relationships. *International Interactions* 8:171–187.
    (1982) Alliance Norms and War: A New Piece to an Old Puzzle. *International Studies Quarterly* 26:572–595.
    (1986) Normative Constraints on the Use of Force Short of War. *Journal of Peace Research* 23:213–227.
    (1994) *A Multipolar Peace?: Great-Power Politics in the Twenty-First Century*. New York: St. Martin's Press.
Kelly, Philip (1986) Escalation of Regional Conflict: Testing the Shatterbelt Concept. *Political Geography Quarterly* 5:161–180.
Kelman, Herbert C. (ed.) (1965) *International Behavior*. New York: Holt, Rinehart and Winston.
Kemp, Anita (1977) A Path Analytic Model of International Violence. *International Interactions* 4:53-85.
Kende, Istvan (1978) Wars of Ten Years, 1967–1976. *Journal of Peace Research* 15:227–241.
Kennedy, Paul (1987) *The Rise and Fall of the Great Powers: Economic Change and Military Conflict from 1500 to 2000*. New York: Random House.

References

(1993) *Preparing for the Twenty-First Century.* New York: Vintage Books.

Keohane, Robert O. (ed.) (1986) *Neorealism and Its Critics.* New York: Columbia University Press.

Keylor, William R. (1992) *The Twentieth-Century World: An International History* (2nd edition). New York: Oxford University Press.

Kim, Woosang (1991) Alliance Transitions and Great Power War. *American Journal of Political Science* 35:833–850.

——— (1992) Power Transitions and Great Power War from Westphalia to Waterloo. *World Politics* 45:153–172.

——— (1996) Power Parity, Alliance, and War from 1648 to 1975. In Jacek Kugler and Douglas Lemke (eds.), *Parity and War: Evaluations and Extensions of The War Ledger.* Ann Arbor: University of Michigan Press, pp. 93–105.

Kim, Woosang and James D. Morrow (1992) When Do Power Shifts Lead to War? *American Journal of Political Science* 36:896–922.

Kirby, Andrew and Michael Ward (1987) The Spatial Analysis of War and Peace. *Comparative Political Studies* 20:293–313.

Kissinger, Henry A. (1957) *Nuclear Weapons and Foreign Policy* (abridged edition). New York: W.W. Norton & Co.

Köhler, Gernot (1975) Imperialism as a Level of Analysis in Correlates of War Research. *Journal of Conflict Resolution* 19:48–62.

Kugler, Jacek and Marina Arbetman (1989) Choosing Among Measures of Power: A Review of the Empirical Record. In Richard J. Stoll and Michael D. Ward (eds.), *Power in World Politics.* Boulder, CO: Lynne Rienner, pp. 49–77.

Kugler, Jacek and Douglas Lemke (eds.) (1996) *Parity and War: Evaluations and Extensions of The War Ledger.* Ann Arbor: University of Michigan Press.

Kugler, Jacek, Lewis W. Snider and William Longwell (1994) From Desert Shield to Desert Storm: Success, Strife, or Quagmire? *Conflict Management and Peace Science* 13:113–148.

Lakatos, Imre (1970) Falsification and the Methodology of Scientific Research Programmes. In Imre Lakatos and Alan Musgrave (eds.), *Criticism and the Growth of Knowledge.* Cambridge: Cambridge University Press, pp. 91–195.

Lave, Charles A. and James G. March (1975) *An Introduction to Models in the Social Sciences.* New York: Harper and Row.

Layne, Christopher (1994) Kant or Cant: The Myth of the Democratic Peace. *International Security* 19:5–49.

——— (1995) On the Democratic Peace. *International Security* 19:175–177.

Lebow, Richard Ned (1984) The Paranoia of the Powerful: Thucydides on World War III. *PS* 17:10–17.

Lemke, Douglas (1995) The Tyranny of Distance: Redefining Relevant Dyads. *International Interactions* 21:23–38.

Lemke, Douglas and Jacek Kugler (1996) The Evolution of the Power Transition Perspective. In Jacek Kugler and Douglas Lemke (eds.), *Parity and War: Evaluations and Extensions of The War Ledger.* Ann Arbor: University of Michigan Press, pp. 3–33.

Leng, Russell J. (1980) Influence Strategies and Interstate Conflict. In J. David Singer (ed.), *The Correlates of War: II. Testing Some Realpolitik Models.* New York: The Free Press, pp. 124–157.

(1983) When Will They Ever Learn? Coercive Bargaining in Recurrent Crises. *Journal of Conflict Resolution* 27:379–419.

(1984) Reagan and the Russians: Crisis Bargaining Beliefs and the Historical Record. *American Political Science Review* 78:338–355.

(1993) *Interstate Crisis Behavior, 1816–1980: Realism Versus Reciprocity.* Cambridge: Cambridge University Press.

Leng, Russell J. and Stephen G. Walker (1982) Comparing Two Studies of Crisis Bargaining: Confrontation, Coercion, and Reciprocity. *Journal of Conflict Resolution* 26:571–591.

Lenin, Vladimir I. ([1916], 1939) *Imperialism: The Highest Stage of Capitalism.* New York: International Publishers.

Levy, Jack S. (1981) Alliance Formation and War Behavior: An Analysis of the Great Powers, 1495–1975. *Journal of Conflict Resolution* 25:581–613.

(1982a) Historical Trends in Great Power War, 1495–1975. *International Studies Quarterly* 26:278–300.

(1982b) The Contagion of Great Power War Behavior, 1495–1975. *American Journal of Political Science* 26:562–582.

(1983) *War in the Modern Great Power System.* Lexington: University of Kentucky Press.

(1984) Size and Stability in the Modern Great Power System. *International Interactions* 11:341–358.

(1987) Declining Power and the Preventive Motivation for War. *World Politics* 40:82–107.

(1988) Domestic Politics and War. *Journal of Interdisciplinary History* 18:653–673.

(1989a) The Diversionary Theory of War: A Critique. In Manus I. Midlarsky (ed.), *Handbook of War Studies.* Boston: Unwin Hyman, pp. 259–288.

(1989b) The Causes of War: A Review of Theories and Evidence. In Philip E. Tetlock, Jo L. Husbands, Robert Jervis, Paul C. Stern and Charles Tilly (eds.), *Behavior, Society, and Nuclear War* (vol. 1). New York: Oxford University Press, pp. 209–333.

(1991) Long Cycles, Hegemonic Transitions, and the Long Peace. In Charles W. Kegley, Jr. (ed.), *The Long Postwar Peace: Contending Explanations and Projections.* New York: Harper Collins, pp. 147–176.

(1992a) An Introduction to Prospect Theory. *Political Psychology* 13:171–186.

(1992b) Prospect Theory and International Relations: Theoretical Applications and Analytical Problems. *Political Psychology* 13:283–310.

(1996) Loss Aversion, Framing, and Bargaining: The Implications of Prospect Theory for International Conflict. *International Political Science Review* 17:179–195.

Levy, Jack S. and T. Clifton Morgan (1986) The War-Weariness Hypothesis: An Empirical Test. *American Journal of Political Science* 30:26–49.

References

Li, Richard P.Y. and William R. Thompson (1975) The "Coup Contagion" Hypothesis. *Journal of Conflict Resolution* 19:63–88.

Lieberson, Stanley and Arnold L. Silverman (1965) The Precipitants and Underlying Conditions of Race Riots. *American Sociological Review* 30:887–889.

Mackinder, Halford (1904) The Geographical Pivot of History. *Geographical Journal* 23:421–444.

Majeski, Stephen J. (1986) Mutual and Unilateral Cooperation in Arms Race Settings. *International Interactions* 12:343–361.

Majeski, Stephen J. and David J. Sylvan (1984) Simple Choices and Complex Calculations: A Critique of *The War Trap*. *Journal of Conflict Resolution* 28:316–340.

Mallery, John C. (1994) Beyond Correlation: Bringing Artifical Intelligence to Events Data. *International Interactions* 20:101–145.

Mandel, Robert (1980) Roots of the Modern Interstate Border Dispute. *Journal of Conflict Resolution* 24:427–454.

Mansfield, Edward D. (1988) Distributions of War Over Time. *World Politics* 41:21–51.

(1994) *Power, Trade, and War.* Princeton: Princeton University Press.

Mansfield, Edward D. and Jack Snyder (1995) Democratization and the Danger of War. *International Security* 20:5–38.

Maoz, Zeev (1982) *Paths to Conflict: International Dispute Initiation, 1816–1976.* Boulder, CO: Westview Press.

(1989) Joining the Club of Nations: Political Development and International Conflict, 1816–1976. *International Studies Quarterly* 33:199–231.

(1993) The Onset and Initiation of Disputes. *International Interactions* 19:27–47.

Maoz, Zeev and Nasrin Abdolali (1989) Regime Types and International Conflict, 1816–1976. *Journal of Conflict Resolution* 33:3–35.

Maoz, Zeev and Bruce Russett (1993) Normative and Structural Causes of Democratic Peace, 1946–1986. *American Political Science Review* 87:624–638.

Maurer, John H. (1992) The Anglo-German Naval Rivalry and Informal Arms Control, 1912–1914. *Journal of Conflict Resolution* 36:284–308.

McClelland, Charles A. (1983) Let the User Beware. *International Studies Quarterly* 27:169–177.

McClelland, Charles A. and Gary D. Hoggard (1969) Conflict Patterns in the Interactions Among Nations. In James N. Rosenau (ed.), *International Politics and Foreign Policy: A Reader in Research and Theory* (revised edition). New York: The Free Press, pp. 711–724.

McGowan, Patrick J. and Howard B. Shapiro (1973) *The Comparative Study of Foreign Policy: A Survey of Scientific Findings.* Beverly Hills: Sage.

Mearsheimer, John J. (1990) Back to the Future: Instability in Europe After the Cold War. *International Security* 15:5–56.

Merritt, Richard L. (1994) Measuring Events for International Political Analysis. *International Interactions* 20:3–33.

Merritt, Richard L. and Dina A. Zinnes (1989) Alternative Indexes of National Power. In Richard J. Stoll and Michael D. Ward (eds.), *Power in World Politics.* Boulder, CO: Lynne Rienner, pp. 11–28.

Midlarsky, Manus I. (1970) Mathematical Models of Instability and a Theory of Diffusion. *International Studies Quarterly* 14:60–84.

(1975) *On War: Political Violence in the International System.* New York: The Free Press.

(1978) Analyzing Diffusion and Contagion Effects: The Urban Disorders of the 1960s. *American Political Science Review* 72:996–1008.

(1984) Preventing Systemic War: Crisis Decision-Making Amidst a Structure of Conflict Relationships. *Journal of Conflict Resolution* 28:563–584.

(1986) A Hierarchical Equilibrium Theory of Systemic War. *International Studies Quarterly* 30:77–105.

(1988) *The Onset of World War.* Boston: Unwin Hyman.

Midlarsky, Manus I., Martha Crenshaw and Fumihiko Yoshida (1980) Why Violence Spreads. *International Studies Quarterly* 24:262–298.

Mihalka, Michael (1976) Hostilities in the European State System, 1816–1970. *Peace Science Society Papers* 26:100–116.

Modelski, George (1972) *Principles of World Politics.* New York: The Free Press.

(1981) Long Cycles, Kondratieffs, and Alternating Innovations: Implications for U.S. Foreign Policy. In Charles W. Kegley, Jr. and Pat McGowan (eds.), *The Political Economy of Foreign Policy Behavior.* Beverly Hills: Sage, pp. 63–83.

(1983) Long Cycles of World Leadership. In William R. Thompson (ed.), *Contending Approaches to World System Analysis.* Beverly Hills: Sage, pp. 115–139.

Morgan, Patrick M. (1977) *Deterrence: A Conceptual Analysis.* Sage Library of Social Research (vol. 40). Beverly Hills: Sage.

Morgan, T. Clifton and Sally Howard Campbell (1991) Domestic Structure, Decisional Constraints, and War: So Why Kant Democracies Fight? *Journal of Conflict Resolution* 35:187–211.

Morgan, T. Clifton and Valerie L. Schwebach (1992) Take Two Democracies and Call Me in the Morning: A Prescription for Peace? *International Interactions* 17:305–320.

Morgenthau, Hans J. ([1948], 1967) *Politics Among Nations: The Struggle for Power and Peace* (4th edition). New York: Alfred A. Knopf.

Morrow, James D. (1989) A Twist of Truth: A Reexamination of the Effects of Arms Races on the Occurrence of War. *Journal of Conflict Resolution* 33:500–529.

(1996) The Logic of Overtaking. In Jacek Kugler and Douglas Lemke (eds.), *Parity and War: Evaluations and Extensions of The War Ledger.* Ann Arbor: University of Michigan Press, pp. 313–330.

Most, Benjamin A. and Harvey Starr (1980) Diffusion, Reinforcement, Geopolitics and the Spread of War. *American Political Science Review* 74:932–946.

Most, Benjamin A., Harvey Starr and Randolph M. Siverson (1989) The Logic

References

and Study of the Diffusion of International Conflict. In Manus I. Midlarsky (ed.), *Handbook of War Studies*. Boston: Unwin Hyman, pp. 111–139.

Moul, William B. (1985) Balances of Power and European Great Power War, 1815–1939: A Suggestion and Some Evidence. *Canadian Journal of Political Science* 43:481–528.

(1988) Balance of Power and the Escalation of Serious Disputes Among European Great Powers, 1815–1939: Some Evidence. *American Journal of Political Science* 32:241–275.

(1989) Measuring the "Balances of Power": A Look at Some Numbers. *Review of International Studies* 15:101–121.

Mueller, John E. (1969) Systematic History. In John E. Mueller (ed.), *Approaches to Measurement in International Relations: A Non-Evangelical Survey*. New York: Meredith Corporation, pp. 5–14.

Naroll, Raoul (1968) Some Thoughts on Comparative Method in Cultural Anthropology. In Hubert M. Blalock, Jr. and Ann B. Blalock (eds.), *Methodology in Social Research*. New York: McGraw-Hill, pp. 236–277.

Neack, Laura, Jeanne A.K. Hey and Patrick J. Haney (1995) Generational Change in Foreign Policy Analysis. In Laura Neack, Jeanne A.K. Hey and Patrick J. Haney (eds.), *Foreign Policy Analysis: Continuity and Change in Its Second Generation*. Englewood Cliffs, NJ: Prentice-Hall, pp. 1–15.

Nicholson, Michael (1987) The Conceptual Bases of *The War Trap*. *Journal of Conflict Resolution* 31:346–369.

(1989) *Formal Theories in International Relations*. Cambridge: Cambridge University Press.

(1992) *Rationality and the Analysis of International Conflict*. Cambridge: Cambridge University Press.

(1995) "The Concept of Preference in Games." Paper presented at the Pan-European Conference of the European Consortium for Political Research, Fondation Nationale des Sciences Politiques, September 13–16, Paris, France.

(1996) *Causes and Consequences in International Relations: A Conceptual Study*. London: Pinter.

Nincic, Miroslav (1990) U.S. Soviet Policy and the Electoral Connection. *World Politics* 42:370–396.

Nye, Joseph S., Jr. (1990) *Bound to Lead: The Changing Nature of American Power*. New York: Basic Books.

O'Loughlin, John and Luc Anselin (1991) Bringing Geography Back to the Study of International Relations: Spatial Dependence and Regional Context in Africa, 1966–1978. *International Interactions* 17:29–61.

Olinick, Michael (1978) *An Introduction to Mathematical Models in the Social and Life Sciences*. Reading, MA: Addison-Wesley.

Oneal, John R., Frances H. Oneal, Zeev Maoz and Bruce Russett (1996) The Liberal Peace: Interdependence, Democracy, and International Conflict, 1950–85. *Journal of Peace Research* 33:11–28.

Organski, A. F. K. (1958) *World Politics*. New York: Alfred A. Knopf.

Organski, A. F. K. and Jacek Kugler (1980) *The War Ledger.* Chicago: University of Chicago Press.

Parsons, Talcott (1951) *The Social System.* New York: The Free Press.

Patomäki, Heikki (1996) How to Tell Better Stories about World Politics. *European Journal of International Relations* 2:105–133.

Paul, T. V. (1994) *Asymmetric Conflicts: War Initiation by Weaker Powers.* Cambridge: Cambridge University Press.

Peterson, Sophia (1975) Research on Research: Events Data Studies, 1961–1972. In Patrick J. McGowan (ed.), *Sage International Yearbook of Foreign Policy Studies* (vol. 3). Beverly Hills: Sage, pp. 263–309.

Popper, Karl R. (1959) *The Logic of Scientific Discovery.* New York: Basic Books.

Pruitt, Dean G. (1965) Definition of the Situation as a Determinant of International Action. In Herbert C. Kelman (ed.), *International Behavior.* New York: Holt, Rinehart and Winston, pp. 393–432.

Quester, George H. (1977) *Offense and Defense in the International System.* New York: John Wiley & Sons.

Ratzel, Friedrich (1899) *Anthropogeographie* (2nd edition). Stuttgart: J. Engelhorn.

Ray, James Lee (1990) Friends as Foes: International Conflict and Wars between Formal Allies. In Charles S. Gochman and Alan Ned Sabrosky (eds.), *Prisoners of War?: Nation-States in the Modern Era.* Lexington, MA: Lexington Books, pp. 73–91.

(1993) Wars Between Democracies: Rare, or Nonexistent? *International Interactions* 18: 251–276.

(1995a) *Democracy and International Conflict: An Evaluation of the Democratic Peace Proposition.* Columbia: University of South Carolina Press.

(1995b) "R.J. Rummel's *Understanding Conflict and War*: An Overlooked Classic?" Paper presented at the 36th Annual Convention of the International Studies Association, February 21–25, Chicago, Illinois.

Ray, James Lee and Bruce Russett (1995) The Future as Arbiter of Theoretical Controversies: Predictions, Explanations, and the End of the Cold War. *British Journal of Political Science* 25:1561–1591.

Ray, James Lee and J. David Singer (1973) Measuring the Concentration of Power in the International System. *Sociological Methods and Research* 1:403–437.

Reichenbach, Hans (1951) *The Rise of Scientific Philosophy.* Berkeley: University of California Press.

Richardson, Lewis F. (1939) Generalized Foreign Policy. *British Journal of Psychology Monographs Supplements* 23.

(1960) *Statistics of Deadly Quarrels.* Pittsburgh and Chicago: Boxwood and Quadrangle.

Rosecrance, Richard N. (1966) Bipolarity, Multipolarity, and the Future. *Journal of Conflict Resolution* 10:314–327.

Rosen, Steven J. (1977) A Stable System of Mutual Nuclear Deterrence in the Arab–Israeli Conflict. *American Political Science Review* 71:1367–1383.

Rosenau, James N. (1966) Pre-theories and Theories of Foreign Policy. In R. Barry Farrell (ed.), *Approaches to Comparative and International Politics.* Evanston: Northwestern University Press, pp. 27–92.

(1990) *Turbulence in World Politics: A Theory of Change and Continuity.* Princeton: Princeton University Press.

Rosenau, James N. and George H. Ramsey, Jr. (1975) External and Internal Typologies of Foreign Policy Behavior: Testing the Stability of an Intriguing Set of Findings. In Patrick J. McGowan (ed.), *Sage International Yearbook of Foreign Policy Studies* (vol. 3). Beverly Hills: Sage, pp. 245–262.

Rousseau, David L., Christopher Gelpi, Dan Reiter and Paul K. Huth (1996) Assessing the Dyadic Nature of the Democratic Peace, 1918–88. *American Political Science Review* 90:512–533.

Rummel, Rudolph J. (1963) Dimensions of Conflict Behavior Within and Between Nations. *General Systems Yearbook* 8:1–50.

(1967) Some Attributes and Behavioral Patterns of Nations. *Journal of Peace Research* 4:196–206.

(1968) The Relationship Between National Attributes and Foreign Conflict Behavior. In J. David Singer (ed.), *Quantitative International Politics: Insights and Evidence.* New York: The Free Press, pp. 187–214.

(1969) Some Empirical Findings on Nations and Their Behavior. *World Politics* 21:226–241.

(1972) *The Dimensions of Nations.* Beverly Hills: Sage.

(1979) *Understanding Conflict and War: War, Power, Peace* (vol. 4). Beverly Hills: Sage.

(1983) Libertarianism and International Violence. *Journal of Conflict Resolution* 27:27–71.

(1985) Libertarian Propositions on Violence Within and Between Nations: A Test Against Published Research Results. *Journal of Conflict Resolution* 29:419–455.

Russett, Bruce M. (1990a) Economic Decline, Electoral Pressure, and the Initiation of Interstate Conflict. In Charles S. Gochman and Alan Ned Sabrosky (eds.), *Prisoners of War?: Nation-States in the Modern Era.* Lexington, MA: Lexington Books, pp. 123–140.

(1990b) *Controlling the Sword: The Democratic Governance of National Security.* Cambridge: Harvard University Press.

(1993) *Grasping the Democractic Peace: Principles for a Post-Cold War World.* Princeton: Princeton University Press.

(1995) The Democratic Peace: And Yet It Moves. *International Security* 19:164–175.

Russett, Bruce M. and R. Joseph Monsen (1975) Bureaucracy and Polyarchy as Predictors of Performance: A Cross-National Examination. *Comparative Political Studies* 8:5–31.

Russett, Bruce and James Lee Ray (1995) Raymond Cohen on Pacific Unions: A Response and a Reply. *Review of International Studies* 21:319–325.

Sagan, Scott D. (1994) The Perils of Proliferation: Organization Theory, Deterrence Theory, and the Spread of Nuclear Weapons. *International Security* 18:66–107.

Sagan, Scott D. and Kenneth N. Waltz (1995) *The Spread of Nuclear Weapons: A Debate.* New York: W.W. Norton & Co.

Salmore, Barbara G. and Stephen A. Salmore (1978) Political Regimes and Foreign Policy. In Maurice A. East, Stephen A. Salmore and Charles F. Hermann (eds.), *Why Nations Act: Theoretical Perspectives for Comparative Foreign Policy Studies.* Beverly Hills: Sage, pp. 103–122.

Salmore, Stephen A. and Charles F. Hermann (1969) The Effect of Size, Development and Accountability on Foreign Policy. *Peace Research Society Papers* 14:15–30.

Schahczenski, Jeffrey J. (1991) Explaining Relative Peace: Major Power Order, 1816–1976. *Journal of Peace Research* 28:295–309.

Schampel, James H. (1993) Change in Material Capabilities and the Onset of War: A Dyadic Approach. *International Studies Quarterly* 37:395–408.

Schelling, Thomas C. (1960) *The Strategy of Conflict.* Oxford: Oxford University Press.

(1966) *Arms and Influence.* New Haven: Yale University Press.

Schrodt, Philip A. (1994) The Statistical Characteristics of Event Data. *International Interactions* 20:35–53.

Schweller, Randall L. (1992) Domestic Structure and Preventive War: Are Democracies More Pacific? *World Politics* 44:235–269.

Singer, J. David (1958) Threat-Perception and the Armament–Tension Dilemma. *Journal of Conflict Resolution* 2:90–105.

(1961) The Level-of-Analysis Problem in International Relations. In Klaus Knorr and Sidney Verba (eds.), *The International System: Theoretical Essays.* Princeton: Princeton University Press, pp. 77–92.

(1963) Inter-Nation Influence: A Formal Model. *American Political Science Review* 57:420–430.

(ed.)(1965) *Human Behavior and International Politics: Contributions from the Social–Psychological Sciences.* Chicago: Rand McNally.

(ed.)(1968) *Quantitative International Politics: Insights and Evidence.* New York: The Free Press.

(1970) From *A Study of War* to Peace Research: Some Criteria and Strategies. *Journal of Conflict Resolution* 14:527–542.

(1972) The "Correlates of War" Project: Interim Report and Rationale. *World Politics* 24:243–270.

(1975) Cumulativeness in the Social Sciences: Some Counter-Prescriptions. *Political Science* Winter:19–21.

(1977) The Historical Experiment as a Research Strategy in the Study of World Politics. *Social Science History* 2:1–22.

(1979) Escalation and Control in International Conflict: A Simple Feedback Model. In J. David Singer (ed.), *The Correlates of War: I. Research Origins and Rationale.* New York: The Free Press, pp. 68–88.

(ed.) (1980) *The Correlates of War: II. Testing Some Realpolitik Models.* New York: The Free Press.

(1981) Accounting for International War: The State of the Discipline. *Journal of Peace Research* 18:1–18.

(1985) The Responsibilities of Competence in the Global Village. *International Studies Quarterly* 29:245–262.

(1989a) System Structure, Decision Processes, and the Incidence of International War. In Manus I. Midlarsky (ed.), *Handbook of War Studies.* Boston: Unwin Hyman, pp. 1–21.

(1989b) The Making of a Peace Researcher. In Joseph Kruzel and James N. Rosenau (eds.), *Journeys through World Politics: Autobiographical Reflections of Thirty-four Academic Travelers.* Lexington, MA: Lexington Books, pp. 213–229.

(1990) *Models, Methods, and Progress in World Politics: A Peace Research Odyssey.* Boulder, CO: Westview Press.

(1992) Nuclear Confrontation: Ambivalence, Rationality and the Doomsday Machine. In Volker Bornschier and Peter Lengyel (eds.), *Waves, Formations and Values in the World System.* New Brunswick, NJ: Transaction Publishers, pp. 257–281.

(1995) Metaphors and Models in the Explanation of War. In Stuart A. Bremer and Thomas R. Cusack (eds.), *The Process of War: Advancing the Scientific Study of War.* Amsterdam: Gordon and Breach Science Publishers.

Singer, J. David and Thomas Cusack (1981) Periodicity, Inexorability, and Steersmanship in International War. In Richard L. Merritt and Bruce M. Russett (eds.), *From National Development to Global Community: Essays in Honor of Karl W. Deutsch.* Boston: Allen and Unwin, pp. 404–422.

Singer, J. David and Melvin Small (1966) National Alliance Commitments and War Involvement, 1815–1945. *Peace Research Society (International) Papers* 5:109–140.

(1968) Alliance Aggregation and the Onset of War, 1815–1945. In J. David Singer (ed.), *Quantitative International Politics: Insights and Evidence.* New York: The Free Press, pp. 247–286.

(1972) *The Wages of War, 1816–1965.* New York: John Wiley & Sons.

(1974) Foreign Policy Indicators: Predictors of War in History and in the State of the World Message. *Policy Sciences* 5:271–296.

Singer, J. David and Michael Wallace (1970) Inter-Governmental Organization and the Preservation of Peace, 1816–1964: Some Bivariate Relationships. *International Organization* 24:520–547.

Singer, J. David, Stuart Bremer and John Stuckey (1972) Capability Distribution, Uncertainty, and Major Power War, 1820–1965. In Bruce M. Russett (ed.), *Peace, War, and Numbers.* Beverly Hills: Sage, pp. 19–48.

Singer, Max and Aaron Wildavsky (1993) *The Real World Order: Zones of Peace/ Zones of Turmoil.* Chatham, NJ: Chatham House Publishers, Inc.

Siverson, Randolph M. and Paul F. Diehl (1989) Arms Races, the Conflict Spiral, and the Onset of War. In Manus I. Midlarsky (ed.), *Handbook of War Studies.* Boston: Unwin Hyman, pp. 195–218.

Siverson, Randolph M. and Ross A. Miller (1993) The Escalation of Disputes to War. *International Interactions* 19:77–97.

Siverson, Randolph M. and Harvey Starr (1990) Opportunity, Willingness, and the Diffusion of War. *American Political Science Review* 84:47–67.

Siverson, Randolph M. and Michael Sullivan (1984) Alliances and War: A New Examination of an Old Problem. *Conflict Management and Peace Science* 8:1–15.

Siverson, Randolph M. and Michael R. Tennefoss (1984) Power, Alliance, and the Escalation of International Conflict, 1815–1965. *American Political Science Review* 78:1057–1069.

Sloan, Geoffrey R. (1988) *Geopolitics in United States Strategic Policy, 1890–1987*. New York: St. Martin's Press.

Small, Melvin and J. David Singer (1970) Patterns in International Warfare, 1816–1965. *Annals of the American Academy of Political and Social Science* 391:145–155.

(1976) The War-Proneness of Democratic Regimes, 1816–1965. *Jerusalem Journal of International Relations* 1:50–69.

(1982) *Resort to Arms: International and Civil Wars, 1816–1980*. Beverly Hills: Sage.

Snyder, Glenn H. and Paul Diesing (1977) *Conflict Among Nations: Bargaining, Decision Making, and System Structure in International Crises*. Princeton: Princeton University Press.

Snyder, Richard C., H.W. Bruck and Burton Sapin (1962) The Decision-Making Approach to the Study of International Politics. In Richard C. Snyder, H.W. Bruck and Burton Sapin (eds.), *Foreign Policy Decision-Making: An Approach to the Study of International Politics*. New York: The Free Press, pp. 60–74.

Sorokin, Pitirim A. (1937) *Social and Cultural Dynamics: Fluctuations of Social Relationships, War, and Revolution* (vol. 3). New York: American Books.

Spiezio, K. Edward (1990) British Hegemony and Major Power War, 1815–1939: An Empirical Test of Gilpin's Model of Hegemonic Governance. *International Studies Quarterly* 34:165–181.

Spilerman, Seymour (1970) The Causes of Racial Disturbances: A Comparison of Alternative Explanations. *American Sociological Review* 35:627–649.

Spiro, David E. (1994) The Insignificance of the Liberal Peace. *International Security* 19:50–86.

(1995) The Liberal Peace: "And Yet It Squirms." *International Security* 19:177–180.

Stallings, Barbara (1972) *Economic Dependency in Africa and Latin America*. Beverly Hills: Sage.

Starr, Harvey (1991) Joining Political and Geographic Perspectives: Geopolitics and International Relations. *International Interactions* 17:1–9.

(1994) Revolution and War: Rethinking the Linkage Between Internal and External Conflict. *Political Research Quarterly* 47:481–507.

Starr, Harvey and Benjamin Most (1976) The Substance and Study of Borders in International Relations Research. *International Studies Quarterly* 20:581–620.

References

(1978) A Return Journey: Richardson, "Frontiers," and Wars in the 1946–1965 Era. *Journal of Conflict Resolution* 22:441–467.

(1983) Contagion and Border Effects on Contemporary African Conflicts. *Comparative Political Studies* 16:92–117.

(1985) The Forms and Processes of War Diffusion: Research Update on Contagion in African Conflict. *Comparative Political Studies* 18:206–229.

Stoll, Richard J. (1982) Major Power Interstate Conflict in the Post-World War II Era: An Increase, Decrease, or No Change? *Western Political Quarterly* 35:587–605.

(1984) The Guns of November: Presidential Reelections and the Use of Force, 1947–1982. *Journal of Conflict Resolution* 28:231–246.

(1992) Steaming in the Dark? Rules, Rivals, and the British Navy, 1860–1913. *Journal of Conflict Resolution* 36:263–283.

Sullivan, Michael (1974) Escalatory and Non-Escalatory Systems. *American Journal of Political Science* 18:549–558.

Sunkel, Osvaldo (1972) National Development Policy and External Dependence in Latin America. In Yale Ferguson (ed.), *Contemporary Inter-American Relations*. Englewood Cliffs, NJ: Prentice-Hall, pp. 465–492.

Swinburne, Richard (ed.) (1974) *The Justification of Induction*. Oxford: Oxford University Press.

Taylor, Charles Lewis and David A. Jodice (1983) *World Handbook of Political and Social Indicators* (3rd edition). New Haven: Yale University Press.

Thompson, William R. (1982) Phases of the Business Cycle and the Outbreak of War. *International Studies Quarterly* 26:301–311.

(1983a) Cycles, Capabilities, and War: An Ecumenical View. In William R. Thompson (ed.), *Contending Approaches to World System Analysis*. Beverly Hills: Sage, pp.141–163.

(1983b) Succession Crises in the Global Political System: A Test of the Transition Model. In Albert Bergesen (ed.), *Crises in the World System*. Beverly Hills: Sage, pp.93–116.

(1986) Polarity, the Long Cycle, and Global Power Warfare. *Journal of Conflict Resolution* 30:587–615.

(1988) *On Global War: Historical–Structural Approaches to World Politics*. Columbia: University of South Carolina Press.

(1995) Principal Rivalries. *Journal of Conflict Resolution* 39:195–223.

(1996) Balances of Power, Transitions, and Long Cycles. In Jacek Kugler and Douglas Lemke (eds.), *Parity and War: Evaluations and Extensions of The War Ledger*. Ann Arbor: University of Michigan Press, pp. 163–185.

Tversky, Amos and Daniel Kahneman (1986) The Framing of Decisions and the Psychology of Choice. In Jon Elster (ed.), *Rational Choice*. New York: New York University Press, pp. 123–141; reprinted from *Science* 211 (1981):453–458.

United States Arms Control and Disarmament Agency (ACDA) (1976) *World Military Expenditures and Arms Transfers, 1966–1975*. Washington, DC: U.S. Government Printing Office.

224

(1984) *World Military Expenditures and Arms Transfers, 1972–1982.* Washington, DC: U.S. Government Printing Office.

Vasquez, John A. (1987) The Steps to War: Toward a Scientific Explanation of Correlates of War Findings. *World Politics* 40:108–145.

(1993) *The War Puzzle.* Cambridge: Cambridge University Press.

(1995) Why Do Neighbors Fight? Proximity, Interaction, or Territoriality. *Journal of Peace Research* 32:277–293.

(1996a) When Are Power Transitions Dangerous?: An Appraisal and Reformulation of Power Transition Theory. In Jacek Kugler and Douglas Lemke (eds.), *Parity and War: Evaluations and Extensions of The War Ledger.* Ann Arbor: University of Michigan Press, pp. 35–56.

(1996b) The Causes of the Second World War in Europe: A New Scientific Explanation. *International Political Science Review* 17:161–178.

Vasquez, John A. and Marie T. Henehan (eds.) (1992) *The Scientific Study of Peace and War: A Text Reader.* New York: Lexington Books.

Verba, Sidney (1961) Assumptions of Rationality and Non-Rationality in Models of the International System. In Klaus Knorr and Sidney Verba (eds.), *The International System: Theoretical Essays.* Princeton: Princeton University Press, pp. 93–117.

Vincent, Jack (1981) Internal and External Conflict: Some Previous Operational Problems and Some New Findings. *Journal of Politics* 43:128–142.

(1983) WEIS vs. COPDAB: Correspondence Problems. *International Studies Quarterly* 27:161–168.

Vincent, Jack, Roger Baker, Susan Gagnon, Keith Hamm and Scott Reilly (1973) Empirical Tests of Attribute, Social-Field and Status-Field Theories of International Relations. *International Studies Quarterly* 17:405–443.

Wagner, R. Harrison (1984) War and Expected Utility Theory. *World Politics* 36:407–423.

(1994) Peace, War, and the Balance of Power. *American Political Science Review* 88:593–607.

Wallace, Michael D. (1971) Power, Status, and International War. *Journal of Peace Research* 8:23–35.

(1973) Alliance Polarization, Cross-cutting, and International War, 1815–1964. *Journal of Conflict Resolution* 17:575–604.

(1979) Arms Races and Escalation: Some New Evidence. *Journal of Conflict Resolution* 23:3–16.

(1980) Some Persisting Findings: A Reply to Professor Weede. *Journal of Conflict Resolution* 24:289–292.

(1981) Old Nails in New Coffins: Para Bellum Hypothesis Revisited. *Journal of Peace Research* 18:91–96.

(1982) Armaments and Escalation: Two Competing Hypotheses. *International Studies Quarterly* 26:37–51.

(1983) Arms Races and Escalation – A Reply to Altfeld. *International Studies Quarterly* 27:233–235.

(1990) Racing Redux: The Arms Race-Escalation Debate Revisited. In Charles

S. Gochman and Alan Ned Sabrosky (eds.), *Prisoners of War?: Nation-States in the Modern Era*. Lexington, MA: Lexington Books, pp. 115–122.

Wallensteen, Peter (1984) Universalism vs. Particularism: On the Limits of Major Power Order. *Journal of Peace Research* 21:243–257.

Wallensteen, Peter and Karin Axell (1993) Armed Conflict at the End of the Cold War, 1989–92. *Journal of Peace Research* 30:331–346.

Wallerstein, Immanuel (1984) *The Politics of the World-Economy*. Cambridge: Cambridge University Press.

Waltz, Kenneth N. (1959) *Man, the State, and War*. New York: Columbia University Press.

(1967) International Structure, National Force, and the Balance of World Power. *Journal of International Affairs* 21:215–231.

(1979) *Theory of International Politics*. Reading, MA: Addison-Wesley.

(1981) *The Spread of Nuclear Weapons: More May Be Better*. Adelphi Papers, no. 171. London: International Institute of Strategic Studies.

(1990) Nuclear Myths and Political Realities. *American Political Science Review* 84:731–745.

(1993) The Emerging Structure of International Politics. *International Security* 18:44–79.

Wang, Kevin and James Lee Ray (1994) Beginners and Winners: The Fate of Initiators of Interstate Wars Involving Great Powers Since 1495. *International Studies Quarterly* 38:139–154.

Wayman, Frank W. (1982) "Power Transitions, Rivalries, and War, 1816–1970." Paper presented at the Institute for the Study of Conflict Theory and International Security Meeting, September 22–24, Urbana–Champaign, Illinois. Correlates of War Project (mimeo).

(1984) Bipolarity and War: The Role of Capability Concentration and Alliance Patterns Among Major Powers, 1816–1965. *Journal of Peace Research* 21:61–78.

(1996) Power Shifts and the Onset of War. In Jacek Kugler and Douglas Lemke (eds.), *Parity and War: Evaluations and Extensions of The War Ledger*. Ann Arbor: University of Michigan Press, pp. 145–162.

Wayman, Frank W. and Paul F. Diehl (eds.) (1994) *Reconstructing Realpolitik*. Ann Arbor: University of Michigan Press.

Wayman, Frank W. and Daniel M. Jones (1991) "Evolution of Conflict in Enduring Rivalries." Paper presented at the 32nd Annual Convention of the International Studies Association, March 19–23, Vancouver, Canada.

Wayman, Frank W. and J. David Singer (1991) Evolution and Directions for Improvement in the Correlates of War Project Methodologies. In J. David Singer and Paul F. Diehl (eds.), *Measuring the Correlates of War*. Ann Arbor: University of Michigan Press, pp. 247–267.

Weede, Erich (1970) Conflict Behavior of Nation-States. *Journal of Peace Research* 7:229–237.

(1975) World Order in the Fifties and Sixties: Dependence, Deterrence and Limited Peace. *Peace Science Society Papers* 24:49–80.

(1976) Overwhelming Preponderance as a Pacifying Condition Among Contiguous Asian Dyads, 1950–1969. *Journal of Conflict Resolution* 20:395–411.

(1980) Arms Races and Escalation: Some Persisting Doubts. *Journal of Conflict Resolution* 24:285–287.

(1984) Democracy and War Involvement. *Journal of Conflict Resolution* 28:649–664.

(1989) Extended Deterrence, Superpower Control, and Militarized Interstate Disputes, 1962–1976. *Journal of Peace Research* 26:7–17.

(1994) Constraints, States, and Wars. *European Journal of Political Research* 26:171–192.

(1995) Economic Policy and International Security: Rent-Seeking, Free Trade and Democratic Peace. *European Journal of International Relations* 1:519–537.

(1996a) Correspondence. *International Security* 20:180–183.

(1996b) *Economic Development, Social Order, and World Politics.* Boulder, CO: Lynne Rienner.

Wendt, Alexander (1987) The Agent–Structure Problem in International Relations Theory. *International Organization* 41:335–370.

Wesley, James Paul (1962) Frequency of Wars and Geographical Opportunity. *Journal of Conflict Resolution* 6:387–389.

Whittlesey, Derwent (1966) Haushofer: The Geopoliticians. In Edward Meade Earle (ed.), *Makers of Modern Strategy: Military Thought from Machiavelli to Hitler.* New York: Atheneum, pp. 388–411.

Wilkenfeld, Jonathan (1969) Some Further Findings Regarding the Domestic and Foreign Conflict Behavior of Nations. *Journal of Peace Research* 6:147–156.

(1971) Domestic and Foreign Conflict Behavior of Nations. In William D. Coplin and Charles W. Kegley, Jr. (eds.), *A Multi-Method Introduction to International Politics.* Chicago: Markham, pp. 189–204.

Wilkinson, David (1980) *Deadly Quarrels: Lewis F. Richardson and the Statistical Study of War.* Berkeley: University of California Press.

Wish, Naomi Bailin (1980) Foreign Policy Makers and Their National Role Conceptions. *International Studies Quarterly* 24:532–554.

Wolf, Fredric M. (1986) *Meta-Analysis.* Sage University Papers Series: Quantitative Applications in the Social Sciences, no. 59. Beverly Hills: Sage.

Wright, Quincy ([1942], 1964) *A Study of War* (revised edition). Chicago: University of Chicago Press.

Zagare, Frank C. (1982) Review of *The War Trap. American Political Science Review* 76:738–739.

(1990) Rationality and Deterrence. *World Politics* 42:238–260.

Zinnes, Dina A. (1968) The Expression and Perception of Hostility in Prewar Crisis: 1914. In J. David Singer (ed.), *Quantitative International Politics: Insights and Evidence.* New York: The Free Press, pp. 85–119.

Zinnes, Dina A. and Jonathan Wilkenfeld (1971) An Analysis of Foreign Conflict Behavior of Nations. In Wolfram F. Hanrieder (ed.), *Comparative Foreign Policy: Theoretical Essays.* New York: David McKay Co., Inc., pp. 167–213.

Index

Abdolali, Nasrin, 55, 85, 86, 123, 126, 198, 199, 202
alliances, 26, 44, 68, 78 n.7, 90 n.14, 130
  asymmetric, 83–4
  and expansion of war, 63–4, 80–1, 120 n.5, 131–33, 156 n.1
  external to dyads, 83–4
  findings on, 27–8, 64, 84–5, 120–21, 137–39, 167 n.5, 193–94
  flexibility of, 114–15
  formation of, 101 n.1
  and onset of war, 27, 189, 193
  reliability of, 115 n.3
  and seriousness of war, 63, 138, 139, 189
  and similarity of interests, 82
  symmetric, 83–4
  and uncertainty, 114–15, 136
  and war-prone dyads, 27, 77, 82–4, 93, 95–6, 193, 199
  and war-prone states, 27, 47, 48, 62–4, 67, 193, 198
  and war-prone systems, 28, 102, 114–15, 117–19, 137–39, 194, 202
  within dyads, 82–3, 84–5
  and World War I, 29–30, 157, 159, 184, 186–89, 190
  see also polarization
Allison, Graham T., 21 n.10, 39, 41
Altfeld, Michael F., 80–1, 199
anarchy, 7, 26
Anderson, Paul A., 73, 76, 89, 91–2, 149, 199
Andriole, Stephen J., 46
Anselin, Luc, 102–03, 104, 111, 201
Arbetman, Marina, 57 n.5
arms race, 22–3, 26, 79 n.8, 199
  findings on, 60, 81, 95
  and rivals, 23

and tension, 80, 81 n.9
and war, 68, 79–81
see also military buildups
Asia, 24–5, 72, 98–101, 102 n.1, 102 n.3, 103, 107, 110–11, 157–58, 160, 187
see also regional factors and war
Austria-Hungary, 48, 170
  alliances, 186–89
  enduring rivalry, 153, 154, 186
  hierarchy, 168–69, 172, 177, 178
  political system, 182–83, 184
  power cycle, 165–66
  power status, 161–63
  proximity/contiguity, 157–61
  and World War I, 190
autocracy, 21, 24, 52 n.4, 53, 55–6, 85, 88, 90 n.14, 123, 126, 138, 155, 179, 181–83, 188, 190
Axell, Karin, 52 n.4, 126, 202
Azar, Edward, 98–9, 127, 201, 202

Babst, Dean V., 86, 199
Baker, Roger, 51
balance of power, 165–66
  theory, 68–71
  parity, 72–3
  preponderance, 71–2
  see also capability
Banks, Arthur S., 53, 143–44, 145–46, 183, 198
Barbieri, Katherine, 94, 199
Batt, James, x
battle-deaths, 27 n.16, 28 n.17, 123, 124, 162–63, 195 n.1
  see also severity of war
beliefs, 33, 34–5, 134
Bennett, D. Scott, 23, 74, 90–1, 185, 199
Bentham, Jeremy, 85

Index

dyadic factors and war, 22–4, 27, 29–30, 68, 199–200
  alliances, 82–5
  arms race, 79–81
  capability balance, 68–76
  contiguity, 76–8
  economic factors, 92–5
  findings on, 27, 75–6, 78, 81, 84–5, 87–9, 92, 94–5, 95–6, 193
  proximity, 76–8
  regimes, 85–9
  status quo orientation, 89–92
dyads
  enduring rivalries, 23–4, 153, 154, 186
  factors, 68, 69–71, 76, 79, 81–2, 85, 89, 92–3
  findings on, 27, 95–6, 193
  number in system, 1, 73

East, Maurice A., 49, 51, 55–6, 66, 95, 123, 198, 202
Eberwein, Wolf-Dieter, 50, 58, 110, 198
Eckhardt, William, 98–9, 127, 201, 202
economic cycles, 49 n.2, 121, 124–25, 126–27
economic development, 22, 24–5, 27, 46, 47, 48–9, 51–2, 67, 68, 92–3, 94–5, 145–47, 193
economic factors and war, 48–9, 51–2, 92–5, 124–25, 127–28, 145–47, 158, 199
election cycles, 22, 46, 53–4, 56
  see also regimes
empirical patterns, x, 7, 13–4, 28, 141, 142, 145, 147, 150, 155, 157, 161, 163, 166, 179, 184, 186, 190, 192, 195
  summary on, 27–8, 192–95
empiricism, 5–6, 7, 8–9, 12–20
enduring rivalries, 23–4, 29, 75, 140, 157
  comparability of databases, 23 n.13, 23 n.14, 150–52, 184–85
  conceptualization of, 23–4, 150–52, 184–85
  list of, 153, 154, 186
  and war, 23, 27, 73, 74–5, 81, 91–2, 152, 154, 185–86, 190
Enterline, Andrew J., 56, 198
epistemology, 2–5, 7–8, 9, 13–20, 191–92, 195
equilibrium, 109–10, 115, 130, 166, 187
errors, Types I and II, 5
escalation, 70 n.3, 71, 72, 75, 77, 78 n.7, 80–1, 83–5, 91, 92
Eurasia, 159–61
  see also regional factors and war
Europe, 24–5, 32, 48, 72, 77, 83, 97–101, 103–05, 107, 108–12, 116–17, 124, 128–29, 135, 157–61, 166–68, 169–71, 180, 181–82, 186–88, 190
  see also regional factors and war
event-data, 65–7
expected-utility theory, 33, 36, 42–4, 45, 71, 81, 84
  see also decision models; rational choice
experiments, 3–4, 8–9, 37–8
explanandum, 14–5, 16–7
explanans, 14–5, 16–7
explanation, 12, 14 n.3, 20 n.9, 28, 140, 155, 156–57, 190, 191–92
  and causality, 13–4, 18–20
  deductive-nomological, 14–6
  and laws, 15–6, 17
  and patterns, 13–4
  and prediction, 15 n.4, 16 n.6, 30, 45, 195
  probabilistic, 16

Faber, Jan, 106, 107–08, 131, 201, 202
factor analysis, 61
  and foreign behavior data sets, 66
Farber, Henry S., 87 n.11, 199
Farkas, Andrew, 32 n.1
Farrar, L.L., Jr., 108–09, 201
Fashoda Crisis, 90
Feierabend, Ivo K., 50–1, 58, 198
Feierabend, Rosalind L., 50–1, 58, 198
Ferdinand, Archduke Franz, 161, 189
Festinger, Leon, 34
forecasting, 30, 45 n.14, 195, 195 n.1
  see also prediction
foreign behavior, 21–2, 46, 49, 50–2, 56–7, 58, 63, 64
  dimensions of, 65–6
foreign policy, 7, 20–2, 25, 31–2, 34 n.2, 35–6, 39, 42, 44, 46–8, 51, 56, 59, 64–7, 71 n.4, 78 n.7, 85, 90, 93, 96, 111, 134, 156 n.1, 164, 165, 180–81, 186–87
formal model, 5, 7, 10, 33, 79 n.8, 87 n.11
France, 1, 29, 48, 90, 101 n.2, 109, 120 n.4, 146, 157
  alliances, 186–89
  enduring rivalry, 153, 154, 184–86
  hierarchy, 166–67, 169–70, 172–79
  political system, 180, 183–84
  power cycle, 163–66
  power status, 161–63
  proximity/contiguity, 157–61
  and World War I, 190
Franco-Prussian War, 186
Frank, André Gunder, 146
free trade, 68, 94 n.16, 193
  advocacy of, 92–3
  see also economic factors and war

Index

Hoffmann, Stanley, 95, 199
Hoggard, Gary, 65, 66 n.9
Hollis, Martin, 20 n.9
Holsti, Kalevi J., 20 n.9, 68 n.1, 101 n.1,
  137, 201, 202
Holsti, Ole R., 47, 115, 202
Hoole, Francis W., 122–23, 202
Hopf, Ted, 103–04, 111, 116–17, 201, 202
Hopmann, P. Terrence, 115, 202
Hopple, Gerald W., 46
hostility, 33, 36 n.5, 47, 53, 56, 64, 67, 81
  n.9, 151 n.7
Houweling, Henk, 29 n.19, 59 n.6, 73, 99,
  106–07, 119, 125, 131–32, 138 n.13, 164
  n.3, 167, 198, 199, 202
Howell, Llewellyn, 66 n.9
Hower, Gretchen, 107–08, 114, 133 n.11
Hsu, Chi-Feng, x
Huang, Chi, 122–23, 202
Hubner-Dick, Gisela, 50
Hudson, Valerie M., 66 n.9
Hume, David, 13–4
Huntington, Samuel P., 80, 82, 105 n.4,
  199, 201
Hussein, Saddam, 142, 143
Huth, Paul, 22–3, 35, 36 n.3, 66 n.10, 74,
  90–1, 185, 199

idealism, 6
  see also liberalism
inductive logic, 8, 12, 14, 16–8, 28–30, 140,
  155, 156–57, 190, 192, 195
industrialization, 6, 9, 59, 70, 92, 145, 149,
  159, 163, 164, 167, 168, 169, 170, 171,
  172–73, 189
initiation of war
  and capabilities, 68–72, 80, 90 n.14, 91
    n.15, 115 n.3, 140, 149–50
  and contenders, 69–70, 89–90, 119–20
  defined, 27 n.16
  findings on, 27, 29, 45, 49, 53, 55, 60, 63,
    65, 67, 74, 75, 82, 91–2, 96, 129–30, 132,
    137–38, 140, 163, 164, 193–94, 195
  and status quo, 64, 89–90, 140
  and subwar disputes, 58, 89–91
  theory of, 21, 44, 70–1
instability, 24–5, 51, 109–10, 146, 174–75,
  178–79
instrumental rationality, 31, 32–3, 36–7,
  41–4, 192
  see also decision models
intensity of war
  defined, 49, 124, 129
  findings on, 49, 124, 129, 134–35, 136,
    163

interactive effects, 51–2, 123, 166–67
interdependence, 92–3, 94–5
intergovernmental organizations (IGOs),
  26, 133–34, 135–37, 139, 202
International Crisis Behavior (ICB)
  Project, 99, 116, 118, 196
international order, 105, 119–20, 124 n.7,
  133–34, 136–37
international system, 9, 12, 20, 32, 45,
  69–70, 108, 113, 191
  alliances in, 62–3, 113–15, 117–19, 120
  attributes of, 25–6, 120–27
  contagion in, 131–33
  and intergovernmental organizations,
    133–34, 135–37
  and norms, 134–35
  polarity of, 113–17, 119–20
  and time, 127–31
  war-proneness of, 25–6, 27–8, 137–39,
    194
interests, 6–7, 27 n.16, 31, 32–3, 35, 39–40,
  44, 48, 59, 70, 82, 87 n.11, 92–3, 115
  n.3, 133, 136, 141, 158, 162, 164–65,
  166, 189, 192
internal/external conflict nexus, 27, 50–1,
  52, 122–23, 125–26, 138, 194
intervention, 52, 75, 102 n.3, 188–89
Intriligator, Michael D., 79 n.8, 199
involvement in war
  findings on, 1, 49–50, 53, 55, 56, 57–8,
    59–60, 62, 63–4, 67, 85, 116, 118,
    161–63, 164–66
Iran, 12, 29, 140, 154–55, 192, 194
  capabilities, 147–50
  economic development, 145–47
  enduring rivalry, 150–54
  political system, 142–44
  Shatt al'Arab, 141–42
Iran/Iraq War, 29, 140–55, 194–95
Iraq, 12, 29, 140, 154–55, 192, 194, 195 n.1
  capabilities, 147–50
  economic development, 145–47
  enduring rivalry, 150–54
  political system, 142–44
  Shatt al'Arab, 141–42
issue-areas, 195

Jagodzinski, Wolfgang, 50
James, Patrick, x, 44 n.12, 60 n.7, 87 n.11,
  115 n.2, 116–17, 118, 165, 198, 199, 202
Janis, Irving L., 35, 36 n.3, 47
Japan, 101 n.1, 129 n.9, 146, 153, 154, 160,
  162, 163, 165, 171, 182, 186, 187, 188
Jervis, Robert, 32, 34–5, 40 n.9, 47, 115, 202
Jodice, David A., 144, 146–47

Index

Managing Interstate Conflict (MIC)
database, 72, 196
Mandel, Robert, 72, 199
Mann, Leon, 35
Mansfield, Edward D., 56, 115–16, 121 n.6, 124–25, 198, 202
Maoz, Zeev, 22 n.12, 23 n.13, 54–5, 70 n.3, 85, 86, 88, 90, 93, 95, 100–01, 110, 122–23, 126, 128, 151, 185, 198, 199, 202
March, James G., 43 n.10
Markov process, 163
Marxism, 20 n.9, 48, 121
Maurer, John H., 188 n.16
McClelland, Charles A., 65, 66 n.9
McGowan, Patrick J., 22
McKeown, Timothy J., 73, 76, 89, 91–2, 149, 199
Mearsheimer, John J., 101 n.2, 111, 201
Merritt, Richard L., 57 n.5, 66 n.9
meta-analysis, 4
Metternichean Concert, 104
Middle East, 24–5, 98–101, 102 n.3, 107, 110–11, 146
see also regional factors and war
Midlarsky, Manus I., 61–2, 90, 105–06, 109–10, 115 n.2, 130, 198, 199, 201, 202
Mihalka, Michael, 72, 77, 83–4, 199, 200
Militarized Interstate Disputes (MID), 22 n.12, 23 n.13, 98, 152 n.8, 196
defined, 151 n.7
findings on, 22–3, 54, 56, 58, 73, 74, 75–6, 80–1, 82–3, 86–7, 94, 96, 99–101, 104, 109, 110, 111, 112, 127–28, 130, 131, 134–35, 136–37, 138–39, 150–52, 184–86
military buildups, 57, 58, 60, 78 n.7, 79
see also arms race
militarization, 22, 33, 57, 58, 60, 67, 83–4, 86–7
military capability (Mil. Cap.) scores, 149–50, 173–75, 176
data, 149 n.5
variables, 148–49, 172–73, 174
military expenditures, 48, 58, 74, 80, 102, 147, 148, 149, 171, 173, 189
data, 149 n.5
military personnel, 27 n.16, 28 n.17, 58, 148, 168, 173
data, 149 n.5
Mill, John Stuart, 92
Miller, Ross A., 70 n.3, 75
minor powers, 64, 101 n.2
findings on, 57–8, 66–7, 71–2, 100, 110, 126–27, 153, 154, 161–63

see also power status
misperception, 34–5, 41, 115, 121, 165
Mitchell, Glenn E., II, 87 n.11, 199
Modelski, George, 64–5, 69–70, 73, 108–10, 115–16, 119, 120 n.4, 124–25, 126–27, 166–67, 198, 200, 201, 202
Monsen, R. Joseph, 55, 198
Morgan, Patrick M., 36 n.4, 40–1
Morgan, T. Clifton, 50, 88–9, 106, 129–30, 199, 202
Morgenthau, Hans J., 6, 115, 202
Morrow, James D., 74, 81, 83 n.10, 89, 120 n.5, 199, 200, 202
Moses, Jonathon, 88 n.12, 199
Mossadeq, Muhammad, 147
Most, Benjamin A., 61, 78, 106–07, 108, 123–24, 126, 132, 133 n.11, 198, 199, 201, 202
Moul, William B., 57 n.5., 72, 77, 149 n.5, 199, 200
Mueller, John E., 80
multipolarity, 101 n.2, 103–04, 114, 115, 116, 117, 119–20, 124 n.7, 137–38, 156 n.1, 166–67, 178–79
see also polarity

Napoleonic Wars, 1
Naroll, Raoul, 131, 202
national attributes, 21–2, 46, 47, 198
business cycles, 49
culture, 50
domestic conflict, 50–1
economic development, 49
interaction effects, 51–2
population, 48
war cycles, 49–50
and war, 52, 67
national culture, 22, 46, 47, 50, 52, 67
Neack, Laura, 66 n.9
necessary conditions, 44, 77, 86
neo-realism, 6
Newman, David, 42–3, 45 n.14
Nicholson, Michael, x, 14 n.3, 16 n.6, 20 n.9, 24, 38 n.7, 44 n.12, 47 n.1, 79 n.8, 195
Nincic, Miroslav, 54, 198
nineteenth century, 8, 22–3, 24–5, 63, 68 n.1, 80, 98, 105, 109, 110, 111, 120 n.4, 131, 142, 157, 158, 159, 166, 171, 181, 188
Nomohan War, 186
nonrational models, 12, 31, 33, 34–40, 44, 46–7, 191–92
see also decision models
norms, 3, 26, 78 n.7, 88, 97, 102, 104–05,

Index

CAMBRIDGE STUDIES IN INTERNATIONAL RELATIONS